Introduction

I was very lucky as a child and from a very early age would generally travel with my late father (C. N. 'Jim' Clemens 1922–1987) on his journeys to record the railway network of Britain from Penzance to the north of Scotland (as long as it did not conflict with school). A result over the years was that I also met his railway friends, and all the photographs in this book were taken by one of these old pals—R. E. James-Robertson. Robert Ellis James-Robertson (but always known to my father and I as Ellis) lived in Worcestershire from the mid-1950s until his death in April 2015. However, Ellis was born on 8 July 1922 and grew up in Swansea, moving at the age of eleven with his family to Pen-y-Bryn in Edern, Pwllheli, North Wales, and thus very well placed to photograph the railway scene revealed to us throughout this book—*The Last Years of Steam Around North Wales: From the Photographic Archive of the Late R. E. James-Robertson.*

Ellis's daughters, Louisa and Fiona, remember their dad having a Rolleiflex twin lens camera; this took 120-roll film with twelve exposures to a roll. He would convert the kitchen into a dark room, and the girls would enjoy watching the magic of photography. Ellis did most of his own black and white developing and printing—a typical combination from the era of the photographs in this book being FP3 film with Definol or Promicrol developer. Colour film (from 1955) was mainly Agfa in the early years but later Kodachrome II. The time period covered by this book is from 1955 to 1966.

Ellis had an excellent eye for detail, and his early love of drawing, combined with a passion for trains, led to his thirty-year connection with the Guild of Railway Artists. It will soon become apparent just why I have always held Ellis's black and white photographs in such high esteem—an almost unsurpassed quality and full of detail. Steam is the dominant motive power throughout, but diesels do appear, including the early Derby lightweight DMUs that worked in the area.

There are three main sources for the dates and places given in this book. Ellis kept notebooks (largely for the black and white photos) that list things such as location, exposure settings, if a filter had been used, the type of developer, plus often an indication of the date and time. The negatives themselves are mostly

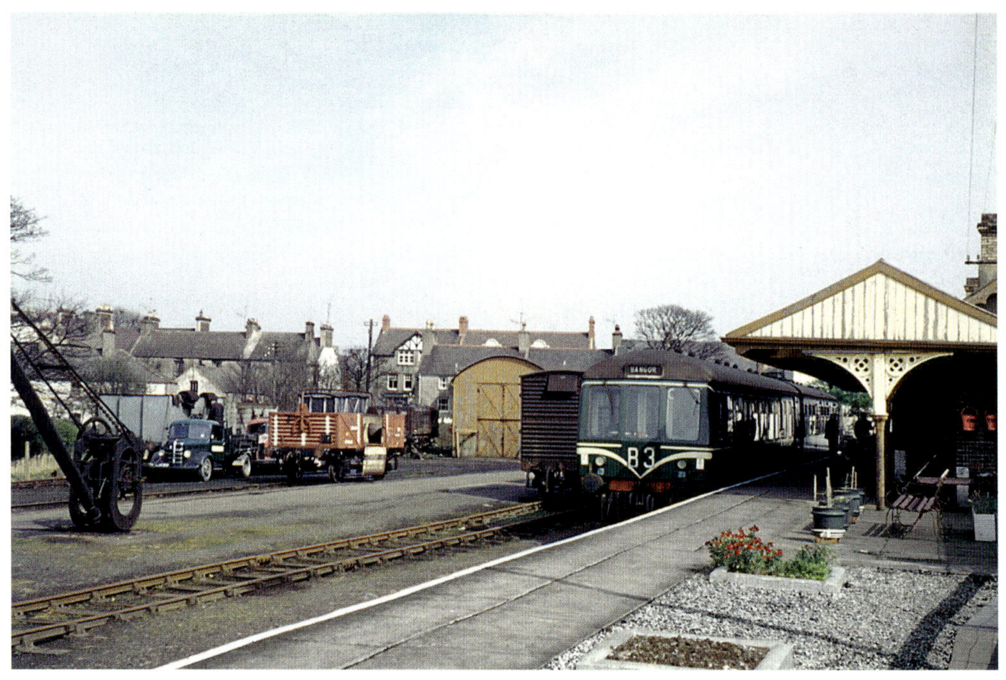

The terminus at Amlwch, Anglesey, was visited by Ellis during April 1961.

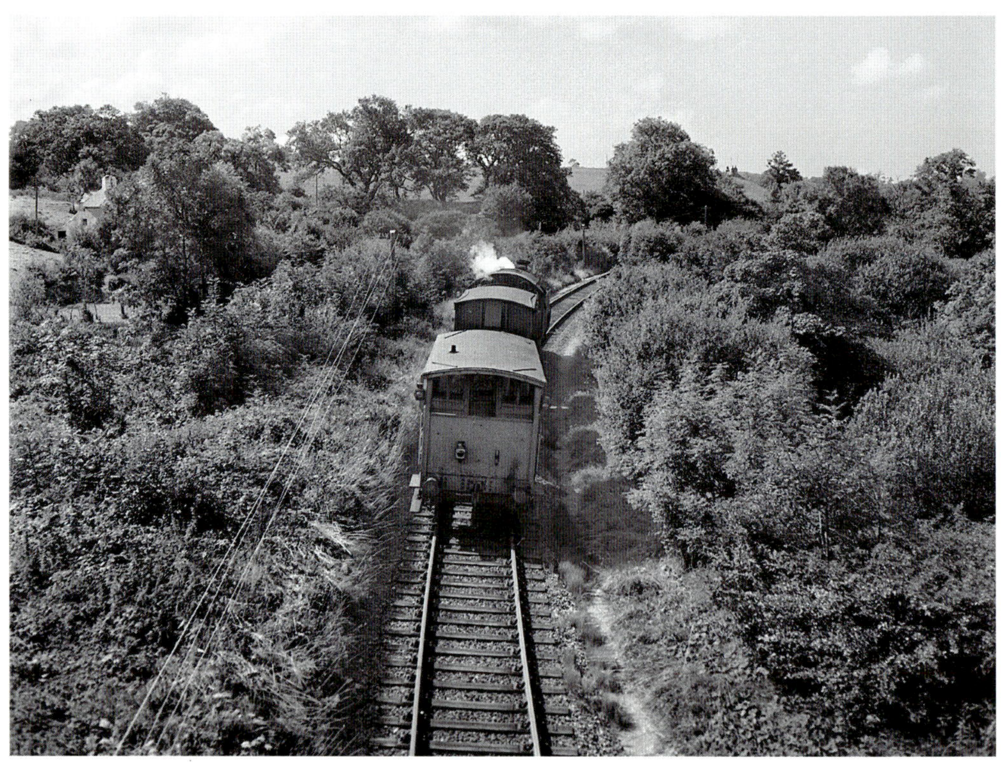

A freight train ambles along the Llanberis branch in August 1964 just before closure.

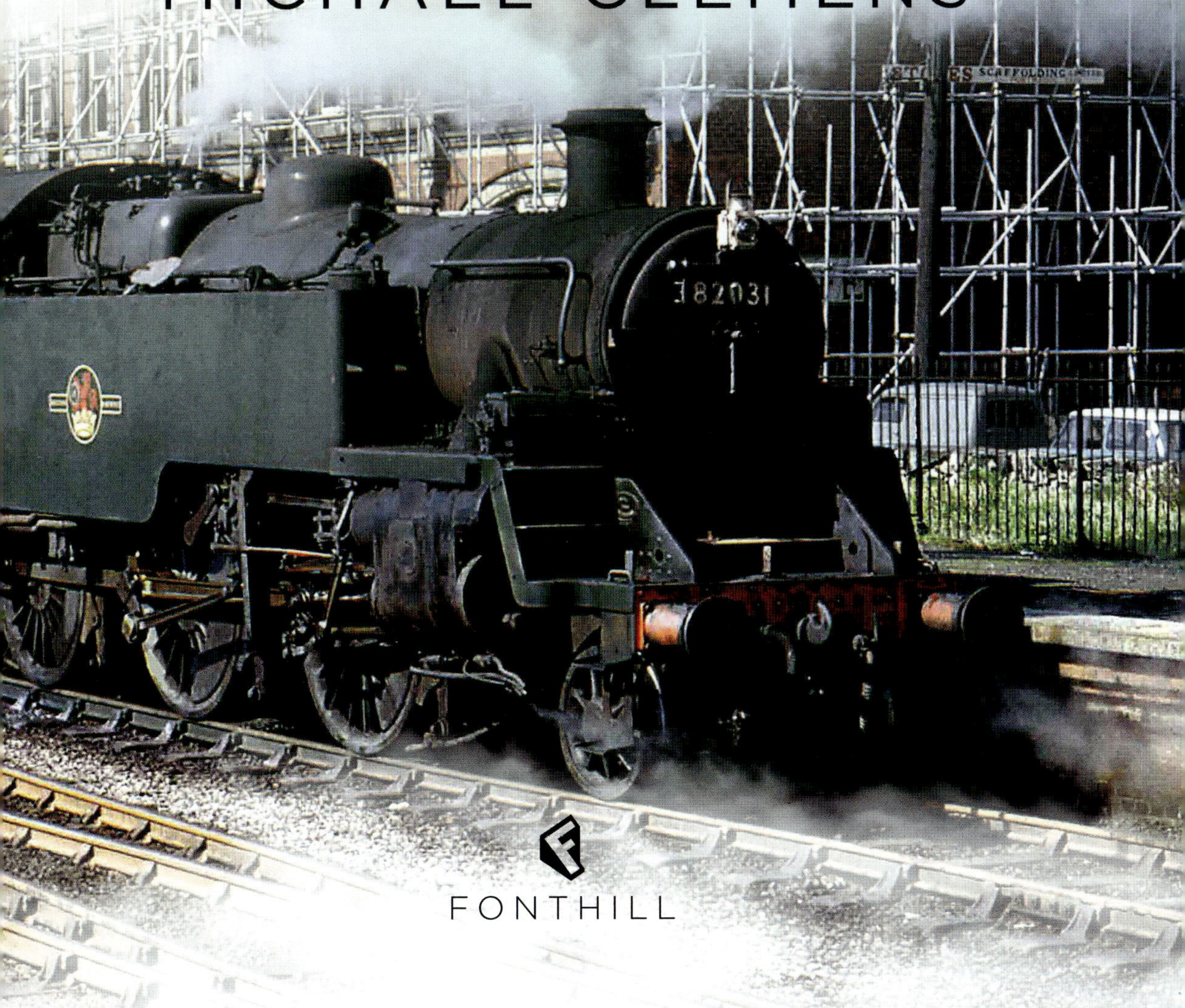

THE LAST YEARS OF STEAM

—AROUND—

NORTH WALES

FROM THE PHOTOGRAPHIC ARCHIVE OF ELLIS JAMES-ROBERTSON

MICHAEL CLEMENS

FONTHILL

Fonthill Media Language Policy

Fonthill Media publishes in the international English language market. One language edition is published worldwide. As there are minor differences in spelling and presentation, especially with regard to American English and British English, a policy is necessary to define which form of English to use. The Fonthill Policy is to use the form of English native to the author. Michael Clemens was born and educated in Worcestershire, England; therefore, British English has been adopted in this publication.

Fonthill Media Limited
Fonthill Media LLC
www.fonthillmedia.com
office@fonthillmedia.com

First published in the United Kingdom and the United States of America 2021

British Library Cataloguing in Publication Data:
A catalogue record for this book is available from the British Library

Typeset in 10.5pt on 13pt Sabon
Printed and bound in England

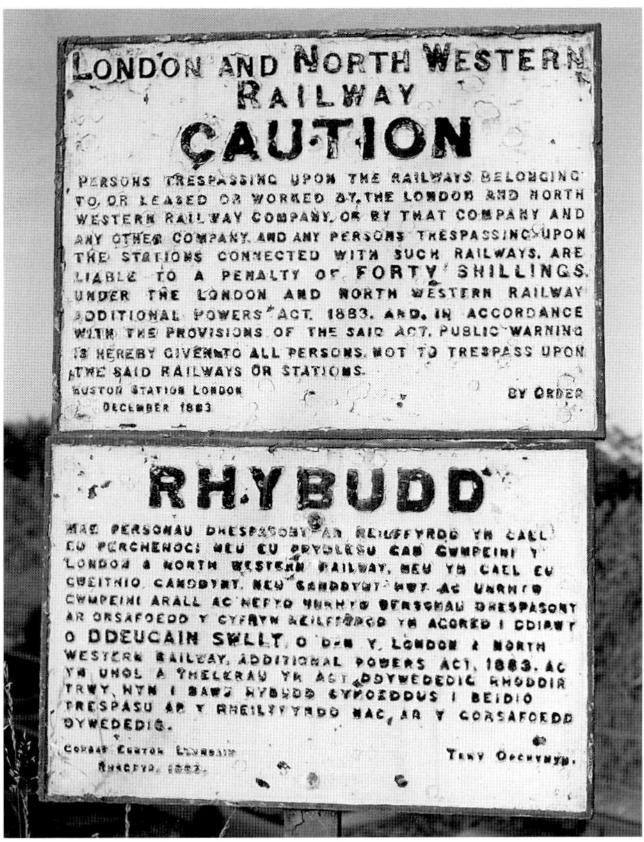

Warning signs near the one-time Dinas Junction during August 1961.

stored inside individual envelopes, a number of which have a precise date stamp on them. Some of the colour slides have a location on their cardboard-type frames plus occasionally a broad indication of date.

Ellis would send some of his best black and white photographs to various railway magazines (both in the UK and the USA) for possible publication, including *Model Railroader*, *Trains*, *Trains Illustrated*, *Railway Magazine*, and *Railway World*; the individual photos concerned are listed in his notebooks. I am not sure how many of Ellis's North Wales photographs have actually appeared in print and am only aware of less than a handful throughout this book; by far, the majority have never been published previously.

In very broad terms, this book moves southwards from the north of North Wales to finish on the border with Central Wales. The main exceptions are the slate quarry systems at Penrhyn and Dinorwic; these are covered separately in some detail at the rear of the book. We begin at the most northerly town in Wales, Amlwch, situated on the north eastern corner of Anglesey at the end of the branch from Gaerwen. Ellis visited the branch in April 1961 and we travel via Llangwyllog, Llangefni, Gaerwen, and Llanfair PG to Bangor. Time is spent at Bangor and we can study the station and engine shed, included are *Duchess of Atholl* plus the unnamed 'Britannia'.

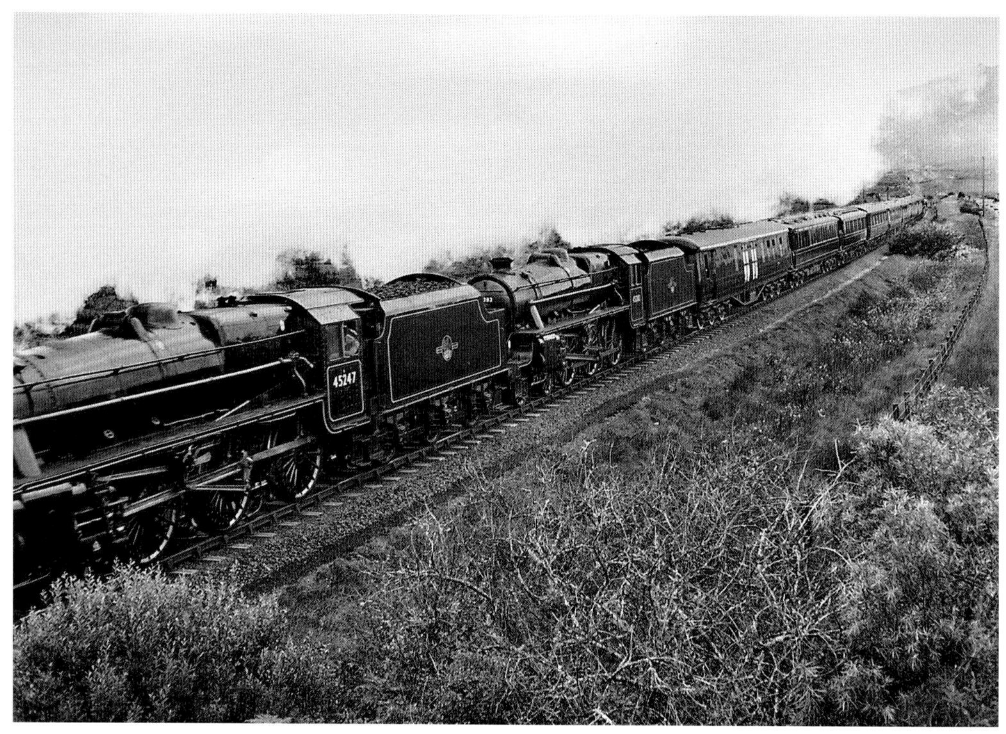

The Royal Train (including twelve-wheeled coaches) is seen just south of Brynkir in August 1963; 'Black 5s' Nos 45247 and 45282 are polished to perfection.

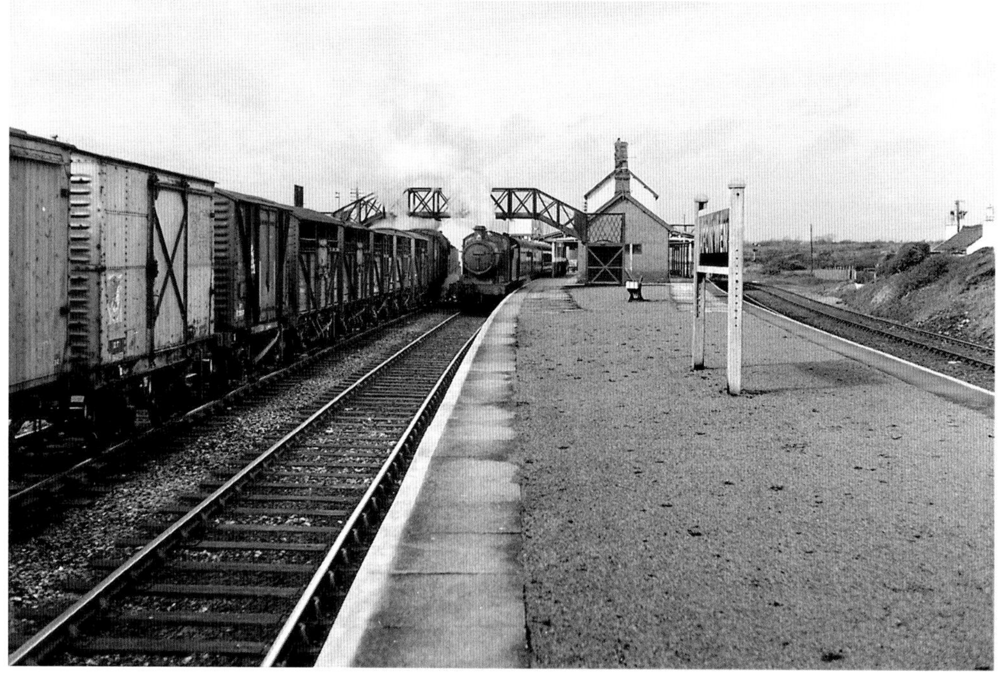

Nos 2287 and 82009 pass at Afon Wen on 7 April 1961.

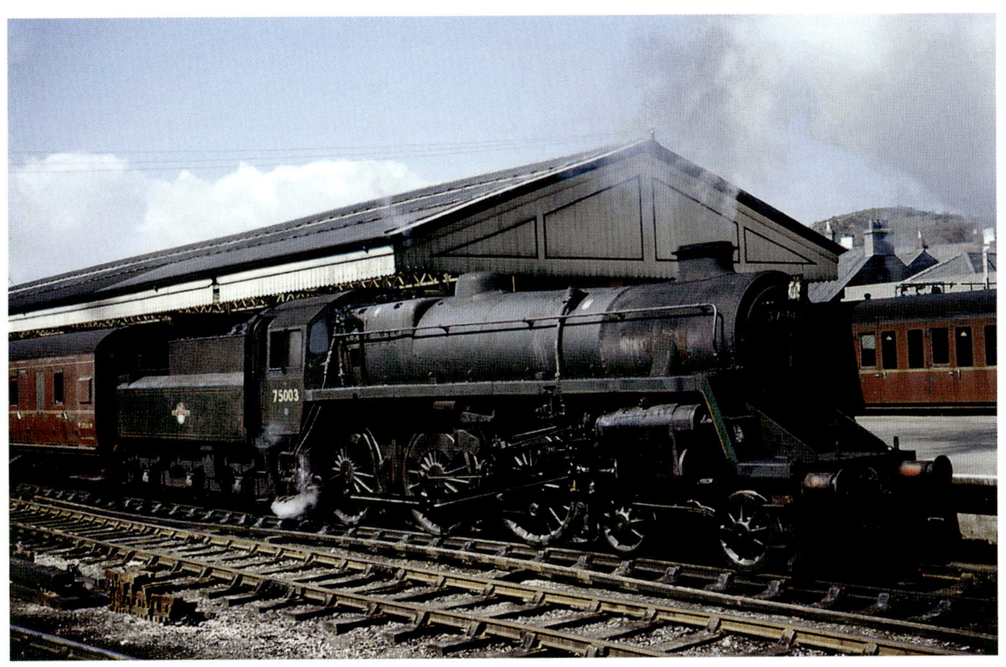

No. 75003 prepares to depart from Pwllheli during the summer of 1963.

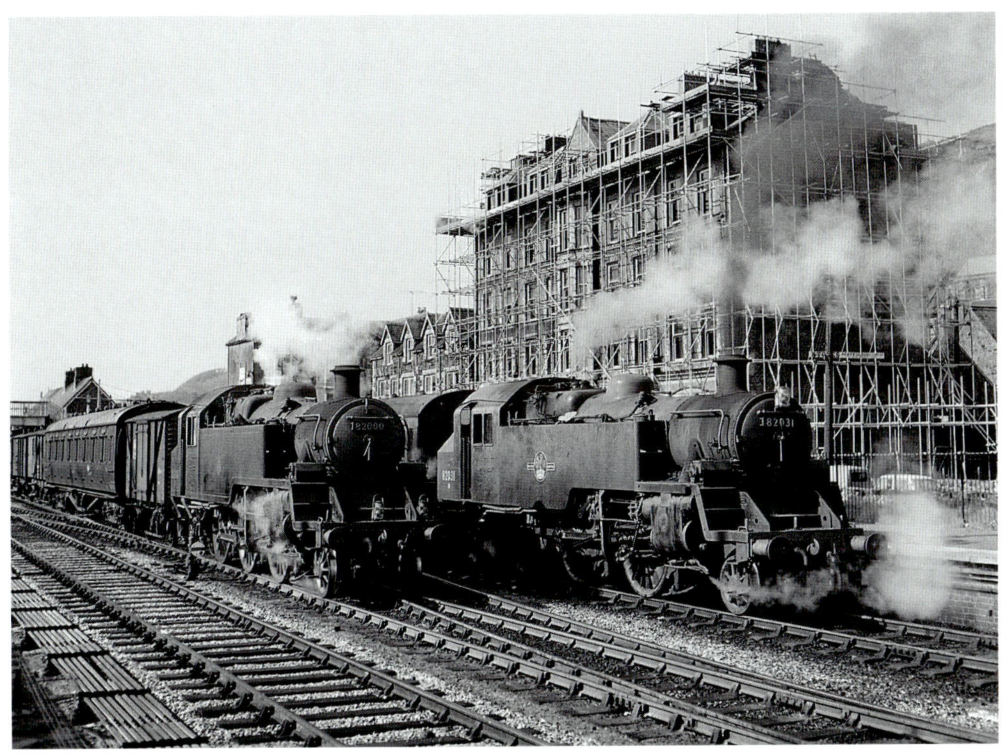

Seeing double; BR Standard Class 3 2-6-2Ts Nos 82000 and 82031 at Barmouth on Friday, 26 April 1963.

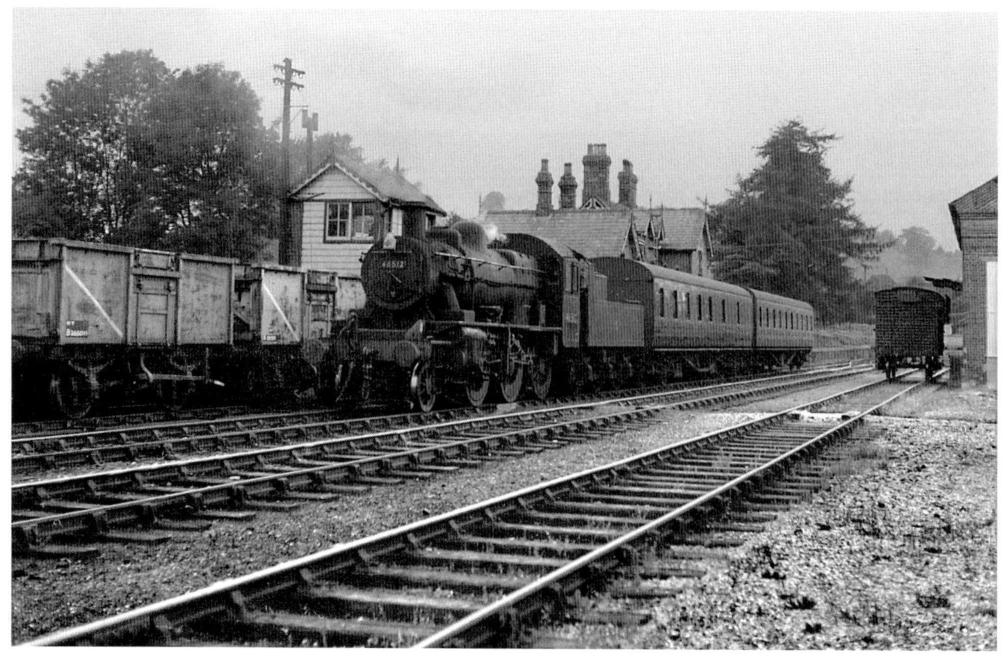

Llanfyllin station during the late summer of 1963 as Oswestry-bound No. 46512 waits for custom.

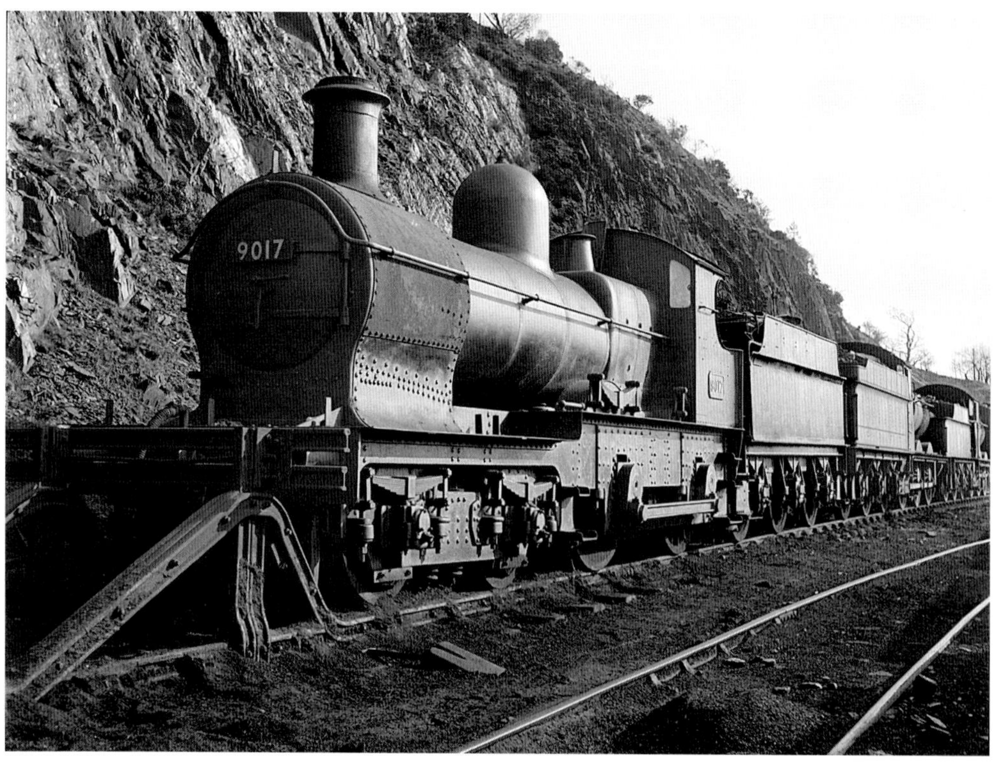

It is April 1960 and No. 9017 *Dukedog* is in store at Machynlleth.

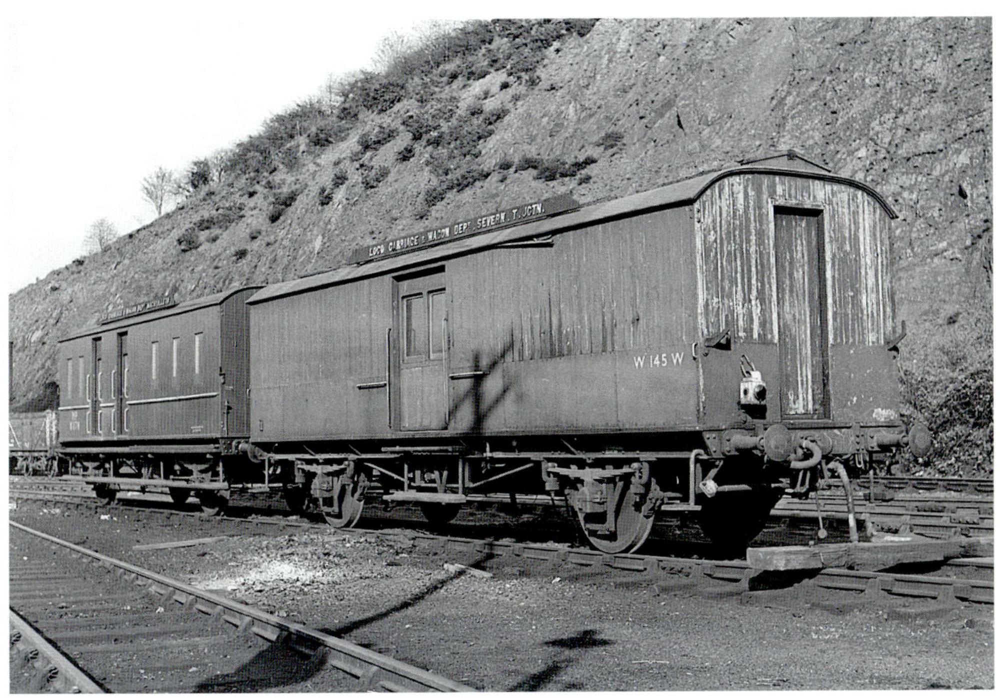

Engineering Department vehicles at Machynlleth shed during April 1960.

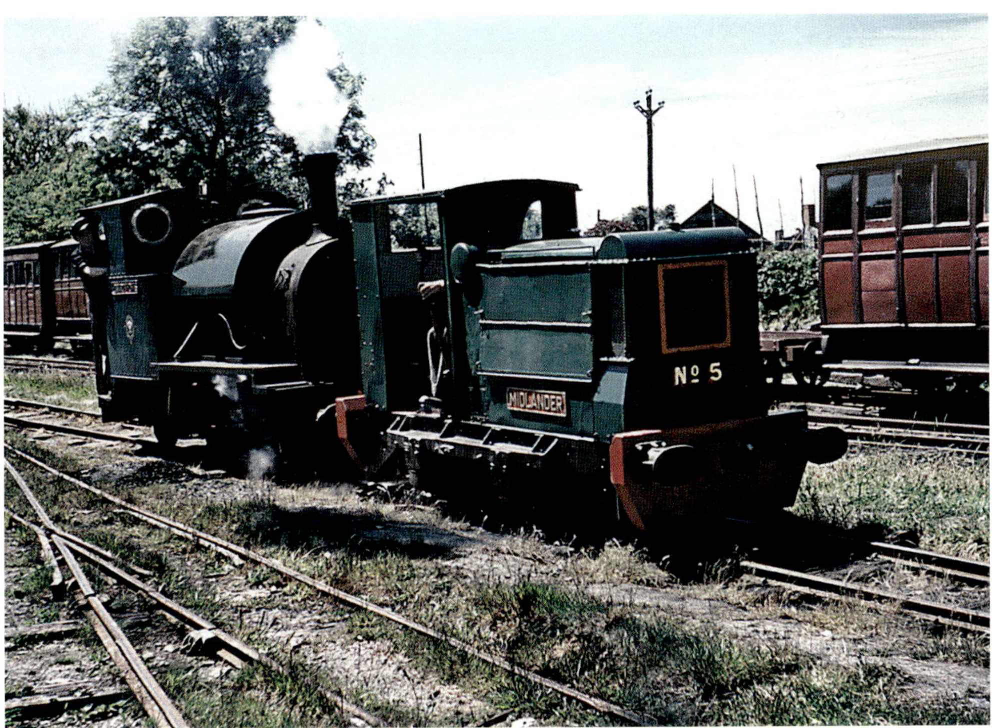

No. 4 *Edward Thomas* and No. 5 *Midlander* are at Towyn Pendre on the Talyllyn Railway in the late 1950s.

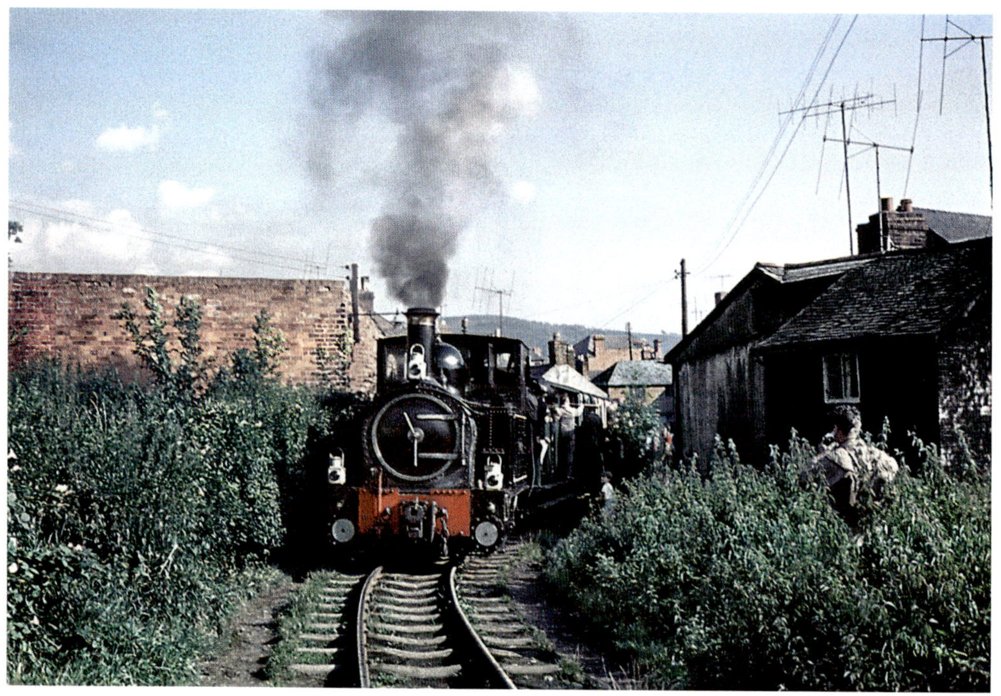

Believed taken on 17 August 1963, the last day services officially worked along the town section of the Welshpool & Llanfair Light Railway; this is No. 823 *The Countess*.

Close to Llandudno Junction, a 'Super D' 0-8-0 is likely bound for Holyhead with a train of cattle wagons. Then, on our way to Caernarvon, the already closed Port Dinorwic station is seen with a 'Jinty' on the link to the quay here. Along the Llanberis branch, we pass close to the one-time terminus at Morfa, Caernarvon; other photographs along this line include Cwm-y-Glo, a local freight train just before closure, 'The Snowdonian' crossing over an arm of Llyn Padarn, and then Llanberis itself.

Following on from two of Ellis's early colour photographs at the top of Snowdon, we visit Penygroes, the Nantlle Tramway, Brynkir, and Llangybi, before an extended exploration of the rather isolated junction station at Afon Wen. Penychain was the station for Butlin's Holiday Camp and boasted bidirectional running, before a series of photographs at Pwllheli. Then we move along the coast via Criccieth, the site of Wern Siding (including the down 'Cambrian Coast Express'), to Portmadoc (Porthmadog since 1974). The early days of the preserved Festiniog Railway at Boston Lodge are relived in a series of colour slides from 1955. After Harlech comes arrival at Barmouth in 1963; BR Standard Class 3 2-6-2Ts abound, and we can enjoy a picture postcard-type view of Barmouth Viaduct.

Then a move inland via Dolgellau, Bonwm, and Berwyn, to Ruabon where the last passenger train to Blaenau Ffestiniog Central is joined on Sunday, 22 January 1961 in very poor weather. The 1860s-closed Llangollen Road station and nearby 1960-closed Whitehurst Halt are visited between Ruabon and Chirk, then the Tanat Valley route near Porthywaen, plus Llangynog, and again including colour

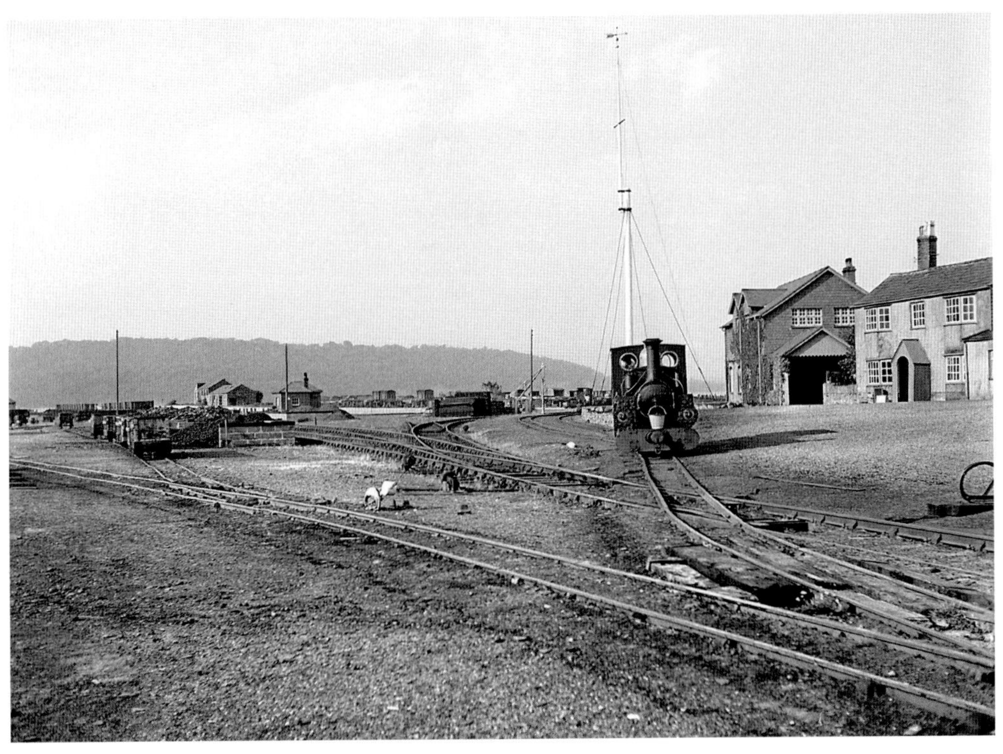

A mixed-gauge crossing is in front of *Blanche* at Port Penrhyn on 1 September 1961.

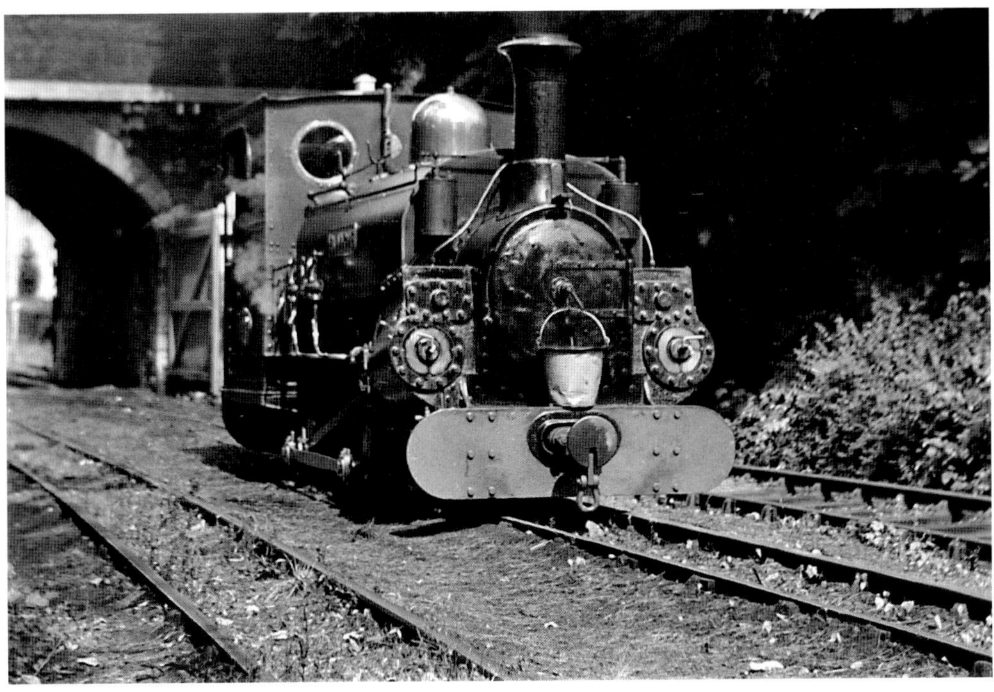

An undated photograph of *Blanche* just to the south of the Regency-style over-bridge at Port Penrhyn.

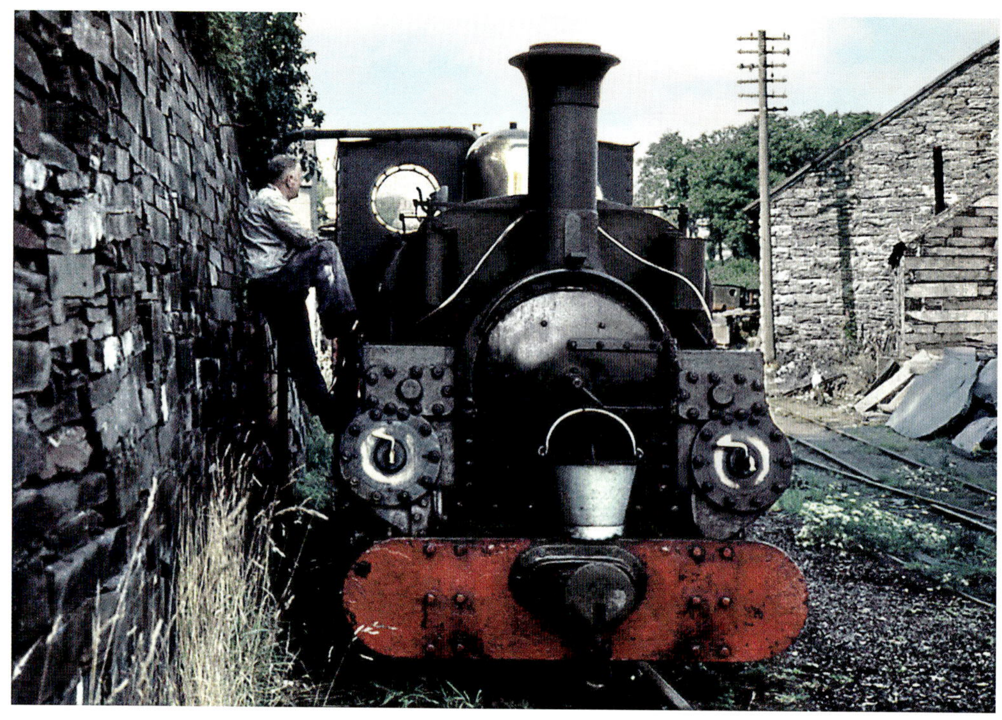

Blanche fills up with water after arrival at Coed-y-Parc on 1 September 1961.

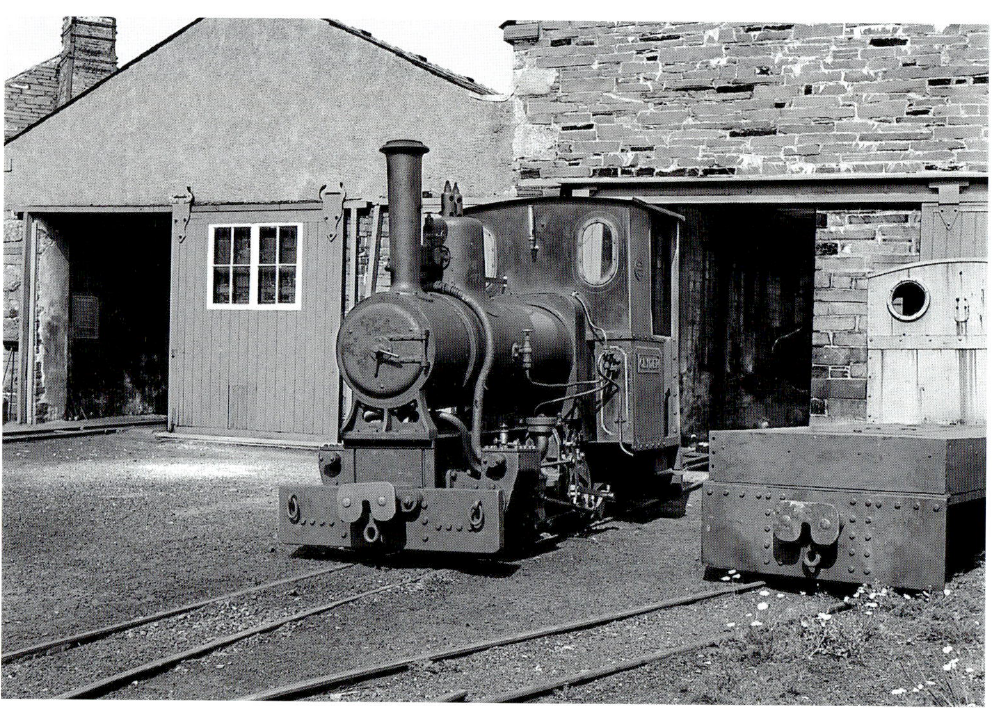

Glyder is seen by the Coed-y-Parc Workshop on 1 September 1961; to its right is a brake van converted in 1956 from the locomotive *Sanford*.

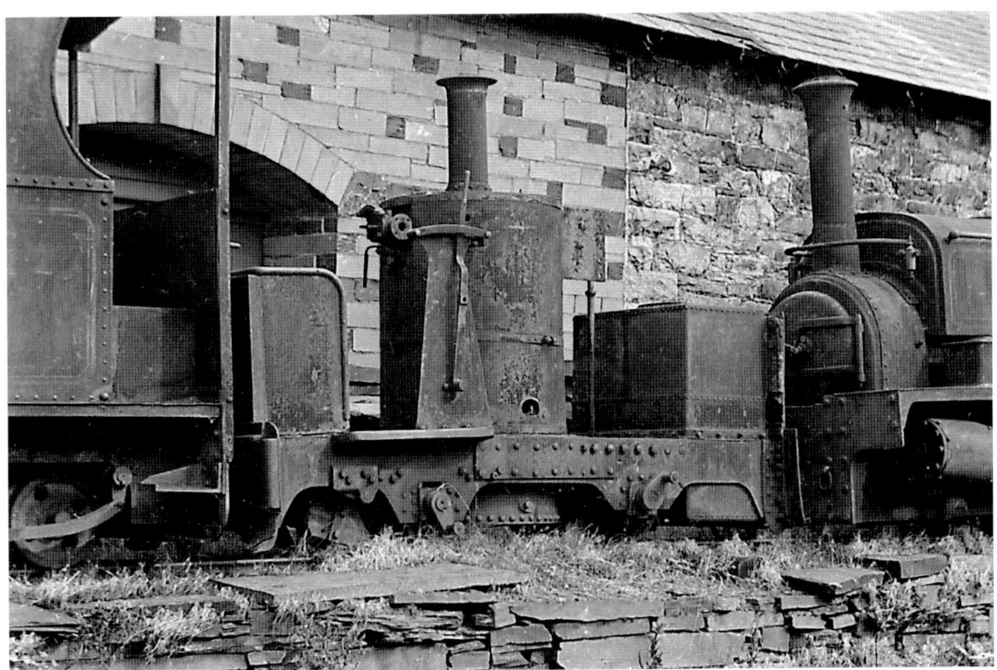

An undated photograph of derelict locomotives at Coed-y-Parc that includes De Winton-built *Kathleen* with its vertical boiler.

from 1955. A quick visit to the Shropshire and Montgomeryshire line follows at Nesscliff & Pentre before moving to Welshpool. The heritage narrow-gauge Welshpool & Llanfair Light Railway had to abandon its town section, and Ellis took a series of photographs here on the last day that services officially worked over this part in August 1963. A visit is made to Machynlleth engine shed during April 1960 and included here in storage is one of the final 'Dukedogs' still in service. The narrow-gauge Vale of Rheidol plus Talyllyn lines are covered and include *Edward Thomas*, both before and after fitting of its Giesl ejector chimney.

Many I am sure will be keen to pore over the photographs of Ellis's visits to the Penrhyn and the Dinorwic slate quarry systems; there are over sixty photographs covering these two networks. *Blanche* was the Penrhyn's main line locomotive at the time, and after studying Port Penrhyn with its mixed-gauge crossing, trips were made in both directions (loaded and unloaded). At Coed-y-Parc, the famous row of stored/derelict locomotives is seen. Coverage of the Dinorwic slate quarry system is even more extensive; gravity-worked inclines, action at the working face including a 'Blondin' aerial wagon transporter, quarry locomotives scurrying about their business, plus shunting by chain or hawser. The Padarn Railway had been famous since early Victorian times for the use of transporter wagons. Four 2-foot quarry-gauge wagons were accommodated on one 4-foot-gauge transporter wagon; these shuttled back and forth between Gilfach Ddu and Pen-Scoins. We follow *Amalthæa* (correctly spelt with a diphthong) making this journey in the late summer of 1961, but not for much longer as the line would be closed within a couple of months.

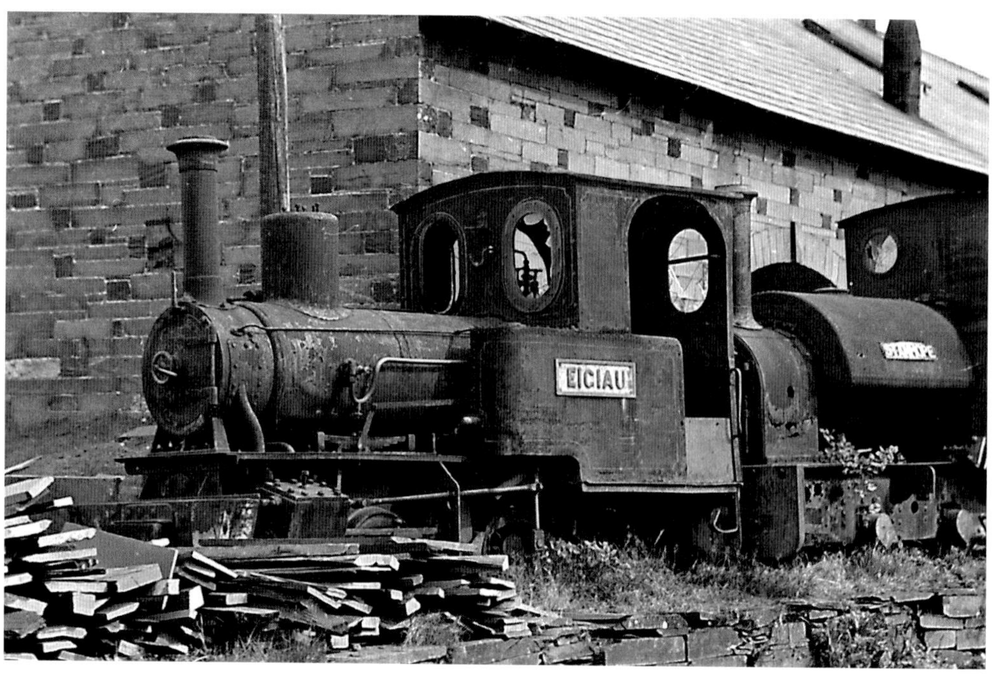

Another undated photograph shows *Eigiau* and *Stanhope* stand together in Coed-y-Parc's row of derelict locomotives.

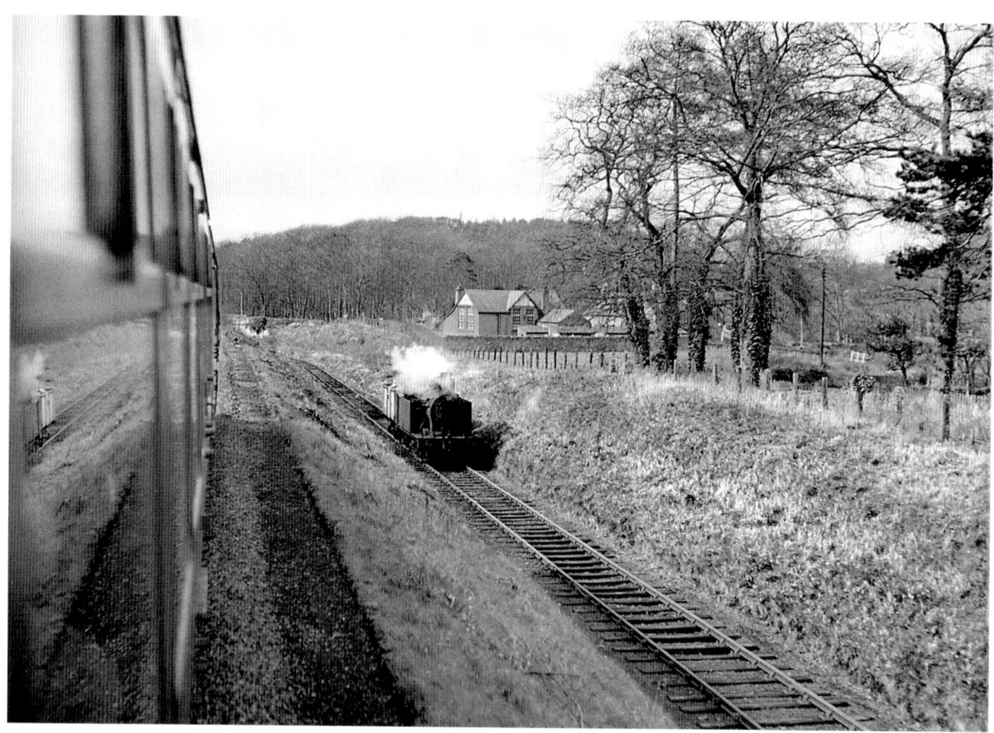

In April 1961, a 'Jinty' is on the connection to Port Dinorwic Quay from the Caernarvon to Bangor line.

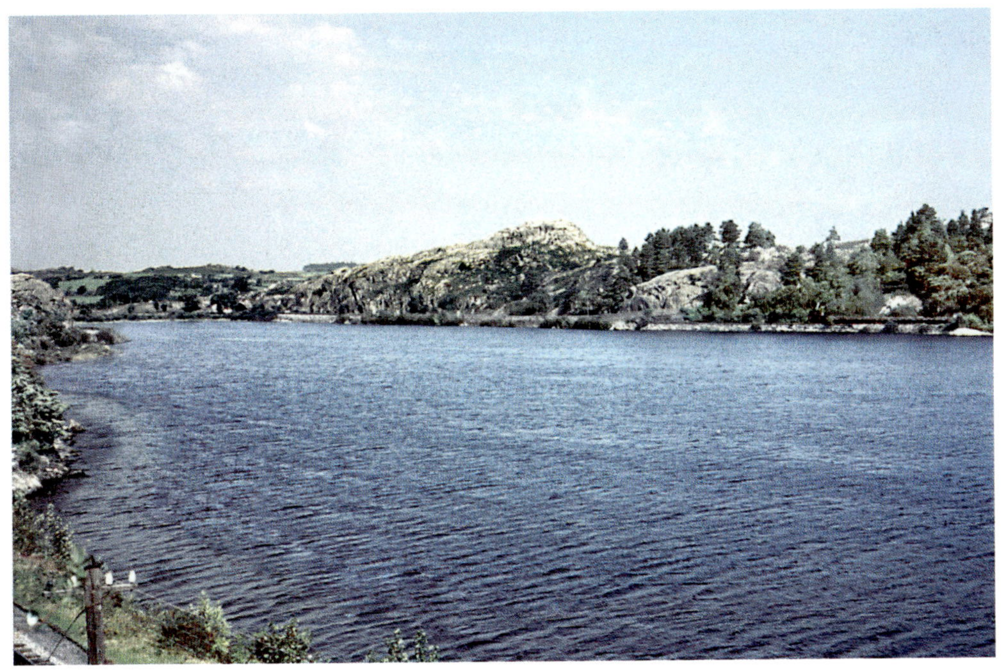

A view across Llyn Padarn in the late summer of 1961; a Padarn Railway slate train is just visible on the far side and the LNWR Llanberis branch on this side.

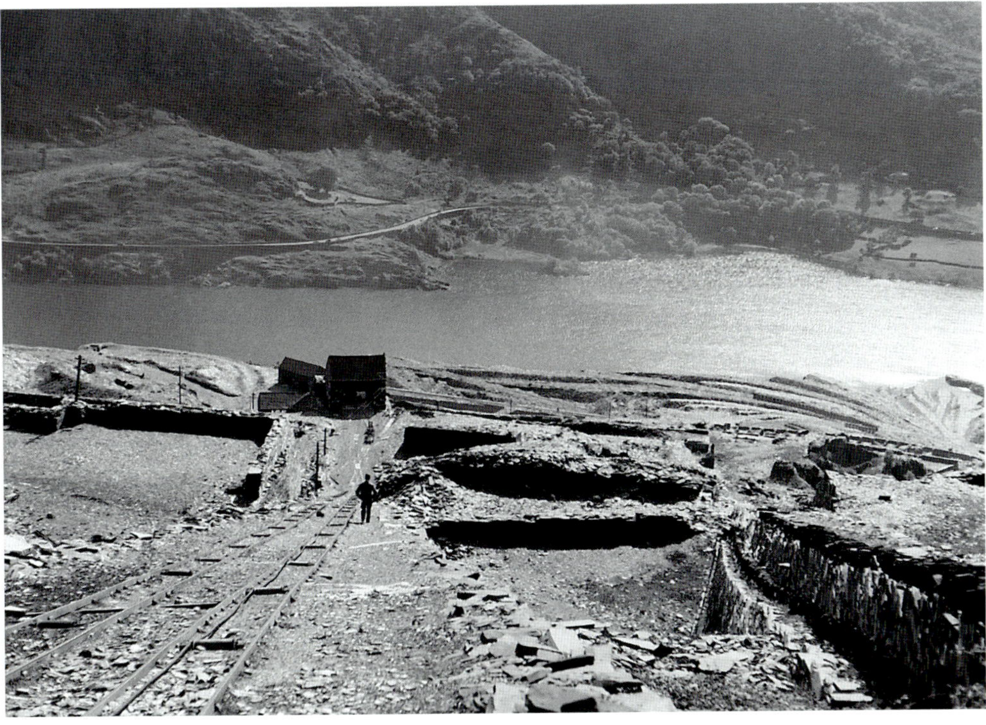

Looking down one of the inclines at the Dinorwic system with Llyn Peris in the background, believed to have been taken on 30 August 1961.

Sadly, one entire reel of colour film that Ellis took at the slate quarries has not been able to be used as all the photographs are out of focus, and he has written across their wrapper 'Duff Lot'. I am something of an armchair astronomer and recalled that the out-of-focus images originally taken by the Hubble Space Telescope before its repair were improved by a technique called deconvolution. A free trial computer programme was downloaded to see if the images could be improved, but the technicalities involved proved beyond my capability.

In the era of these photographs, I was largely ignorant of Welsh pronunciations and spellings. It was many decades before I was instructed in pronunciation by my friend and author of books on the railways of Wales, Gwyn Briwnant-Jones. Thanks to Gwyn, for instance, I no longer pronounce the station name for Butlin's Holiday Camp near Pwllheli as 'Penny-chain' (Penychain), and while my speech is much better now (but still learning), it leaves the problem of Welsh spellings. This is a most difficult area, with both the railway companies and the places concerned using different spellings over the years. A famous example that will appear in this book is Dolgellau (the name adopted by the local RDC in 1958), but the railway has also used Dolgelli, Dolgelly, and Dolgelley. I apologise in advance for any mistakes of this nature that may have been made.

Another debt of gratitude I owe to my father is the massive railway-themed library he built up over the years, and to which I have added over recent decades. It is to these tomes that I always refer when researching for the various books I have written. An author into whose works I have delved again and again for this

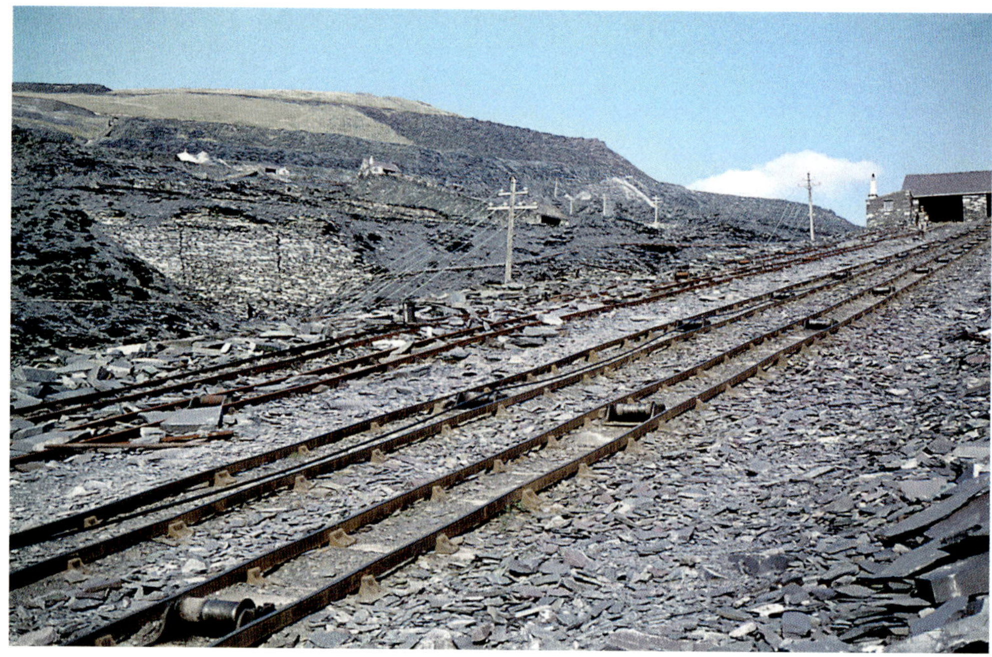

Part of the Dinorwic quarry gravity-worked incline system and thought to date from the late summer of 1961.

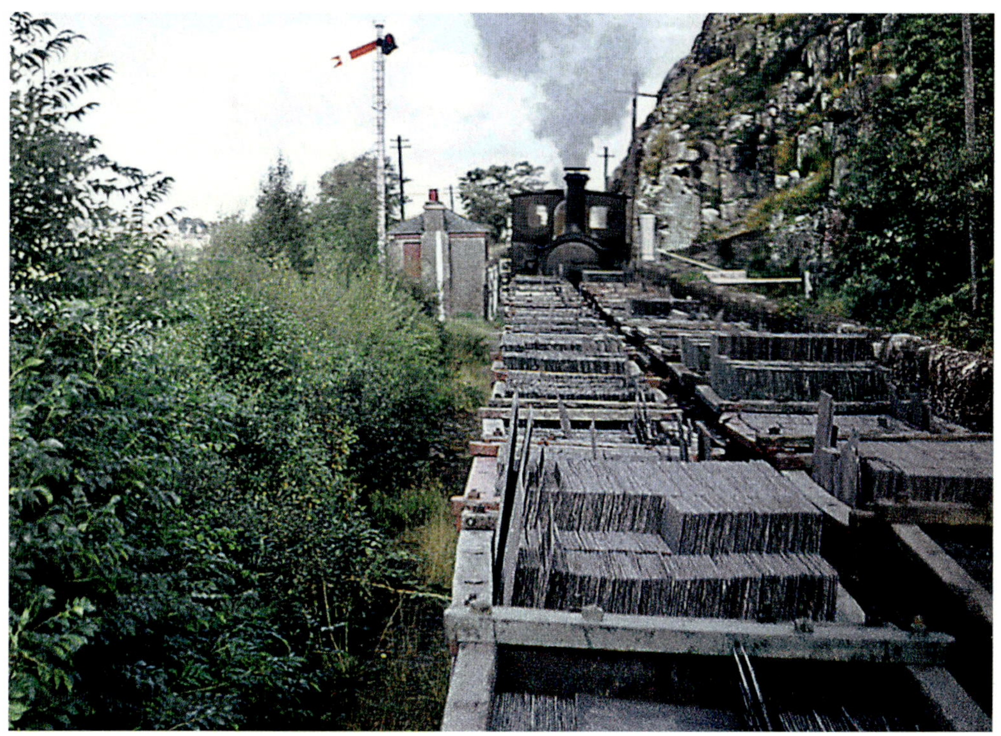

A loaded slate train bound for Pens-Coins hauled by *Amalthæa* is approaching the Pont Pen-y-Llyn level crossing in the late summer of 1961.

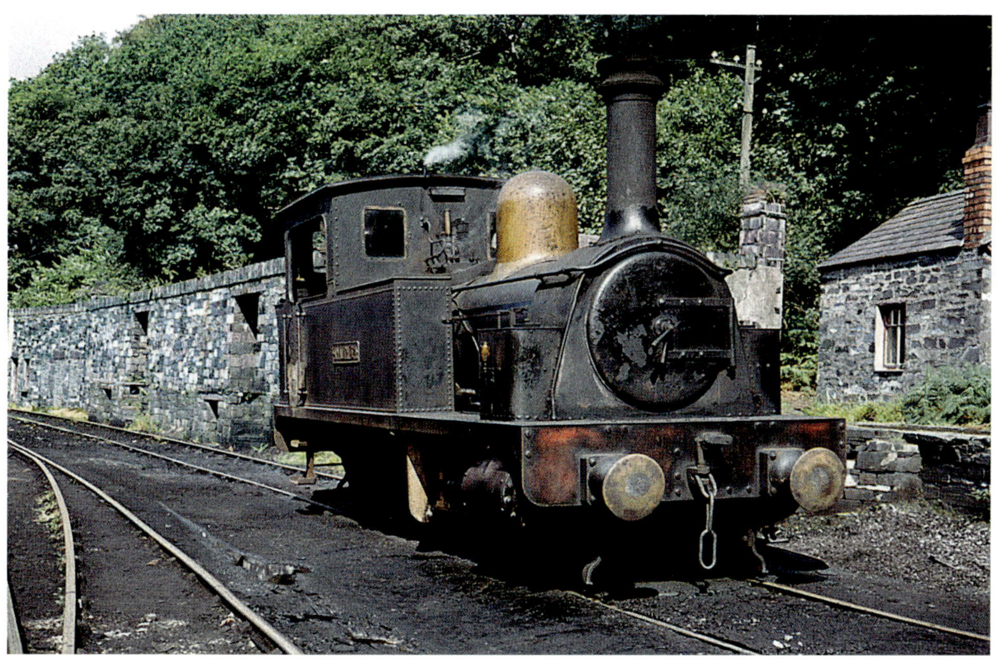

Amalthæa was a 4-foot-gauge locomotive used for hauling slate wagons on transporters to and from Pens-Coins; it is seen at Gilfach-Ddu around the end of August 1961.

book is J. I. C. Boyd, surely the world authority on the slate railways of Wales. J. I. C. and his brother, D. C., lived near Malvern and were both customers of our family company; the connection even continues to this day as our accountant is J. I. C.'s nephew.

The photographs in this book have been used in presentations to various railway societies and individuals who have freely given me their help with things such as dates and locations. I would like to thank in no particular order: Malvern Narrow Gauge Group and their encyclopedic knowledge of the Penrhyn and Dinorwic slate quarry systems, Severn Valley Railway Association (Stourbridge Branch), Chipping Norton Railway Club, Philip Traynor of the Welshpool & Llanfair Light Railway, and Paul Bartlett for his assistance with identification of wagons near Porthywaen. But for the coronavirus shutdown, these photographs would also have been shown at numerous other railway society film shows around the country.

Michael Clemens
Pershore, Worcestershire
December 2020

THE LAST YEARS OF STEAM

— AROUND —

NORTH WALES

FROM THE PHOTOGRAPHIC ARCHIVE OF ELLIS JAMES-ROBERTSON

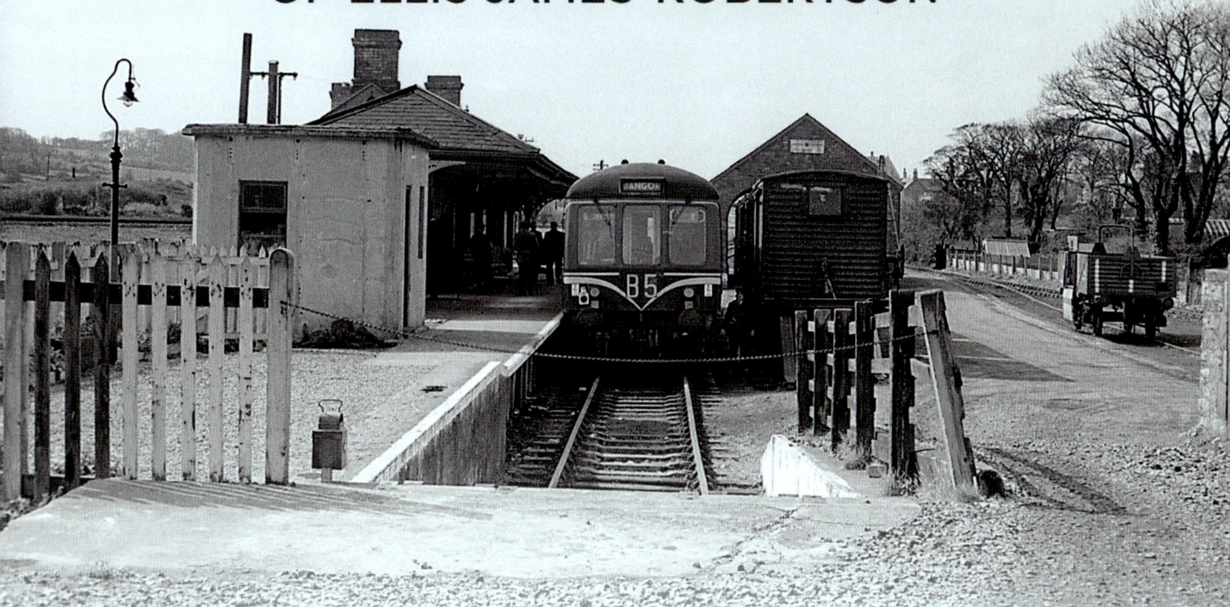

On Friday, 7 April 1961, Ellis made a return trip by rail from Pwllheli via Bangor to here at Amlwch on the Isle of Anglesey. Amlwch is the most northerly town in Wales and a convenient point to begin a circuitous southerly journey through this book to the border with Central Wales, but with the exception of the Dinorwic and Penrhyn quarry systems that are dealt with separately in some detail at the end. As was said in the introduction, Ellis often included technical details about his black and white photographs, and this was taken at 100/11, on FP3 film, with Promicrol as the developer. The two-car DMU—consisting of a power car (M50981) and trailer (incorrectly noted as 56281)—is a member of what would later become Class 108. Amlwch station (see also page 4) opened on the line from Gaerwen for goods traffic in the summer of 1866 before any accommodation had been built. The station and goods warehouse were completed twelve months later, and the line was open throughout for all traffic in June 1867.

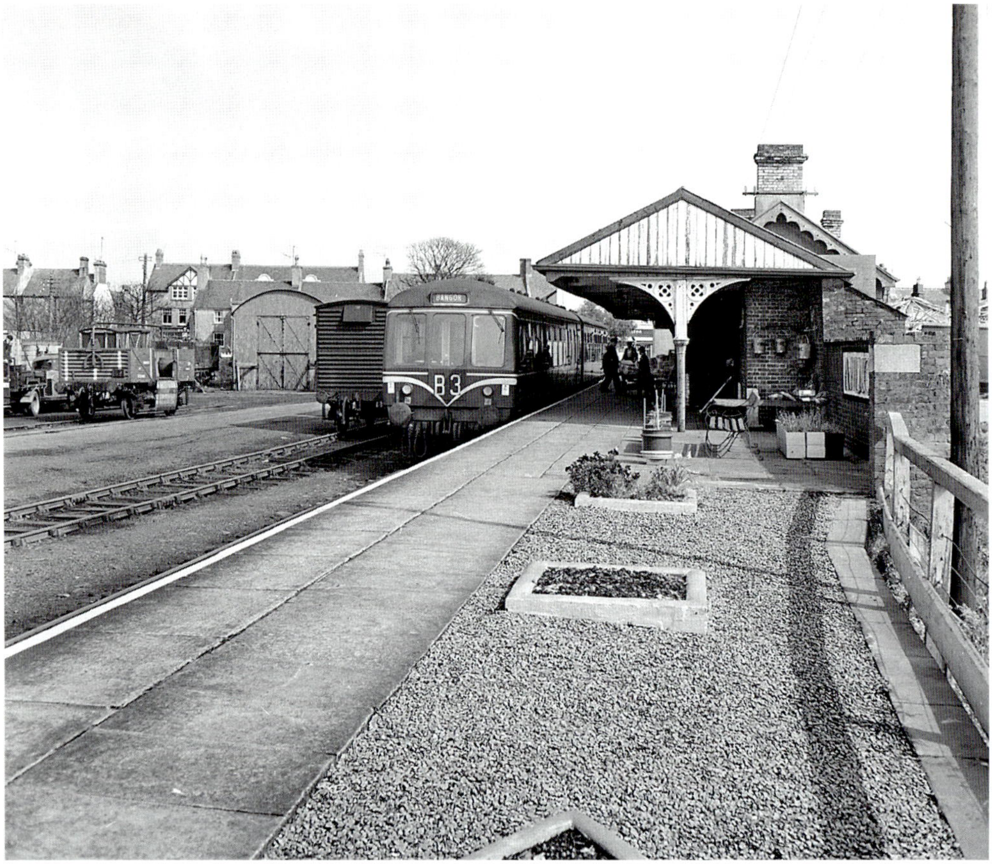

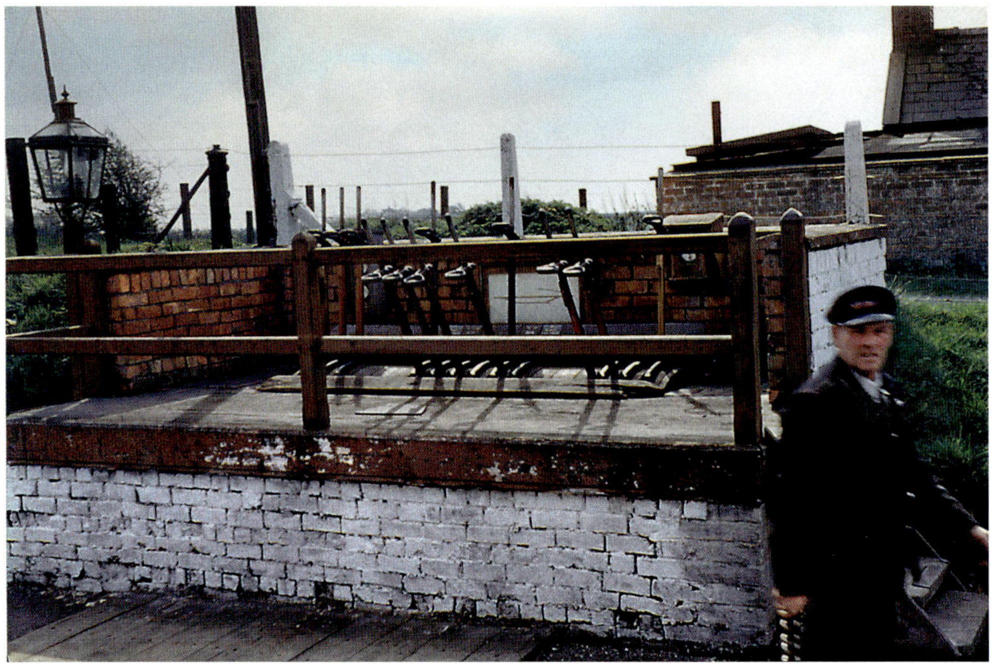

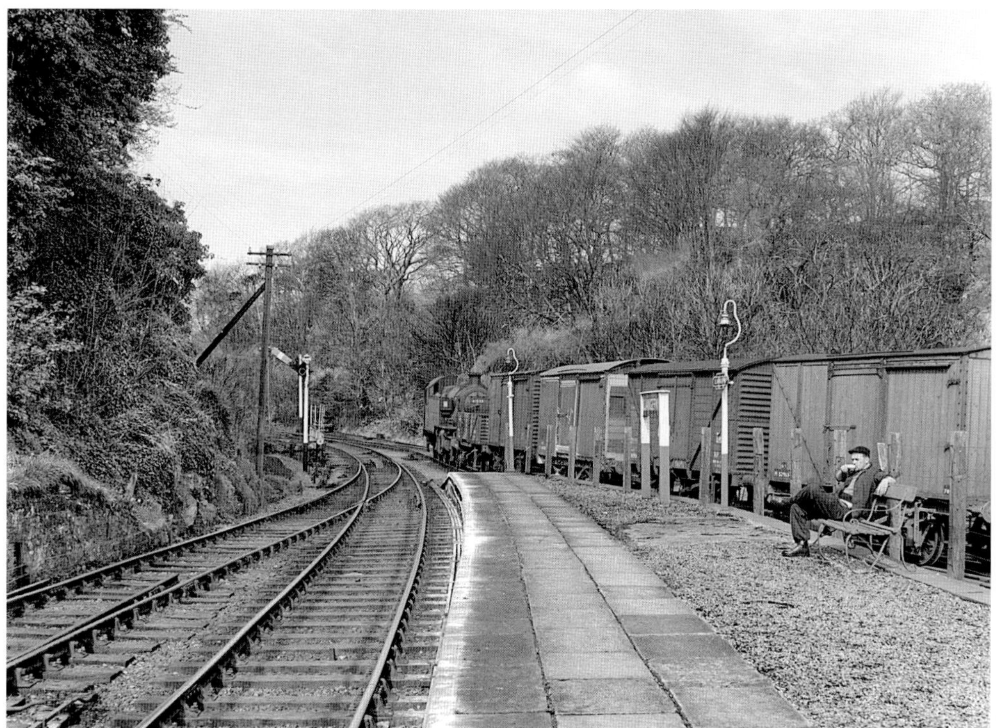

Llangefni, the county town of Anglesey, was served by the one-time Anglesey Central Railway from Gaerwen to Amlwch. This view is looking to the north and dates from 7 April 1961. There was a short loop on the down side opposite the platform (but not used as a passing loop); the goods shed and yard were on the up side with a capacity of fifty-two wagons. The first sod of the ACR was cut here, and the 7 miles from Gaerwen to Llangefni opened for freight at the end of December 1864 to a temporary terminus, with passenger services starting some three months later. The local freight train hauled by Bangor-allocated No. 41233 looks to have been shunted into the sidings out of the way to make way for the DMU Ellis travelled on. While No. 41233 simmers away, a member of the train crew enjoys some refreshment on the station seat.

Opposite above: Amlwch station was a terminus and had just a single platform on the up side, the run-round facilities were outside the station, and the goods yard had a fifty-four-wagon capacity. The date is again 7 April 1961. The branch passenger service had been dieselised in May 1956, and departure back to Bangor will be at 2.05 p.m. Despite the early introduction of DMUs, a 1959 survey showed the line was not paying for itself. The inevitable happened, and the passenger service was withdrawn, with the last trains running on Saturday, 5 December 1964. Although the local goods service ceased, freight to the Associated Ethyl Company works continued until 1993; this was accessed over a short private railway through the town.

Opposite below: The original intention in the late 1850s was to build a line from Gaerwen on the Chester & Holyhead Railway to Amlwch via Llangefni and then continue on through Cemaes and Llanrhyddlad to Valley, where it would rejoin the C&HR. Yet thoughts of an extension were abandoned, and the Act for the Anglesey Central Railway between Gaerwen and Amlwch was passed in 1863. The 18.75-mile-long branch was built as single track throughout; there were no intermediate passing loops. This photograph at Llangwyllog is another taken on 7 April 1961 and shows the station's open-to-the-elements 'signal box' that controlled the passing loop installed here around the beginning of the First World War.

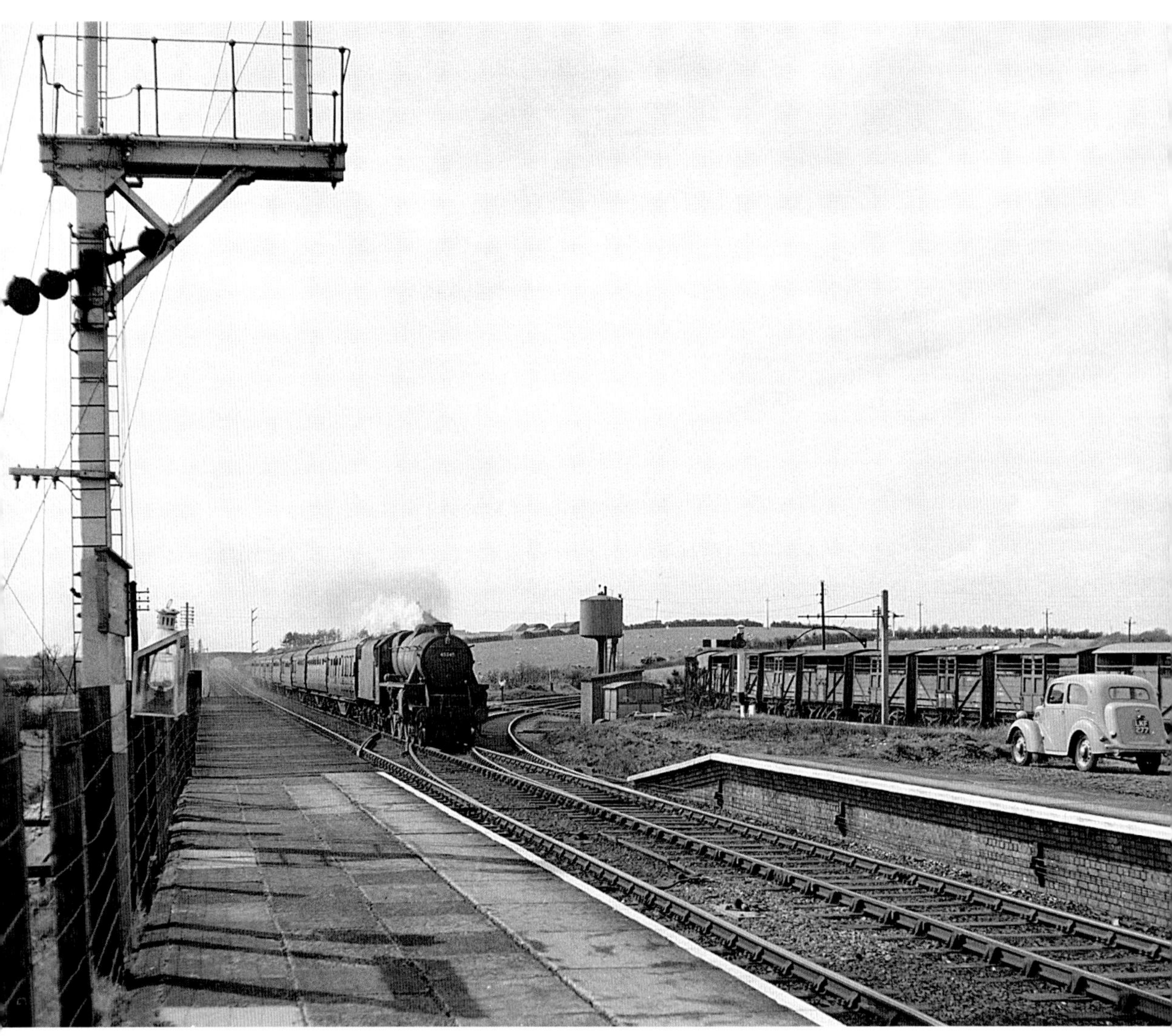

Above and opposite page: Both of these photographs were taken at Gaerwen on 7 April 1961, the first shows the view to the south-west with 'Black 5' No. 45345 approaching over the main line hauling the 12.22 p.m. from Holyhead to Llandudno Junction. The Amlwch branch curves away to the right, there are a string of cattle wagons in the station yard and a Ford Popular (LKF 277) on the up platform. Ellis travelled on the DMU in the second photograph from Bangor, which is awaiting departure for the onward journey to Amlwch. Although the Amlwch branch closed to passengers in December 1964, main line services continued to call at Gaerwen until February 1966.

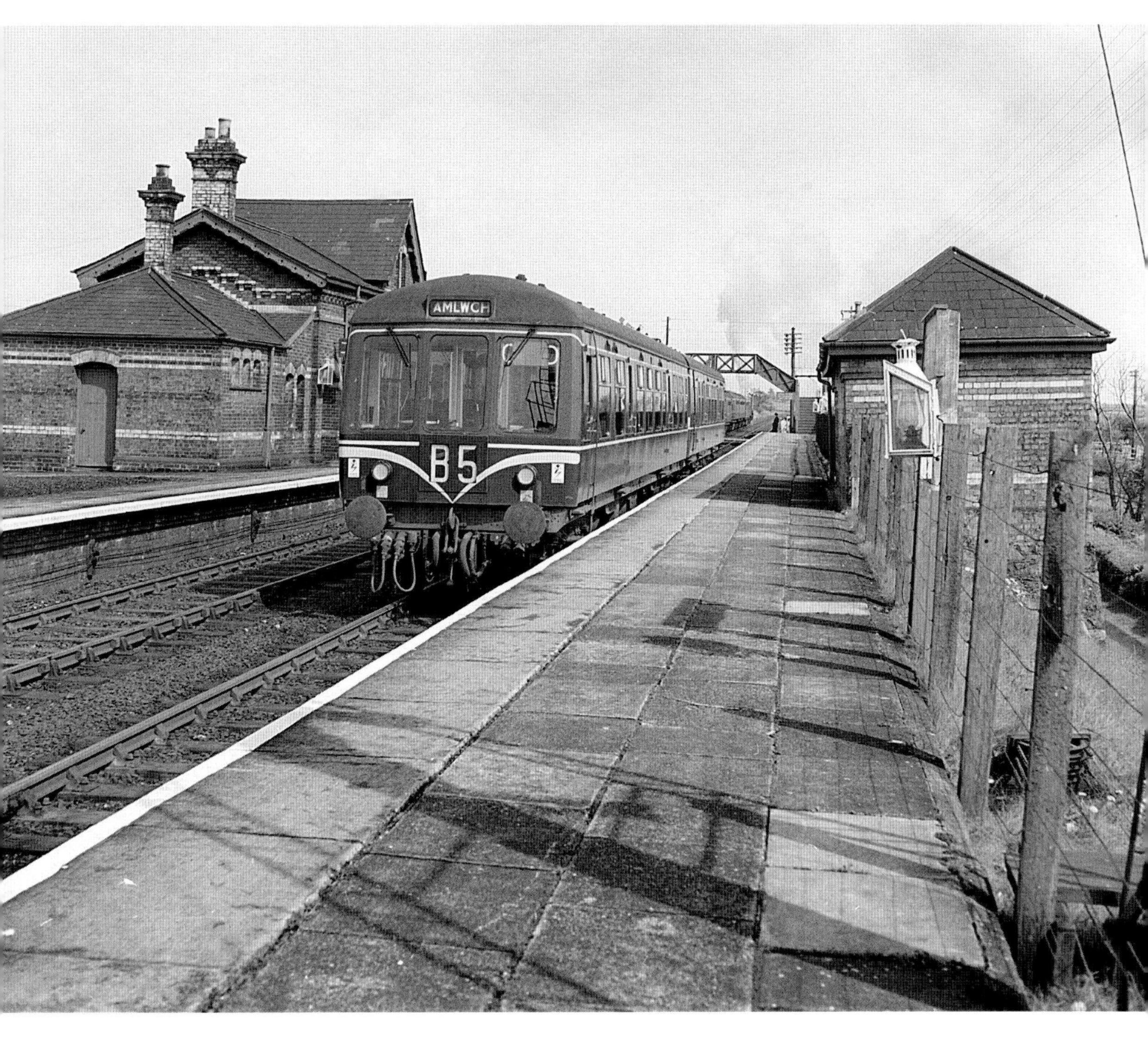

AMLWCH
B5

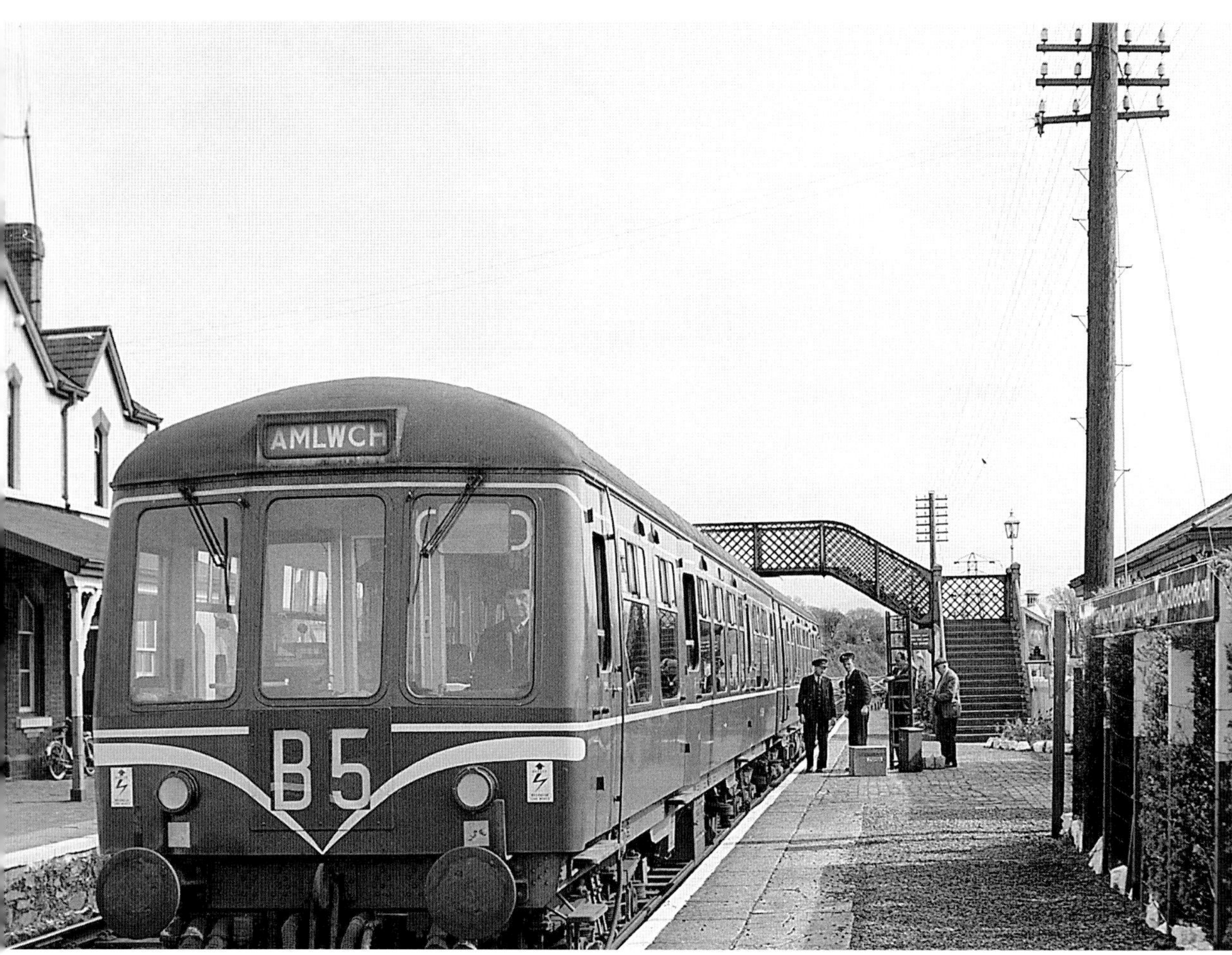

Above and opposite page: The DMU in the initial photograph has stopped for business at the first station in Anglesey. It has just passed over the Britannia Tubular Bridge across the Menai Strait on its 7 April 1961 journey from Bangor to Amlwch. Although the bridge did not open until 1850, a temporary service was run across Anglesey from Holyhead to here from 1848. This station was called Llanfair from 1848 until closure in 1966, but it reopened from 1970 until 1972 following the Britannia Bridge fire so that passengers could use the still-open Holyhead section; during this time, it was called Llanfair PG. It was reopened again in 1973 as Llanfairpwll, permanently this time, and after looking rather run-down for some years, it is now part of a huge visitor centre, fulfilling the aspirations of its Victorian visionaries.

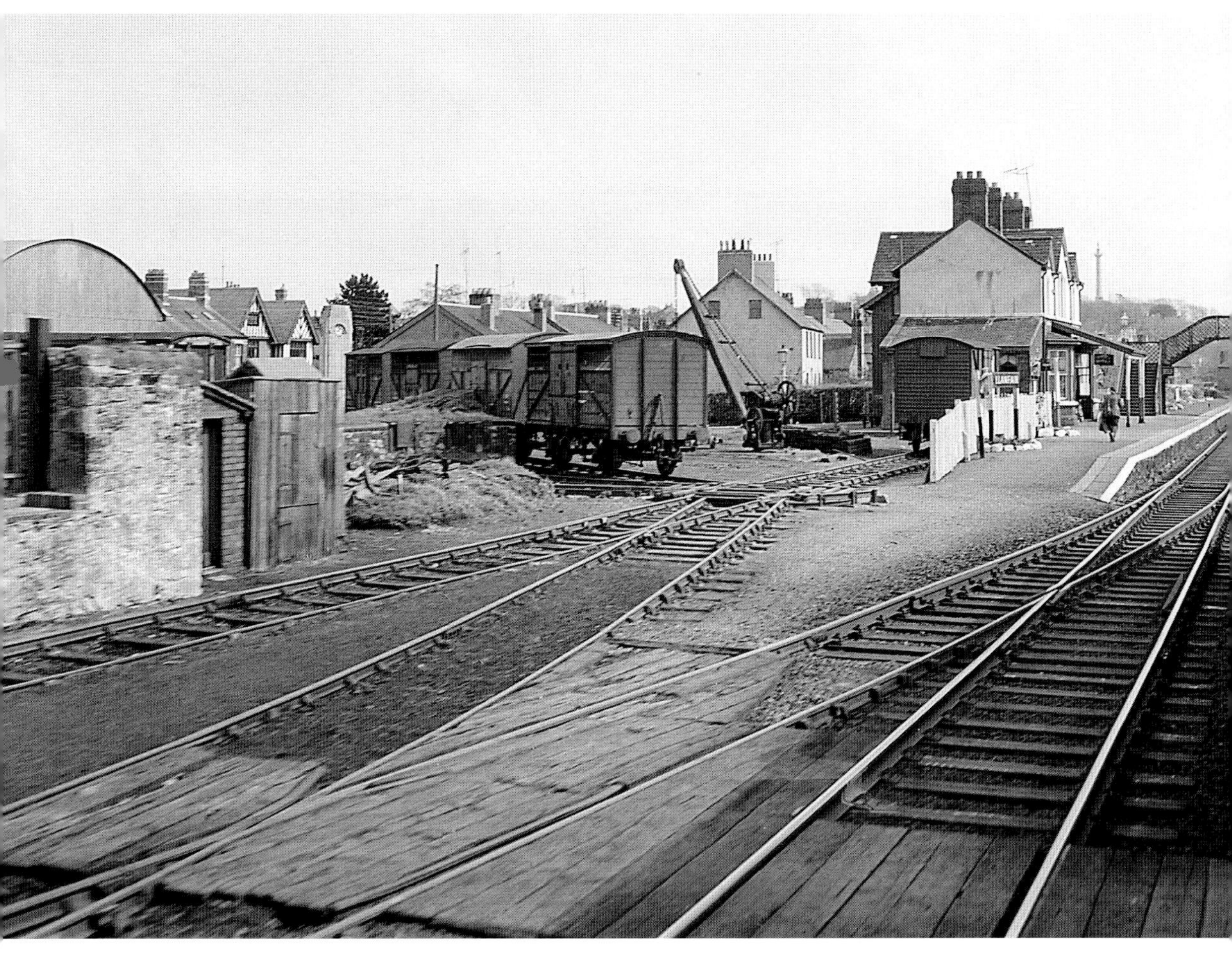

On the right of the first photograph is the famous name this station is often known as—Llanfairpwllgwyngyllgogerychwyrndrobwllllantysiliogogogoch. This lengthy name is officially recognised as the longest in the UK and one of the longest in the world as it comprises fifty-eight letters. Yet it was artificially contrived by the village council in Victorian times for commercial gain and as a tourist attraction. The 20-foot-long enamel station sign dated from 1956 and replaced a rustic one (made by a station porter from tree branches), which, at 78 feet, was claimed to be the longest in the world. The January 1966 edition of *Railway Magazine* stated BR had sold 356,000 souvenir platform tickets at 3*d* each in the previous three years here; these 6-inch tickets were longer than standard to accommodate the fifty-eight letters. The second photograph taken on the same day shows the up platform and goods yard at Llanfair; of particular interest is the wagon turntable.

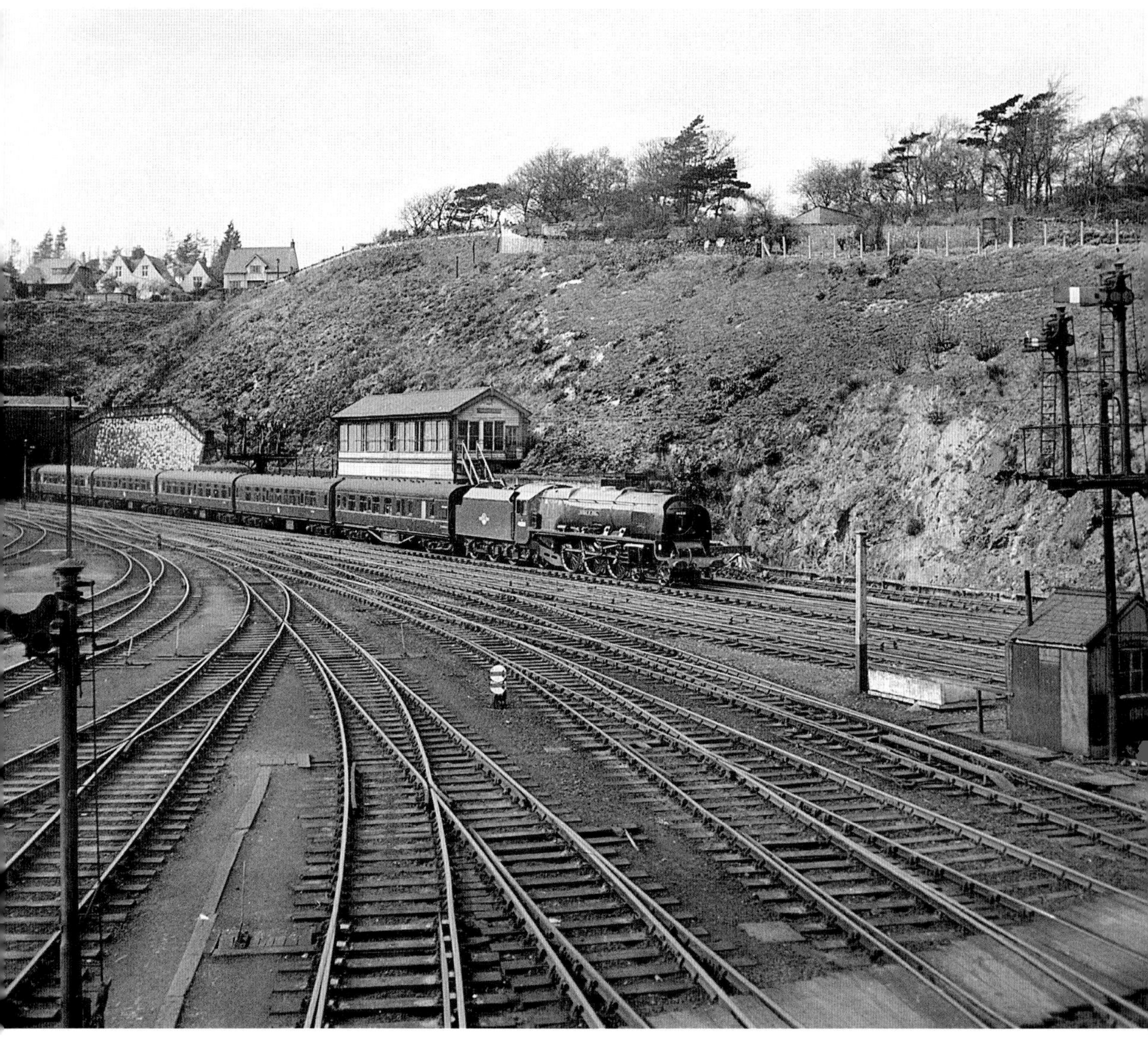

The view from the footbridge connecting Bangor station to the goods yard and engine shed approaches. Ellis took this following his return from Amlwch on 7 April 1961 and it shows 46231 *Duchess of Atholl* approaching with, what is believed to be, the 2.50 p.m. up working from Holyhead. The 648-yard-long Belmont tunnel is at the west end of the station, and the visible signal box is Bangor No. 2. Earlier that day, another photograph was taken here of this same locomotive on its down working to Holyhead (see page 29).

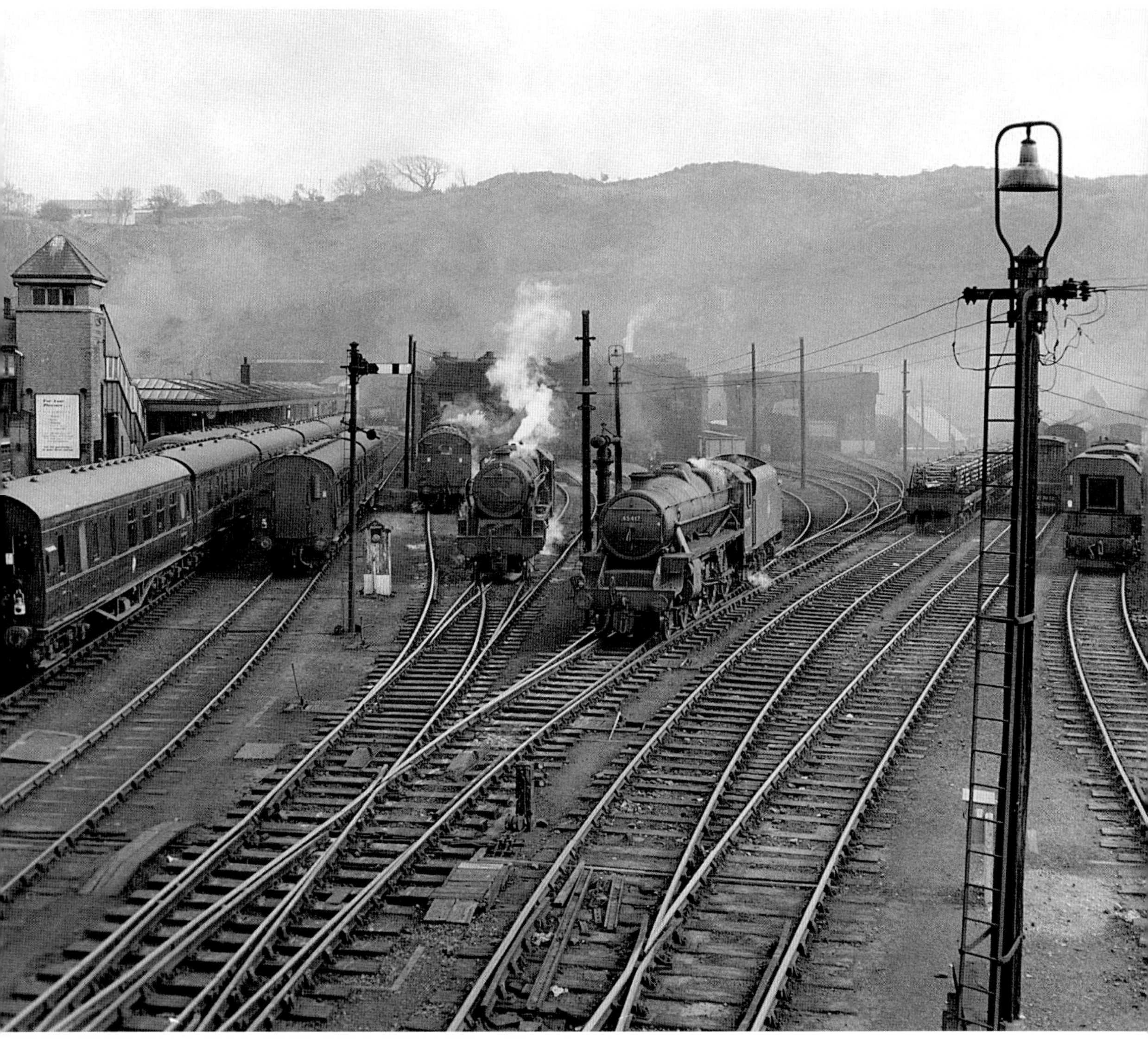

Now the view in the opposite direction from the same bridge on the same day as the previous photograph, this shows Bangor engine shed plus part of the station to its left. Prominent is Bangor-allocated 'Black 5' No. 45417, and the 'Royal Scot' by its side is No. 46149. The one-time locomotive shedmaster at Bangor, John Maxwell Dunn, was also a fellow enthusiast and appeared in the railway press from time to time. He took on the role at Bangor in 1944, transforming a depot with a poor reputation. The September 1951 Stephenson Locomotive Society (SLS) house magazine recalls how he met enthusiasts (with official permission for a visit): 'I will be at the foot of the overbridge on the down platform wearing a fawn raincoat, tweed cap, and carrying a walking stick'. In the author's experience, a welcome like this was rare indeed. In May 1957, when the SLS 'Caernarvonshire' rail tour was at Bangor, he organised a shed visit, a collection of photographs and relics, plus the tour's informative itinerary and historical notes. Apparently, Mrs Dunn said she did not know whether she had married Max or the railway. An appreciation appeared in the May 1969 SLS house magazine following his death. Bangor engine shed closed in June 1965.

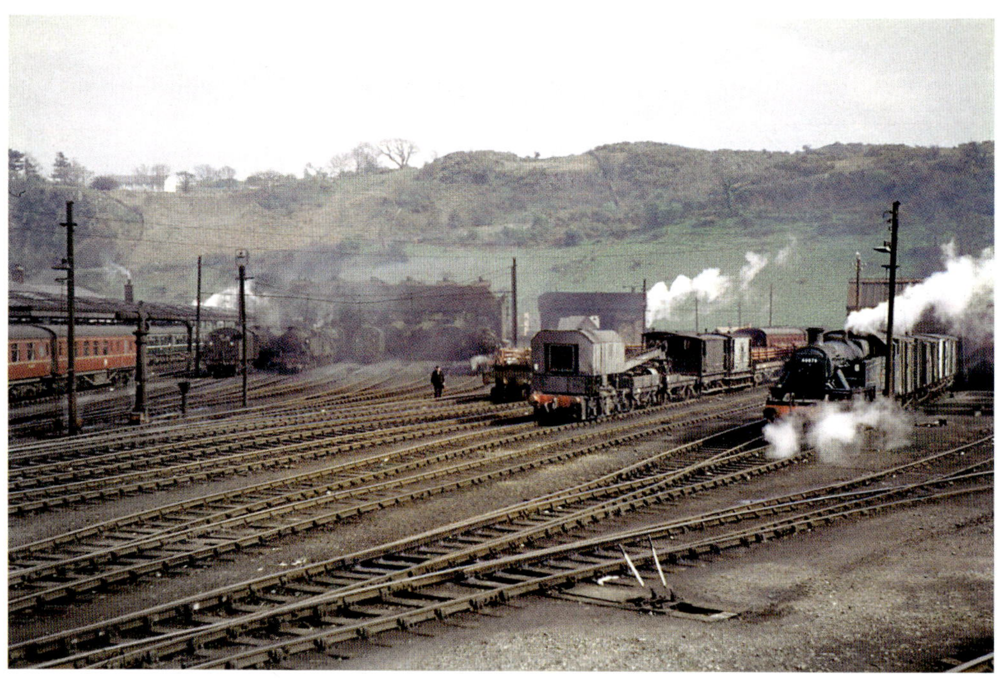

Above and below: A further two views at Bangor taken on 7 April 1961. The engine shed is to the left of the first photograph and the locomotive on the far right is Stanier Class 3 2-6-2T No. 40078. This class used the smallest of Stanier's boilers but were poor performers, unlike the equivalent GWR design (the 45xx 2-6-2Ts) that revolutionised branch line working in the West Country. The second photograph shows 'Rebuilt Royal Scot' No. 46149 *The Middlesex Regiment*, a class of locomotive with an excellent reputation. Rebuilding had started during the darkest days of the Second World War and transformed a powerful but sometimes rather patchy class into one of the finest express 4-6-0s in the country.

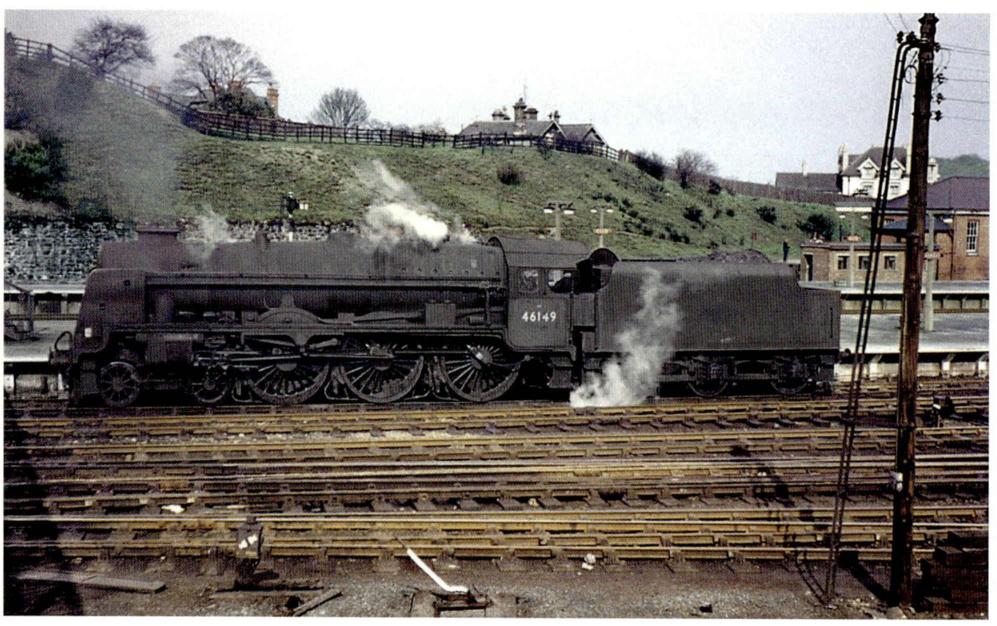

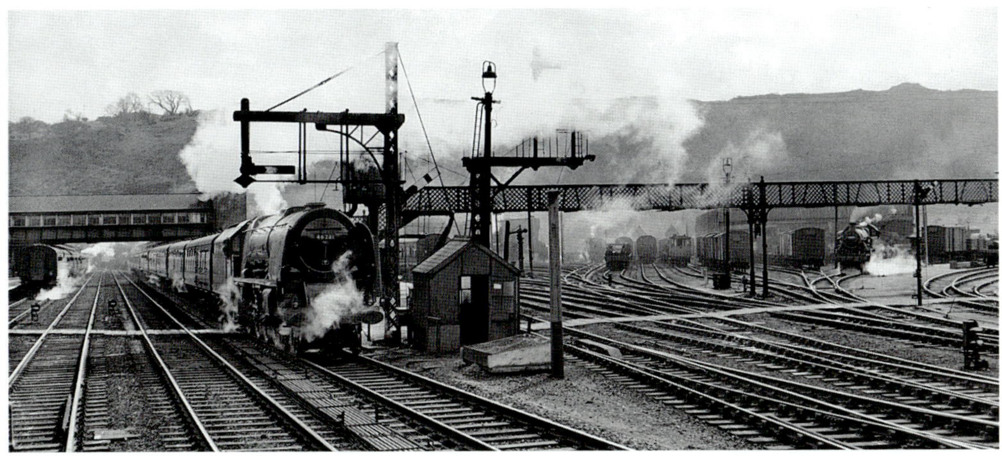

A few pages back, we saw 'Coronation' No. 46231 *Duchess of Atholl* approaching Bangor during the afternoon of 7 April 1961 from the Holyhead direction. This photograph, taken earlier that same day, shows No. 46231 making its way to Holyhead as Ellis arrived from Pwllheli; his train was due here at exactly midday. *Duchess of Atholl* has charge of the 9.20 a.m. from Crewe to Holyhead that was scheduled an extended stop at Bangor from 11.41 a.m. to 12.03 p.m. No. 40078 seen on the previous page can be seen on the right of this photograph. No. 46231 *Duchess of Atholl* is a long way from home (shed code 66A: Polmadie, Glasgow) and heading in the wrong direction. The answer to this conundrum would appear to be that No. 46231 has just received attention at Crewe works and is now 'running in' on a trip to Holyhead and back; it certainly looks very well presented and is in green livery.

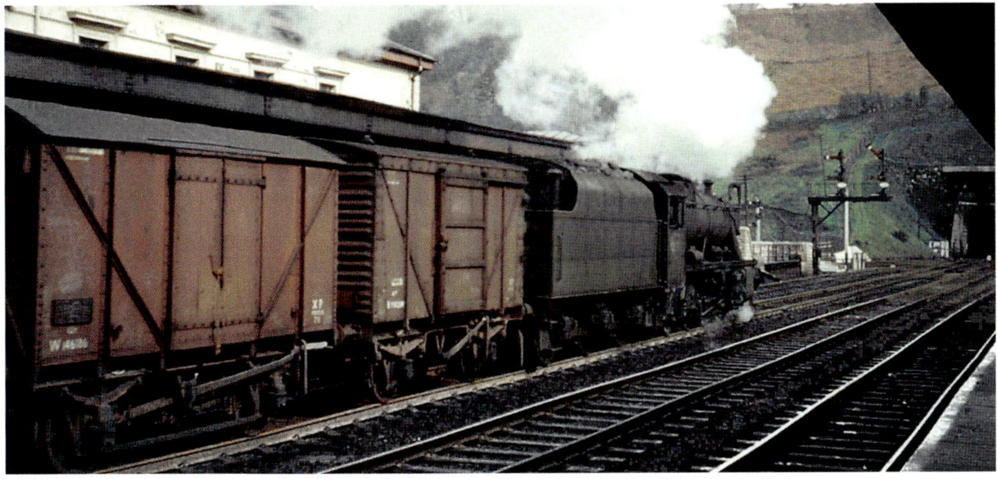

The city of Bangor lies between two prominent hills, and the railway station is located between them; it is a cramped location with tunnels at either end. A few pages earlier, we saw the tunnel at the west end. This view, believed to have been taken on 7 April 1961, shows an unidentified 8F passing through the station. It will soon enter the 890-yard-long Bangor Tunnel at the east end on its way towards Llandudno Junction. Bangor station opened on 1 May 1848 and was, temporarily, the western terminus of the line from Chester. This 8F is passing through on the eastbound fast line, and in total, there were four tracks between the platforms. Not visible is Bangor No. 1 signal box, which was at the east end on the south side; it closed in December 1968 with its functions taken over by Bangor No. 2 seen earlier at the west end.

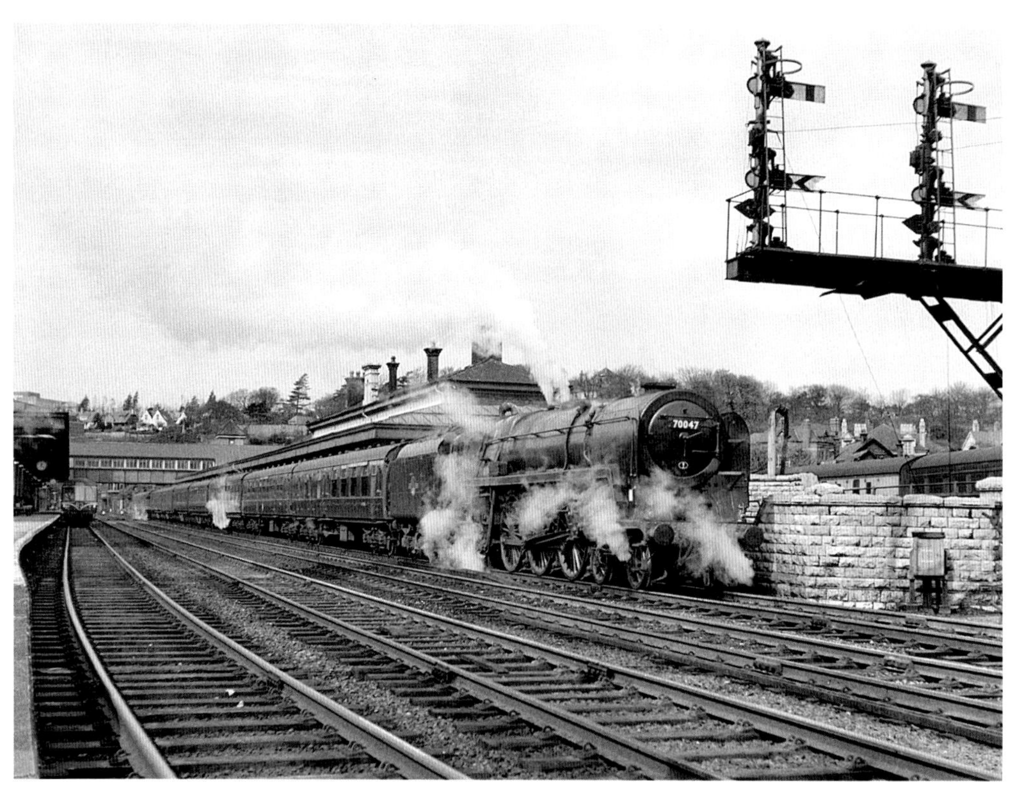

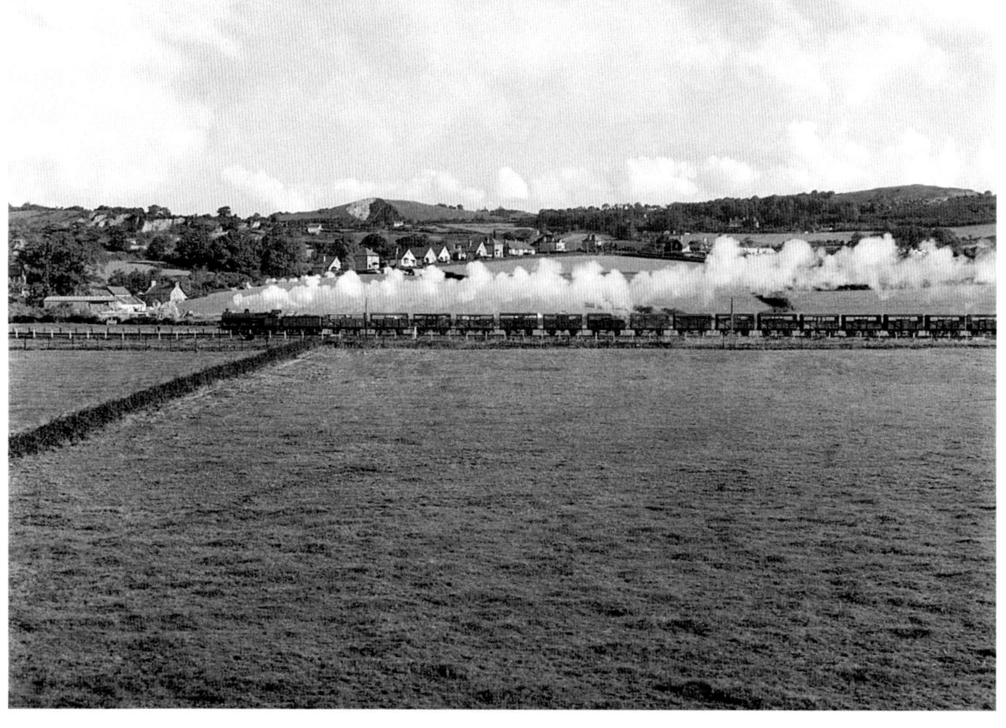

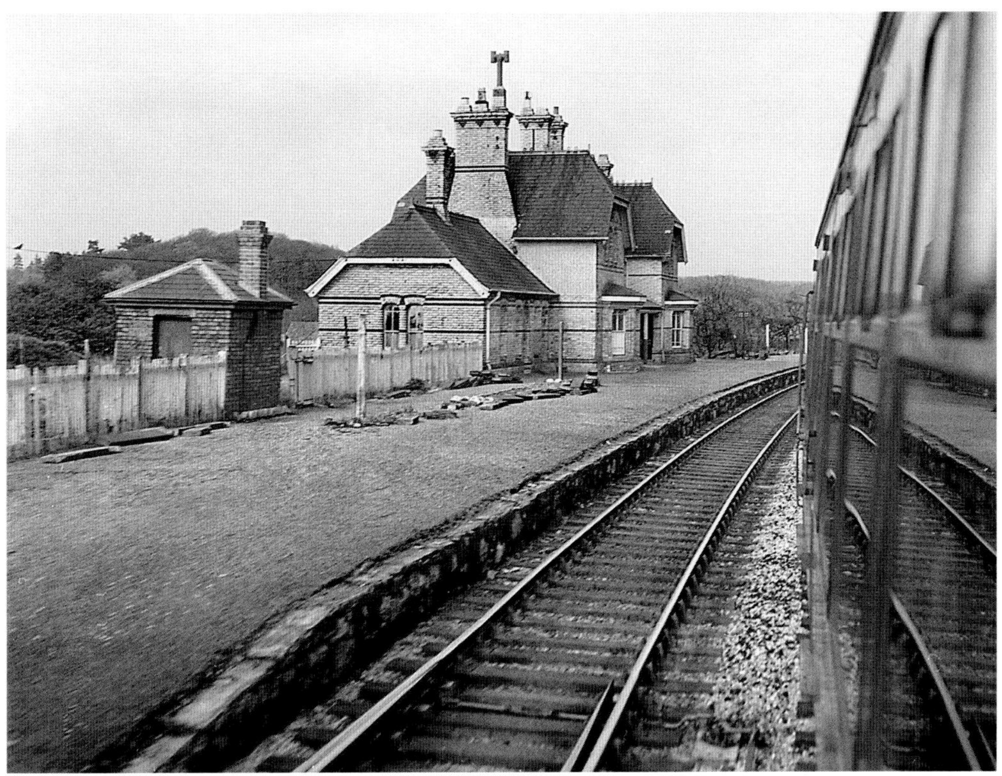

Port Dinorwic station is seen from a passing train travelling from Bangor to Caernarvon on 7 April 1961, although it had closed to passengers the previous year. This was the second station for the village that is today known by its Welsh name of Y Felinheli. Port Dinorwic's first station had opened in 1852 but was replaced by the one in this photograph in 1874, which was closer to the centre of the village. The railway through Port Dinorwic was doubled as far as Caernarvon in 1872. The station building was large for a village and built in yellow brick with red brick string courses; it survives today as a listed building.

Opposite above: A final photograph taken at Bangor on 7 April 1961 shows the unnamed 'Britannia', No. 70047, at the east end of the station awaiting departure with the 12.50 p.m. restaurant car express to London Euston, a journey scheduled to take six hours. The DMU on the left is that on which Ellis travelled to Amlwch and back, having a 12.40 p.m. departure; the station clock to its side says 12.20 p.m. The naming of 'Britannias' was taken very seriously by British Railways, and a small but effective committee of intelligent and well-educated people spent much time trying to get it right. They looked for names that were not ephemeral and were generally successful in their task. It was said that although No. 70047 never received a name, it was not for want of trying.

Opposite below: In August 1960, Ellis travelled by car from North Wales to Sheffield, and this photograph to the east of Llandudno Junction was taken from the A55 main road during that journey. The locomotive is an unidentified LNWR 'Super D' 0-8-0, and the houses in the background are on the strangely named Pabo Lane. The trailing load is entirely made up of empty cattle wagons, likely bound for Holyhead to collect livestock from Ireland. This successful family of locomotives had a long pedigree, stretching back to Victorian times, and many were rebuilt. In the 1930s, it was cheaper to rebuild these 0-8-0s than construct new replacement Stanier 8F 2-8-0s.

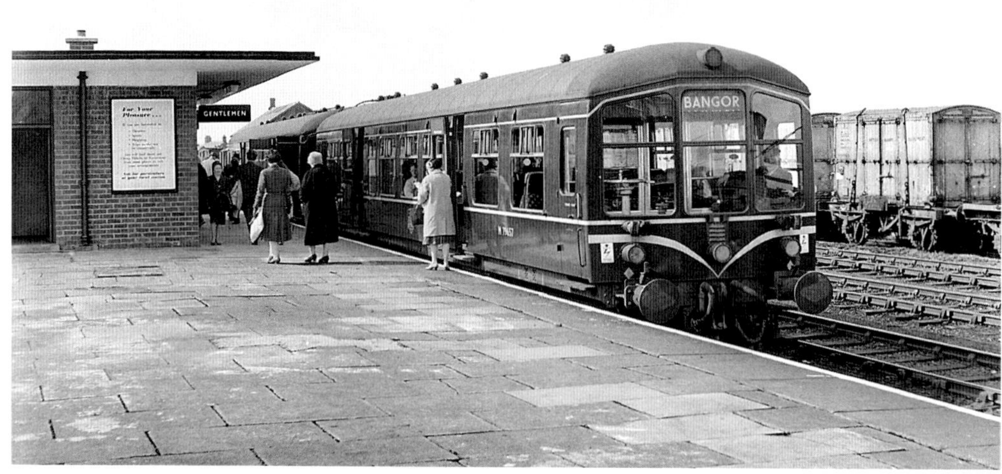

The Derby lightweight DMUs, such as this example at Caernarvon station (first officially spelt with an 'e' by the railway in December 1925) on 7 April 1961 bound for Bangor, were the first of their type to be built in quantity for BR. Their initial use was in West Cumberland, and later orders were allocated to areas such as Lincolnshire and East Anglia. They also came to North Wales on the Llandudno to Blaenau Ffestiniog line from 5 March 1956, with the Bangor to Amlwch route following from 28 May 1956. There was seating for nine first-class and 105 second-class passengers, and they were equipped with toilet facilities. The units were a success, both reducing the cost of operating branch lines and increasing passenger numbers. In their first month working the Blaenau Ffestiniog service in 1956, branch passenger numbers went up by 33 per cent compared with 1955. The front unit is Driving Trailer Composite M79657.

Opposite above: The first sod of the railway from Caernarvon to Llanberis was cut in September 1864; it was single track and 9 miles in length, and a further act authorised an extension to the Caernarvon station, seen in the previous photograph. Things did not go according to plan. The 1866 financial crisis stopped work completely, and the LNWR came in with a deal. The compromise reached was that the line would be jointly owned—C&LR and LNWR. The branch opened for both goods and passenger services in July 1869, although in July 1870, the LNWR took it over completely. The lines to Llanberis and Afon Wen ran together as two single lines side-by-side (not double track) south of Caernarvon for just over 1 mile before diverging. This photograph, taken on 7 April 1961, shows the point of divergence with the Llanberis branch heading off to the left. From July 1869 until the beginning of August 1870, a temporary terminus station on the Llanberis branch was used at Morfa, Carnarvon; its site was by the overbridge in the middle distance.

Opposite below: An undated view looking towards Llanberis of Cwm-y-Glo, the busiest of the intermediate stations along the branch from Caernarvon for passenger traffic. The single low platform on the down side was 320 feet long, and portable wooden steps used to be on-hand to assist passengers. The station included living accommodation, a booking hall, office, waiting room, and toilets. Beyond is the substantial goods shed, and the goods yard had two sidings. Cwm-y-Glo had no signalling, and the points were controlled by a ground frame. *Bradshaw's Guide* for February 1919 shows a passenger service of four trains each way on weekdays but nothing on Sundays. Bus competition became a problem for the branch in the 1920s and although the passenger service was increased to ten trains each way (twelve on Saturdays), it was withdrawn in September 1930. The branch goods service carried on until September 1964 (see page 4); today, the old trackbed here is part of the A4086 road.

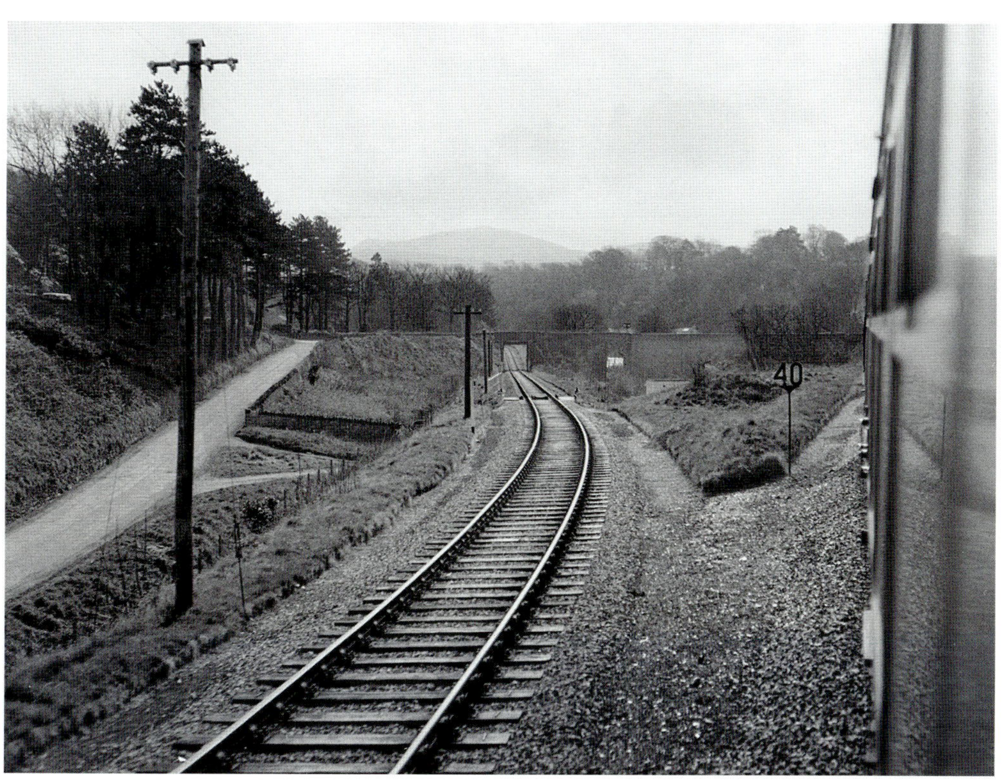

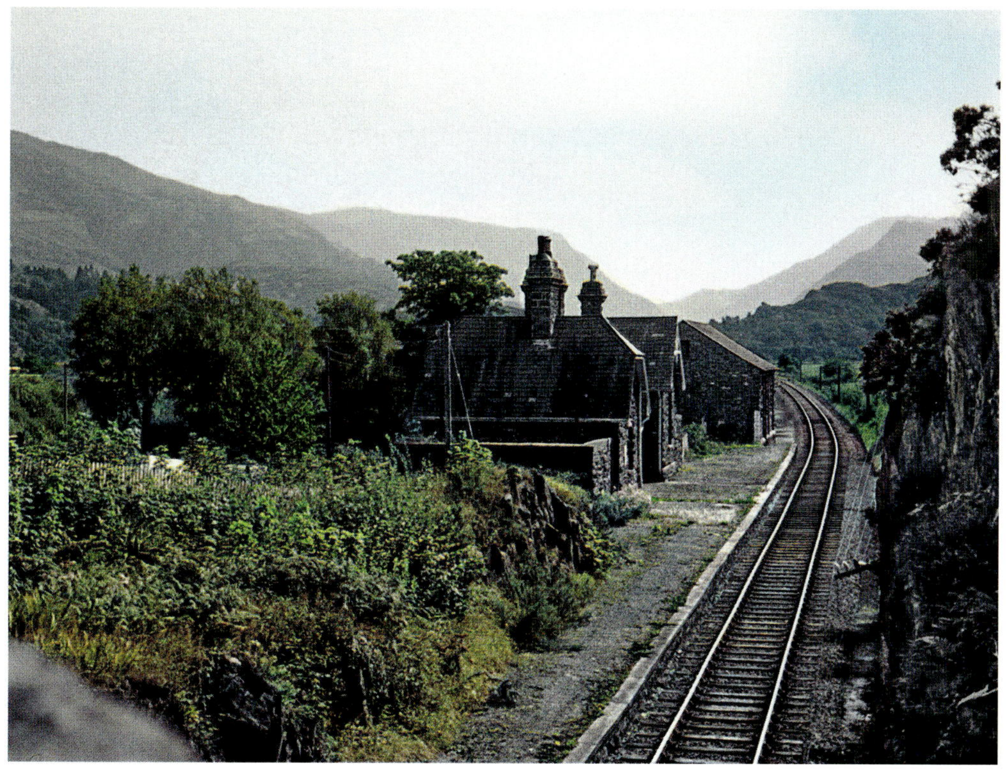

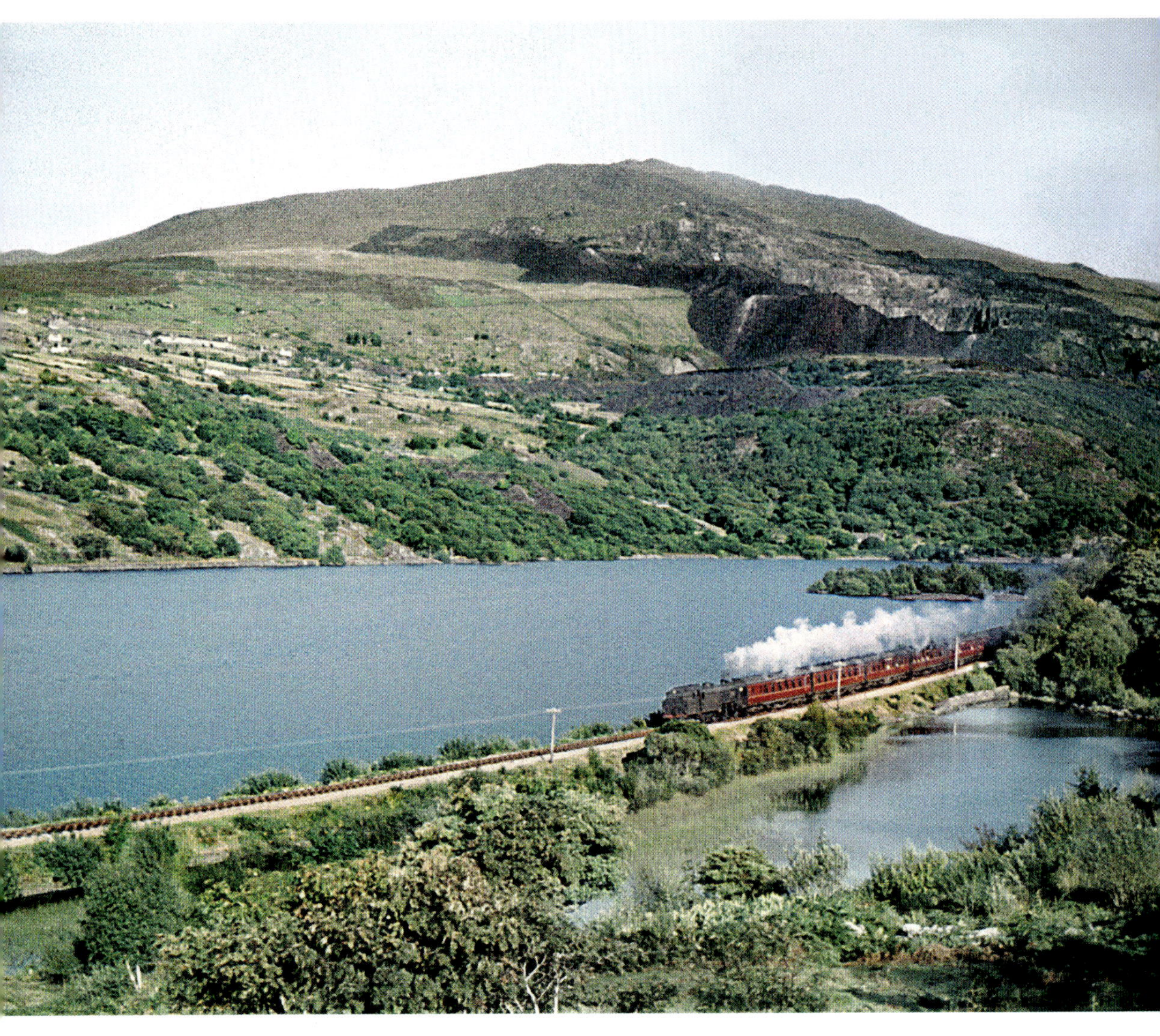

Between Cwm-y-Glo and Llanberis, the railway reaches Llyn Padarn and, for the short distance in this photograph, runs on an embankment with water on each side. Although regular passenger services had ceased in 1930, excursion trains ran during the summer months; also, an all-year-round Saturdays-only market service was introduced in the mid-1930s until the Second World War. The summer excursion service resumed after the Second World War in 1946 (but not the Saturday market service), and in the 1950s, it even acquired a name: *The Snowdonian*. The date this photograph was taken is believed to be 30 August 1961, and an unidentified LMS 2-6-4T is making its way back from Llanberis with *The Snowdonian*, made up of eight coaches. The Padarn Railway ran along an embankment just above the waterline on the opposite side of Llyn Padarn, and in the distance cut into the mountainside is evidence of slate quarrying.

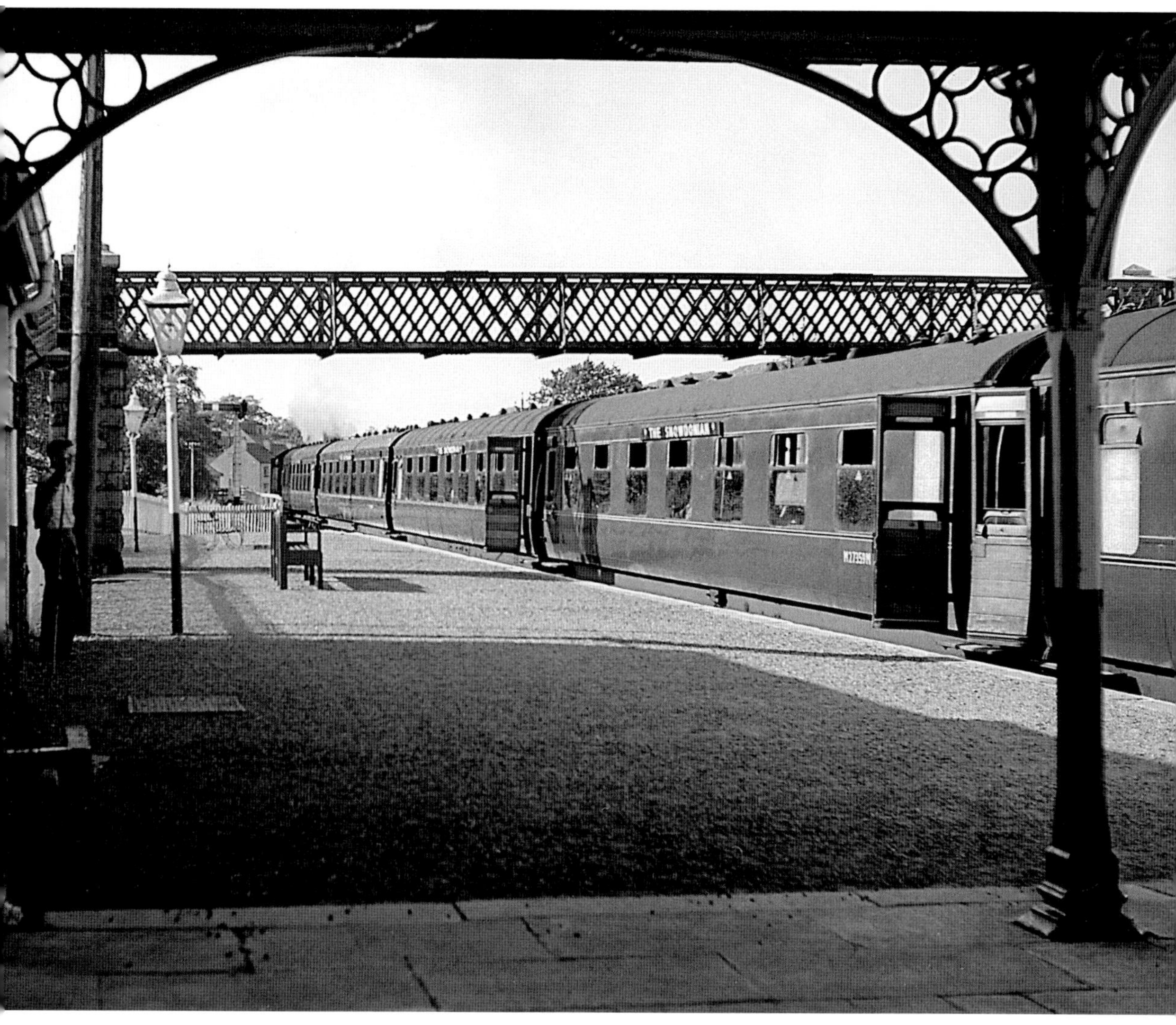

The Snowdonian stands at Llanberis on the same day as the previous photograph. The prominent footbridge provided access between a part of the village and Llyn Padarn. There was just a single platform at Llanberis, and to accommodate eight-coach excursion trains, a narrow wooden extension had been built by the signal. In 1869, when the line opened, Sir Richard Moon, chairman of the LNWR, attended the ceremony and suggested the possibility of extending beyond Llanberis. When this did happen, it was not the LNWR but the Snowdon Mountain Railway in the next photographs, although Sir Richard was a joint founder of the latter. Llanberis station still exists today as an arts and crafts centre, while the rail bed is now used by the A4086.

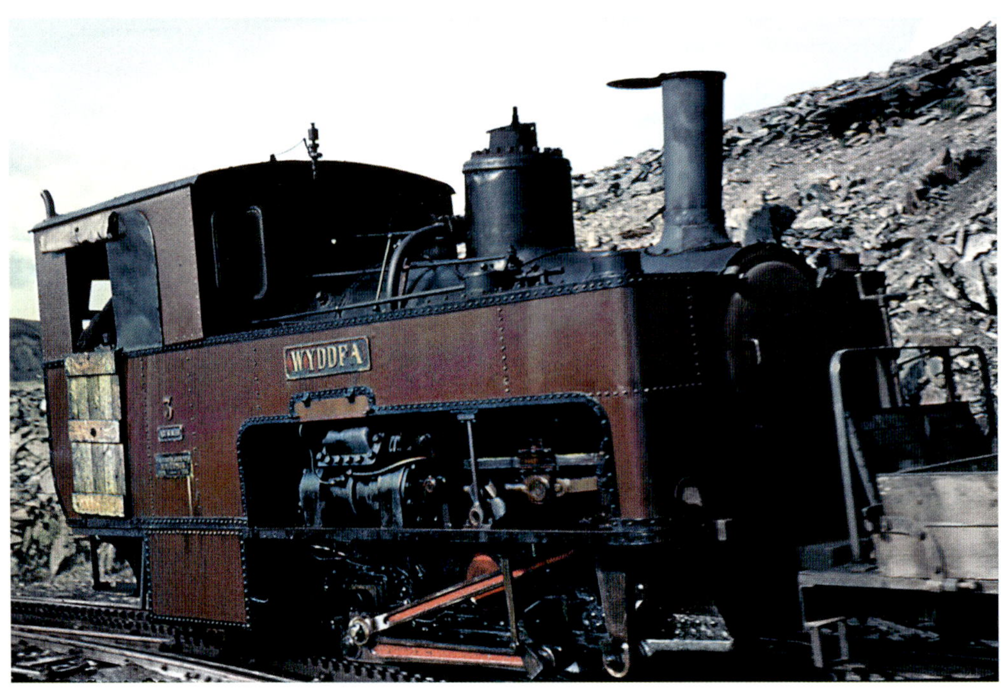

Above and below: Two undated photographs at the summit of the Snowdon Mountain Railway, the first shows No. 3 *Wyddfa* in a brown livery with a supply/engineering train. In the second, No. 2 *Enid* in green livery has a normal service train. Ellis started taking colour photographs (Agfa) from about 1955, and these two, plus others taken that same day, are still in their original Agfa cardboard surrounds. Sadly, the majority of Ellis's colour slides are undated.

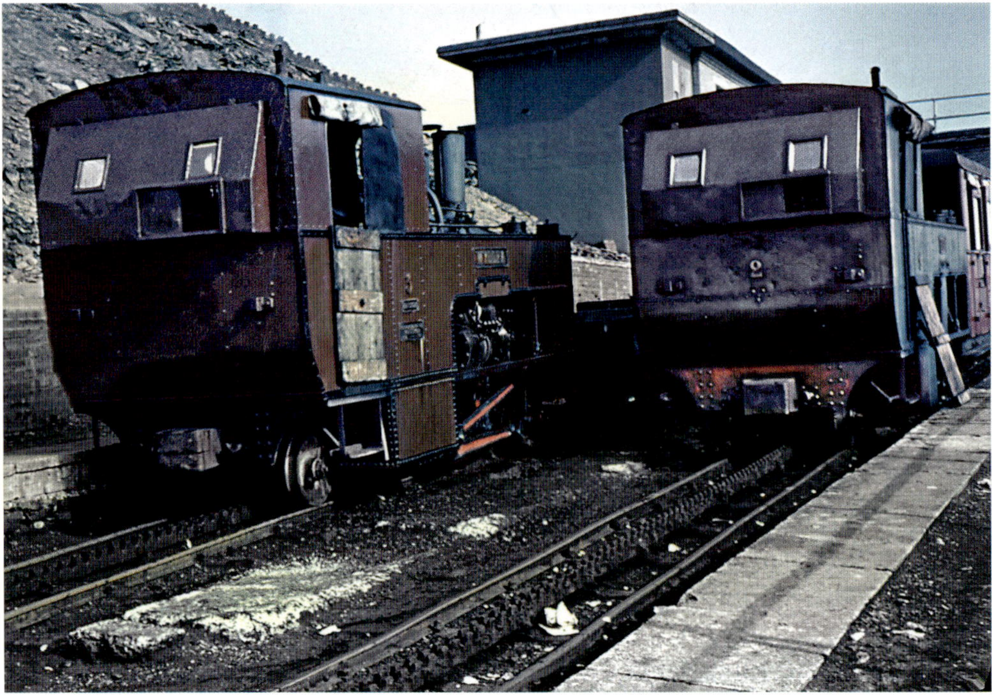

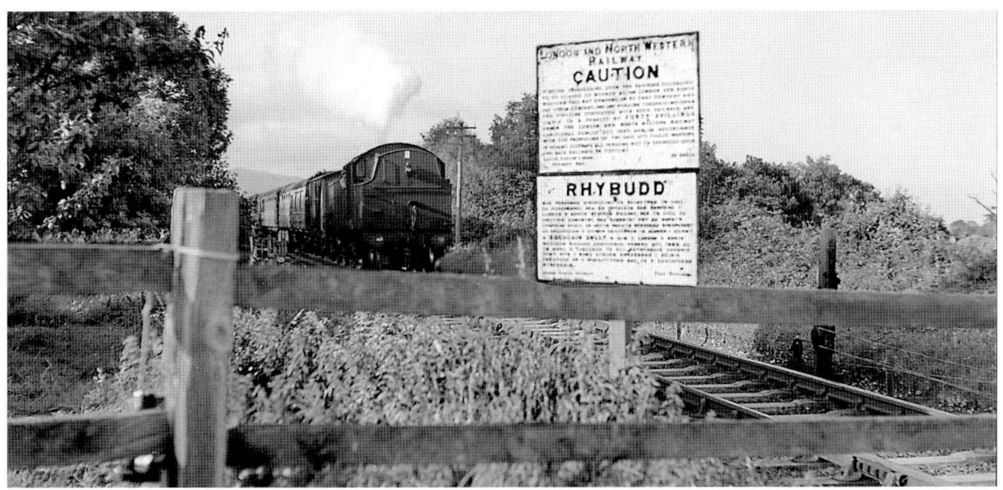

Above: Taken at about 8.50 a.m. on 30 August 1961, Bangor-allocated 2-6-4T No. 42544 approaches the 1951-closed station of Dinas on its journey from Afon Wen to Caernarvon and Bangor; Ellis was on his way to visit the Padarn Railway. These signs can also be seen in the introduction in close-up on page 5. Dinas used to be Dinas Junction (until 1938), where a connection was made in 1877 with the North Wales Narrow Gauge Railways. The NWNGR eventually became the Welsh Highland Railway (incorporated by a Light Railway Order in March 1922) and ultimately extended all the way to Portmadoc, but closure as a through passenger route came about in 1936. Today, the narrow-gauge line has been restored and reopened with a service operating to Portmadoc once again; its headquarters are based at Dinas.

Below: This photograph at Penygroes (Pen-y-Groes until 1904) is another taken on 7 April 1961 during the course of a journey from Pwllheli to Bangor. Branching off from Penygroes's passing loop to the left is the line to Nantlle; this was about 1.5 miles long, and much of it was on the course of the 1828-opened horse-operated Nantlle Railway. By 1922, most passenger services to Nantlle were shuttles to and from Penygroes that started from a bay platform on the track to the left of the passing loop. Passenger services to Nantlle ceased in August 1932, although it had been temporarily closed between 1917 and 1919; excursion traffic continued until 1939. In 2000, a road bypass was built around Penygroes that here is built over the old trackbed.

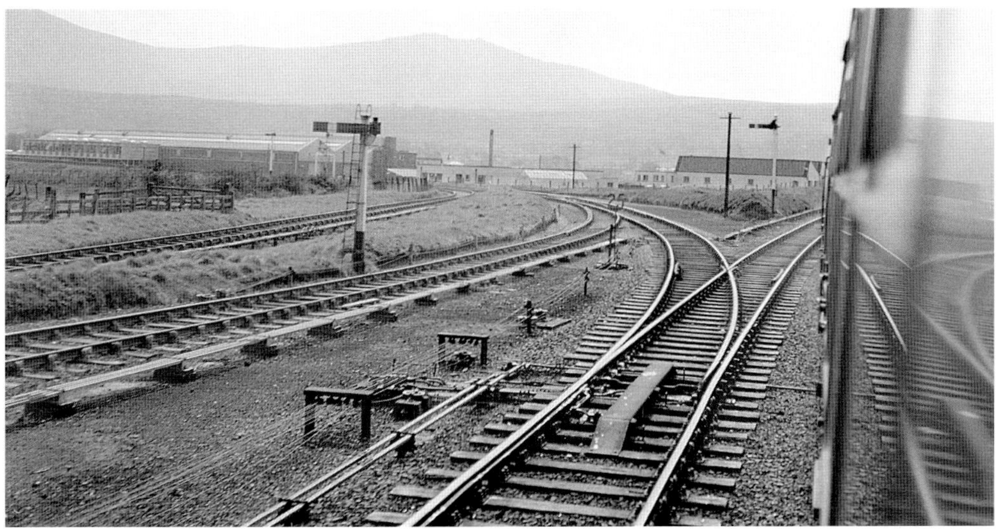

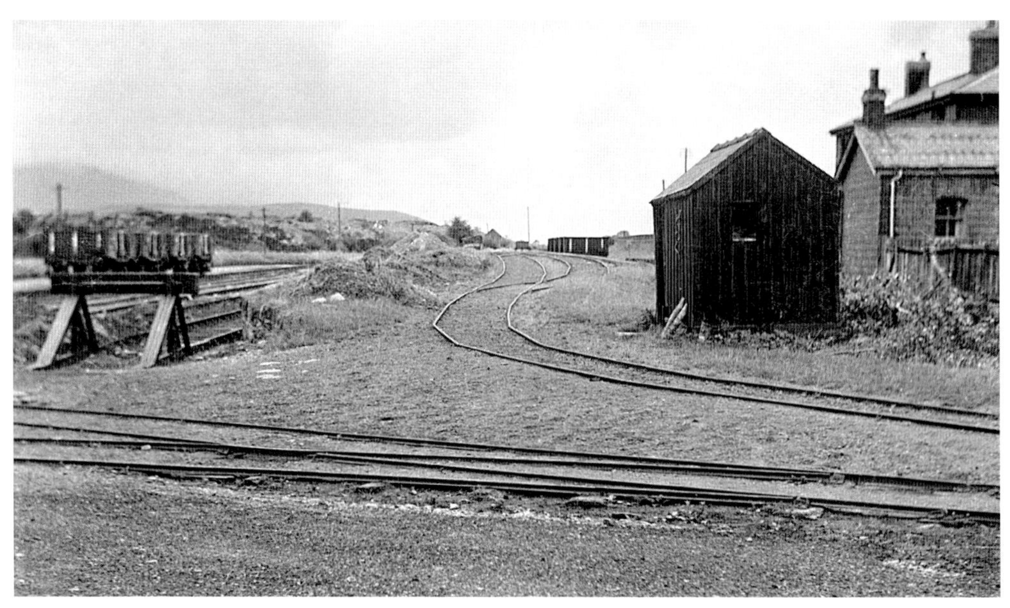

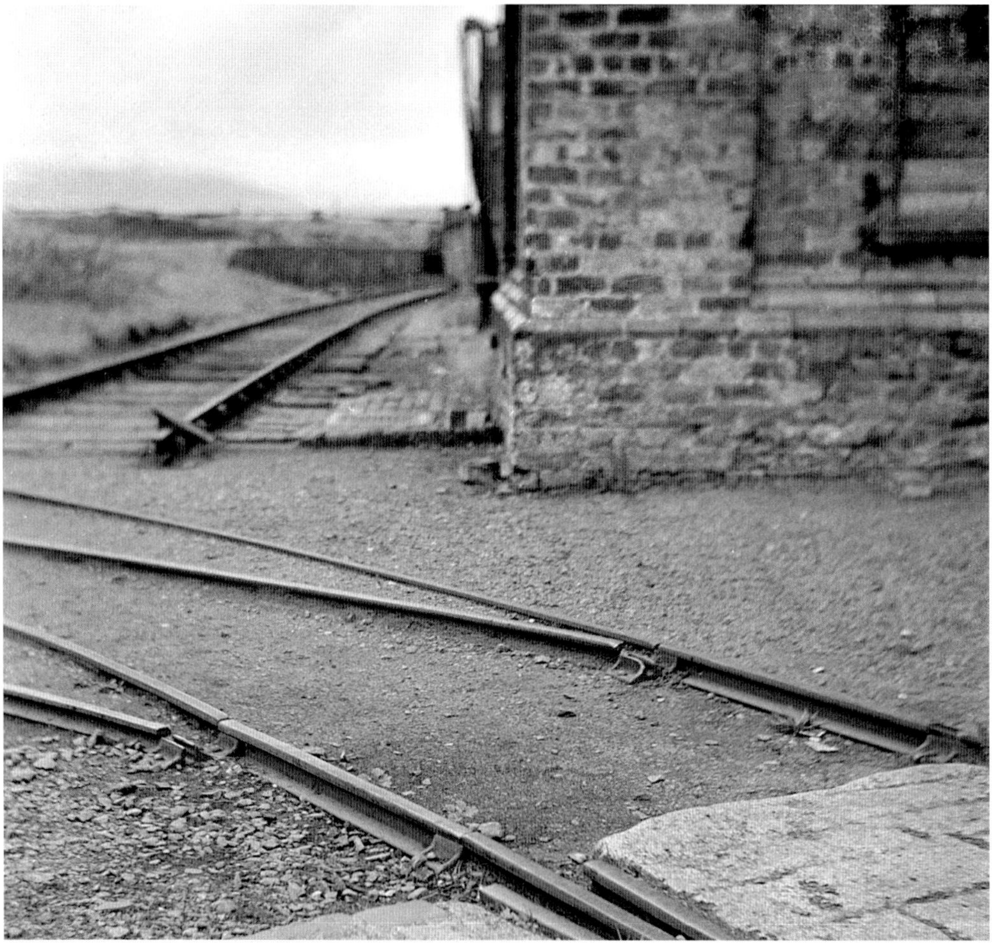

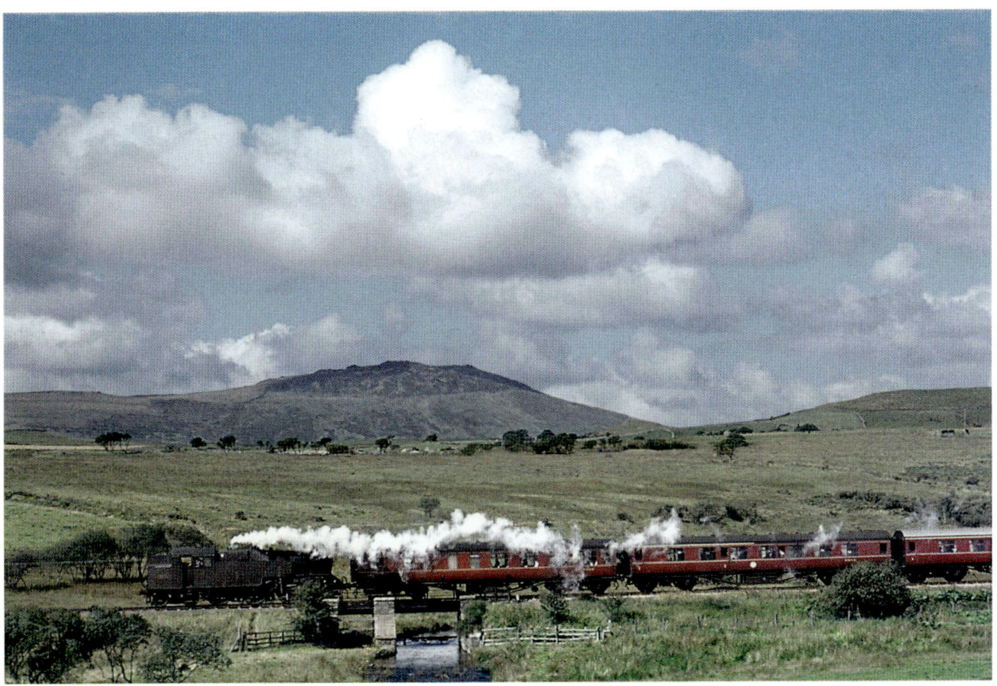

A type of film format not used by the author or his father was '127', producing a square 40 ×
40-mm image mounted in a cardboard holder. Apparently, the name popularised for these was
'Superslides' as there was a larger image area than with the more usual 35-mm slides. Their
holders/mounts were the same size as 'normal' 35-mm slides and thus could be used with a
35-mm projector, and also with modern-day slide scanners as used by the author. Although
the passenger service from Bangor to Afon Wen and Pwllheli was largely dieselised by the late
1950s, steam made something of a comeback latterly. The SLS house magazine for August 1963
reported steam worked most passenger services (plus also the Amlwch branch) and that the
DMUs released were used in multiple (up to eight cars) on the 'Red Dragon' (*sic*.). The location
is a little to the north of Brynkir, the date is believed to be August 1964, and an unidentified
LMS 2-6-4T is making its way southbound crossing the Afon Dwyfach. The last year the line
through Brynkir was open was 1964, closing that December. Nowadays, this part of the railway
has been converted into the Lon Eifion cycleway. More examples of 'Superslides' will follow at
Afon Wen.

Opposite page: The 1828-opened Nantlle Railway was constructed to a 3-foot 6-inch-gauge
and ran from slate quarries to the quayside at Caernarvon. By 1872, the standard-gauge link
seen previously at Penygroes was open to Nantlle; however, that onwards to the quarries
remained at 3 feet 6 inches, and there were transhipment sidings at Nantlle station (actually in
the village of Tal-y-sarn). It was the only section of this gauge owned by BR and was also BR's
last main-line use of horses until closure in 1963; they were supplied under contract by a local
farmer (horse shunting carried on at Newmarket until 1967). Some 3-foot 6-inch-gauge tracks
leading to the transhipment sidings are visible in the first photograph, while in the second is an
example of the basic point work; both are undated.

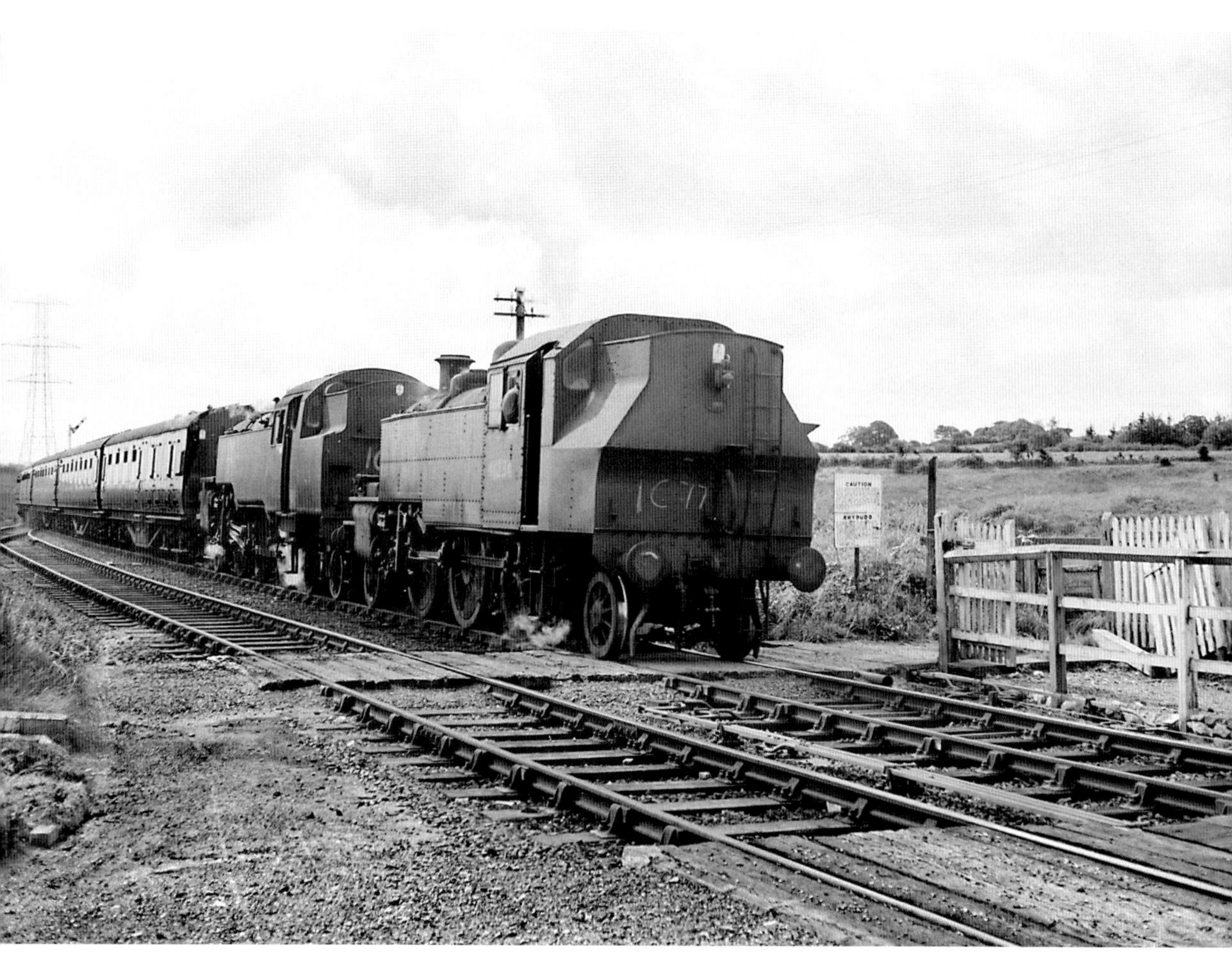

Arriving at Brynkir from Afon Wen on 22 August 1964, with service 1C77 chalked across its coal bunker, is Ivatt Class 2 2-6-2T No. 41234 plus an unidentified BR Standard Class 4 2-6-4T. This is possibly the same locomotive combination as will be seen on page 44, but heading in the opposite direction. The line from Caernarvon to Afon Wen was severely graded, some parts steeper than 1 in 50, and hence the need for double-heading with trains up to ten coaches long. Ellis's notes say this is the 11.12 a.m. from Afon Wen. Many of the summer Saturday extra services served the Butlin's holiday camp at Penychain near Pwllheli, which had opened for business in 1947. To cope with these long trains, the passing loop was extended at Brynkir and other stations along the line.

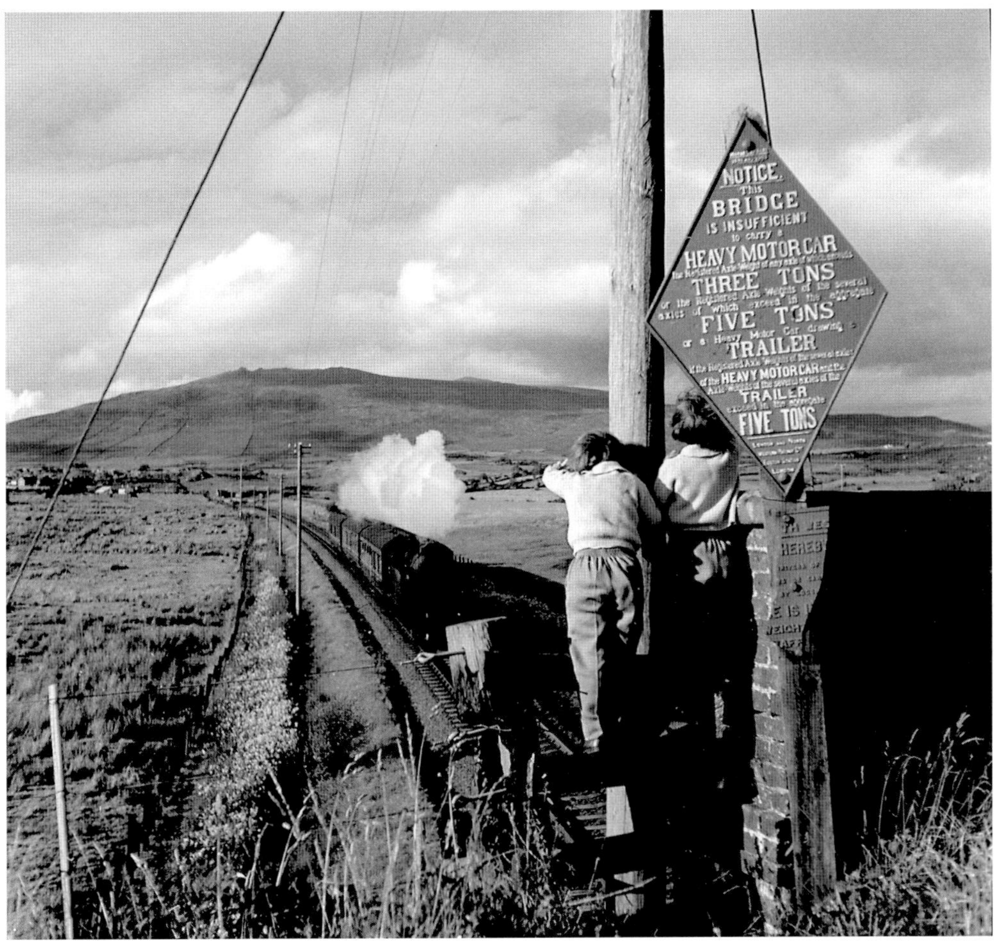

Ellis's daughters, Louisa and Fiona, stand on the first road bridge south of Brynkir with the nearly 2,000-foot-high Mynydd Graig-Goch in the background. It is about 6.45 p.m. on 8 August 1962; however, the locomotive is unidentified. The Carnarvonshire Railway opened between Pant, near Caernarvon, to Afon Wen at the beginning of September 1867, with Brynkir being one of the original stations. A serious accident occurred at Brynkir on 17 September 1920 due to gross carelessness by the porter signalman. A passenger service took the wrong track and collided head-on with a goods train already in the loop; the fireman of the passenger train was killed.

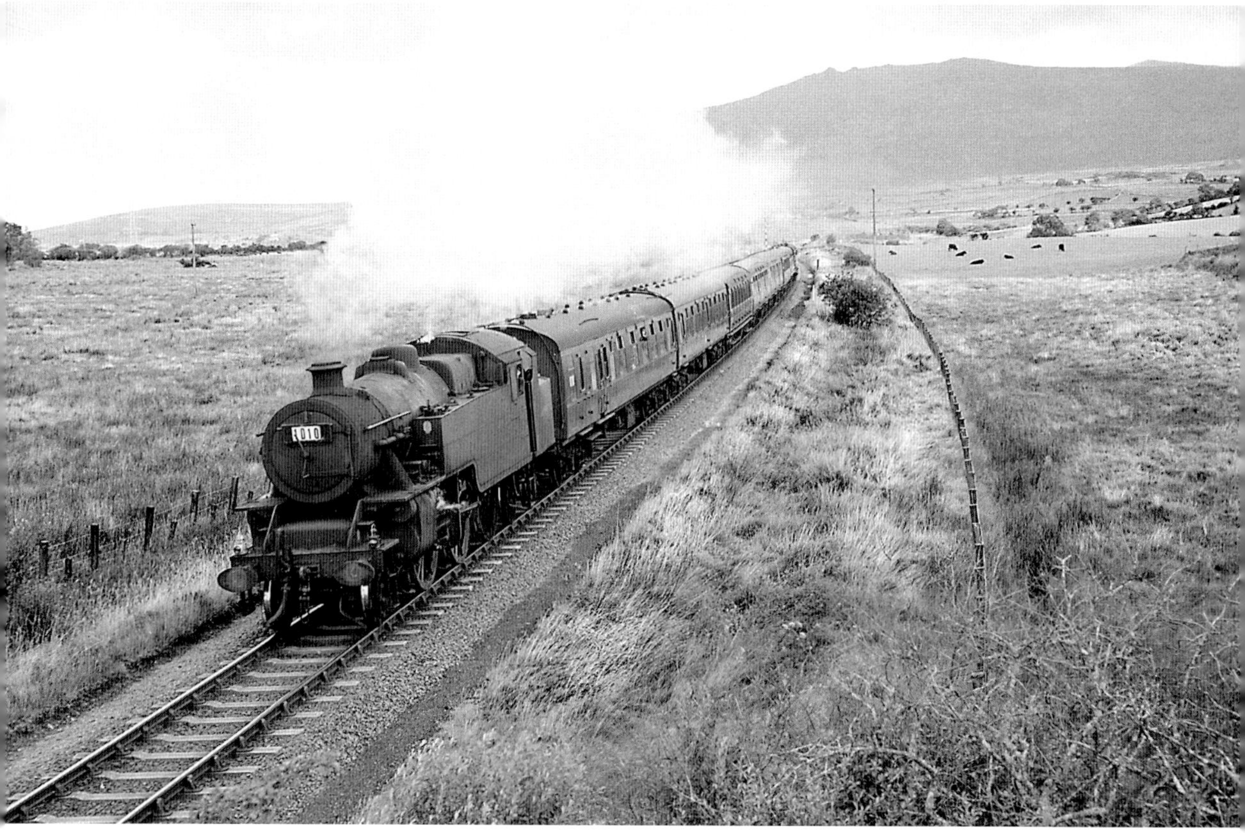

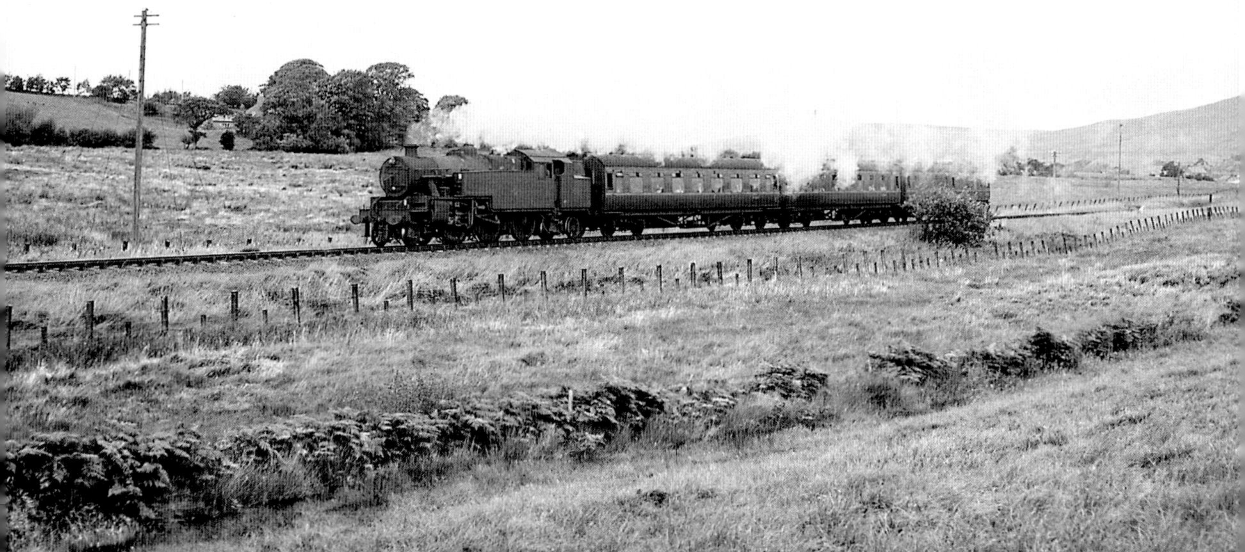

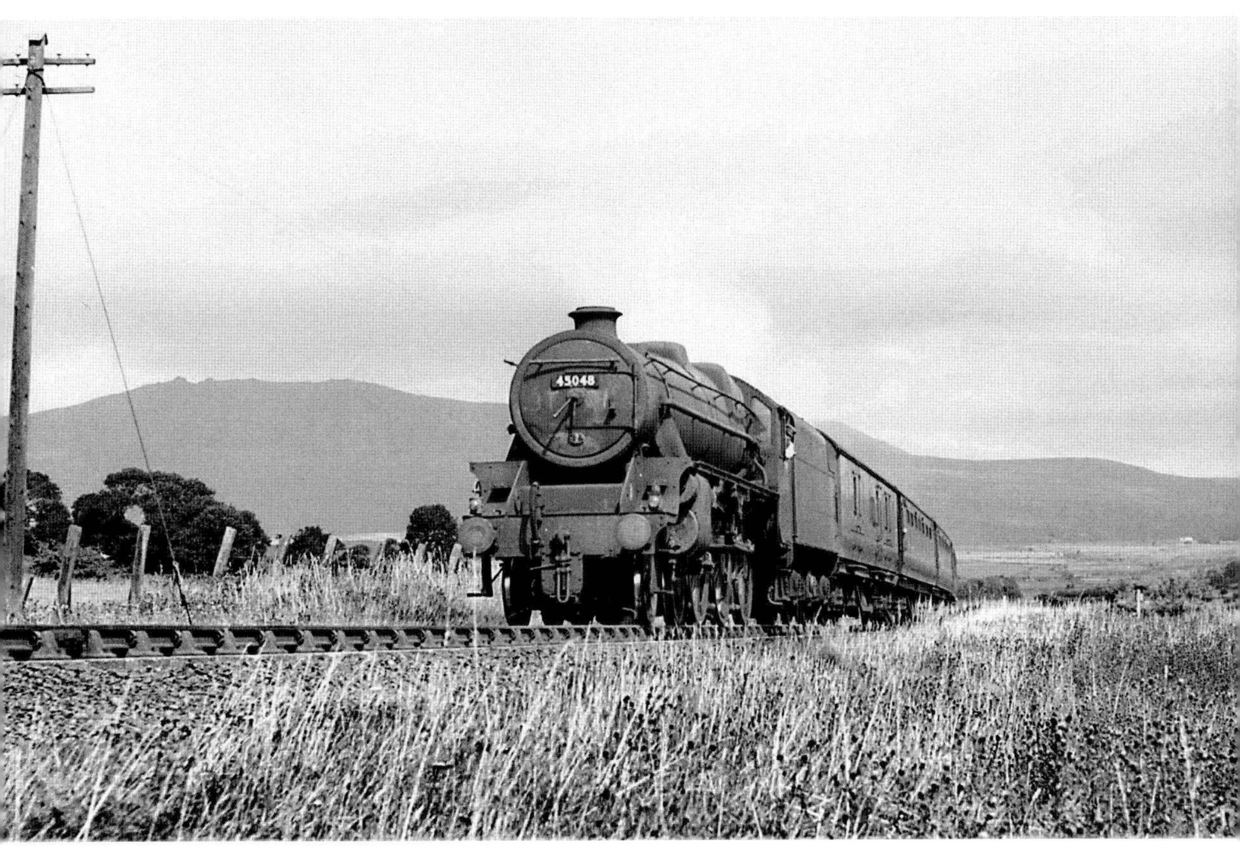

Above and opposite page: Three more photographs taken just to the south of Brynkir, all date from 22 August 1964, and all feature southbound services (see also page 6). The line was substantially built, and the abutments plus bridge piers were made of masonry. Although only single track, there was sufficient land for doubling as can be seen in the first photograph. The locomotive is not identified, but Ellis lists the service as the 8.05 a.m. to Butlin's from Manchester. The second photograph shows the 11.43 a.m. from Caernarvon, but again the locomotive is not identified. The 'Black 5' in the third photograph is Crewe South-allocated No. 45048, and the service listed as the 12.47 p.m. from Caernarvon.

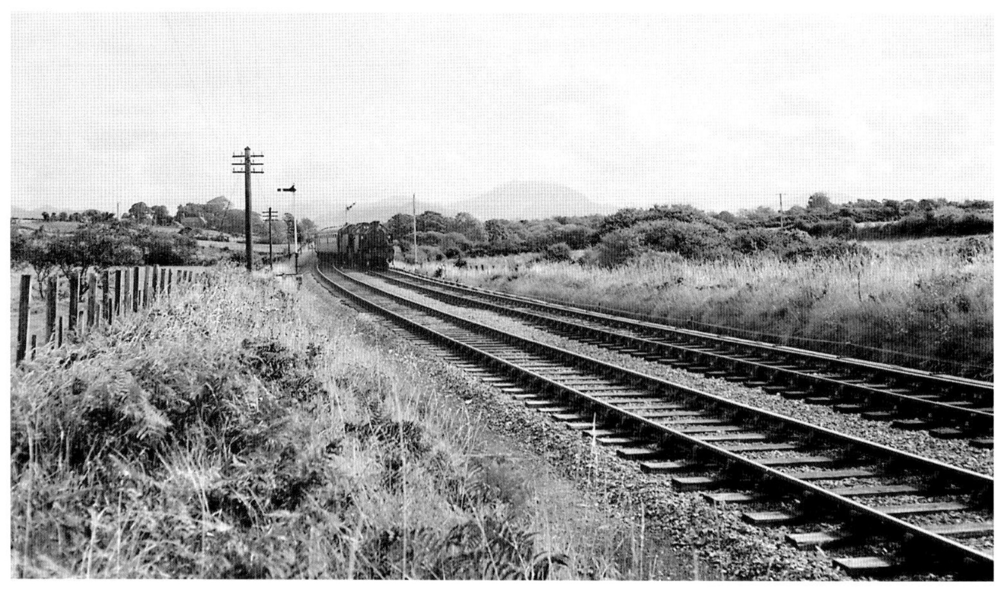

Above and below: Llangybi was 3.75 miles from Brynkir and the next passing place to the south. The loop dates from 1915 and, as at Brynkir, was extended in the late 1940s for the Butlin's trains. These two photographs both date from Saturday, 22 August 1964. In the first, and approaching Llangybi from the north, is a double-headed service of which the leading locomotive is No. 41234; Ellis has listed this as the 9.03 a.m. from Bangor. There is another double-headed combination in the second photograph and held at the signal by the level crossing. It is service 1C71 with an LMS 2-6-4T and 'Black 5'; Ellis's notes say this is the 9.50 a.m. from Afon Wen.

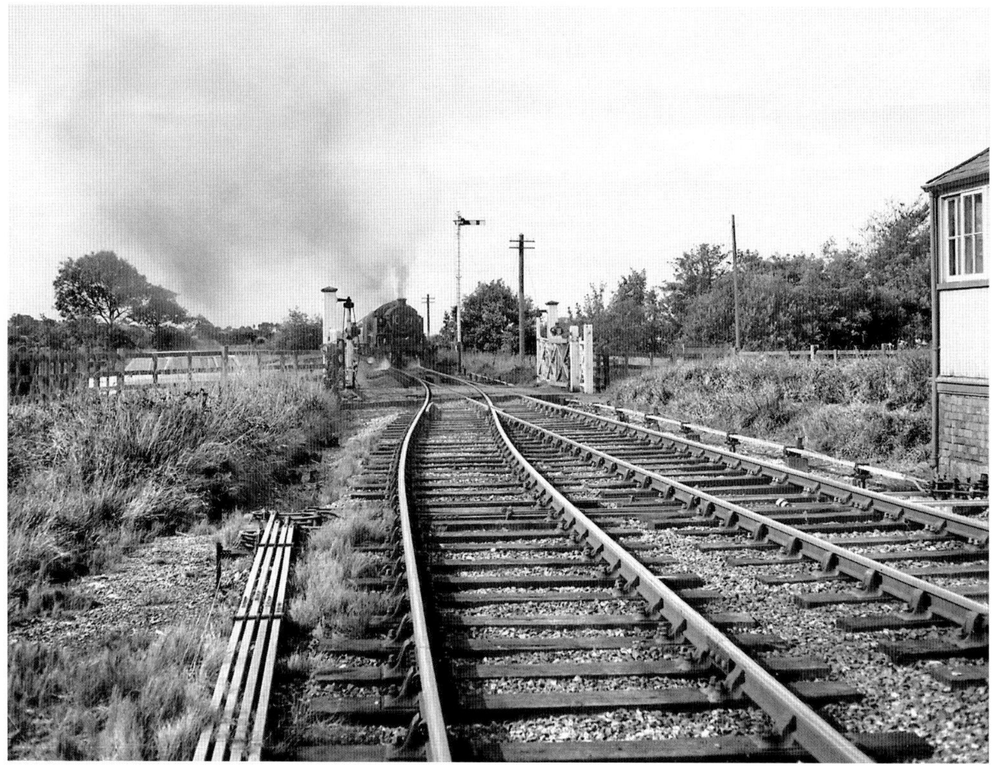

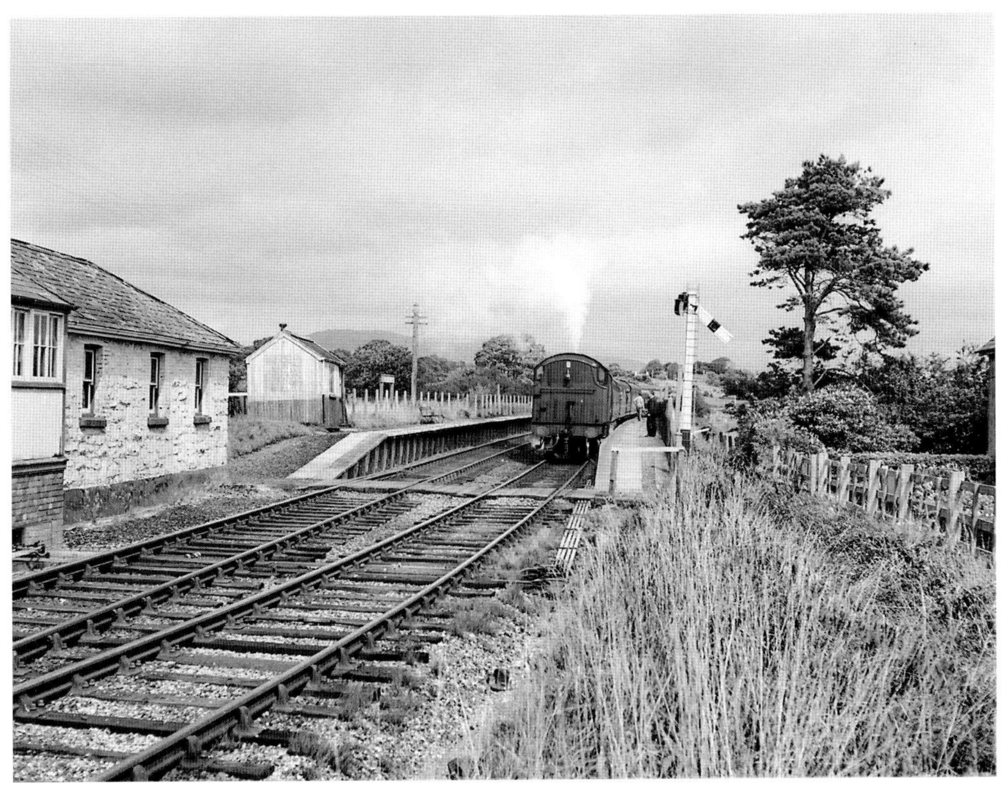

Llangybi was not one of the original stations along the line, and it opened for limited business (markets and fairs only) in 1869. This was an isolated location, and the village of Llangybi was some 2 miles away. A single-story stone building was provided on the north side of the level crossing and west of the line; this contained a booking plus parcels office. When the passing loop was installed during the First World War, an extra platform was added, the new line to the east of the original. On the up platform (towards Brynkir), there was a timber waiting shelter that contained a ladies' waiting room. The connection between the platforms was over a wooden barrow crossing, and the down starter signal was on the down platform to protect passengers using this crossing. When the passing loop was extended during the winter of 1946–47, the platforms were rebuilt with prefabricated concrete sections. The small signal box south of the original station building was a standard LNWR type and had fifteen levers. This photograph at Llangybi is another taken on 22 August 1964. Sadly, neither the locomotive's number nor the service have been listed by Ellis, but, presumably not a Butlin's train as it is composed of just three coaches. The 1963 Beeching Report recommended total closure of the line from Afon Wen to Caernarvon, which duly came to pass on and from 7 December 1964.

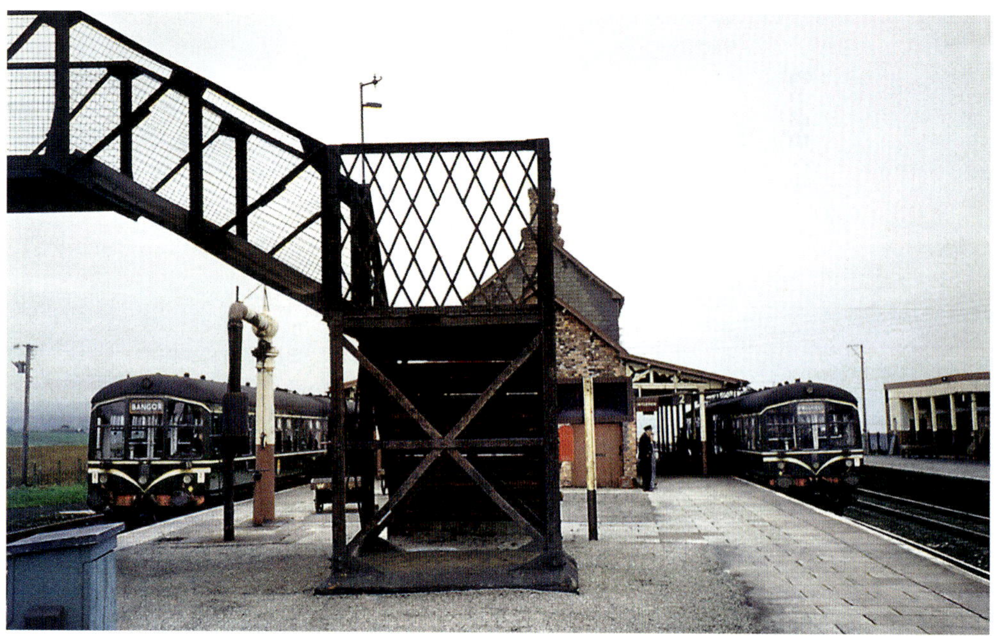

The Aberystwyth & Welsh Coast Railway was authorised in 1861 to build a line around Cardigan Bay from Aberystwyth to, eventually, a terminus at Pwllheli. This is Afon Wen, about 4 miles from the original station at Pwllheli; the A&WCR opened here in October 1867 (although by that time it was part of the Cambrian Railways). The Carnarvonshire Railway that we have been following from the north over the last few pages opened to Afon Wen in September 1867. For that intervening month, the Carnarvonshire services ran through in the direction of Portmadoc, by agreement with the Cambrian. Although undated, this photograph is believed to have been taken on 7 April 1961. Two Derby Lightweight DMUs are at Afon Wen, that on the left with its destination indicator showing 'Bangor' and that on the right 'Pwllheli'. All services from Pwllheli to Caernarvon and Bangor had to reverse at Afon Wen.

Opposite above: Afon Wen was certainly a busy place on this August 1964 Saturday with steam locomotive after steam locomotive; however, this was the final year it would be the case. The DMUs working the old Carnarvonshire line to Bangor had been sent to strengthen services elsewhere, and steam filled the breach. The Butlin's trains to the north could load up to ten or possibly twelve coaches and were steam-hauled, regularly double-headed because of the grades. Yet this line would close during the coming winter. The Cambrian route along Cardigan Bay was also entirely steam-operated but from early 1965, the local passenger services were turned over to DMUs. This is another of the 40 × 40-mm 'Superslides' (as also the next two photographs) and shows No. 82003 on a Cambrian service bound for Pwllheli, while the unidentified LMS 2-6-4T will be used for a train to the north. No. 82003 was one of the last of its class to have a general overhaul—at Crewe works in the spring of 1964.

Opposite below: To the right is the back of Afon Wen signal box with masses of point rodding and signal wires. The front of this box can be seen in the previous photograph taken on the same day. The station had the luxury of two water towers at the west end of the station and also an area where minor locomotive servicing could be carried out, such as disposing of ash and clinker; in earlier times, there was even a turntable at Afon Wen. Although there were sidings at the Portmadoc end of the station, there was no freight handling facility other than for re-marshalling of traffic between the two companies. At its peak, during the summer in later years, there could be over 100 train movements daily here.

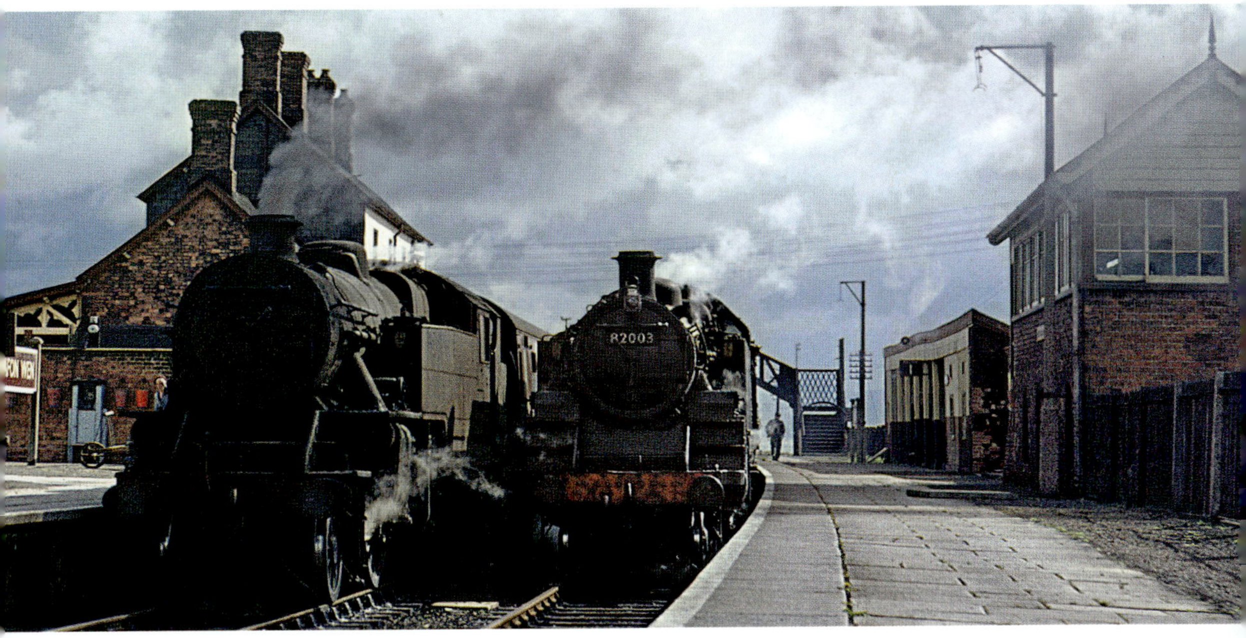

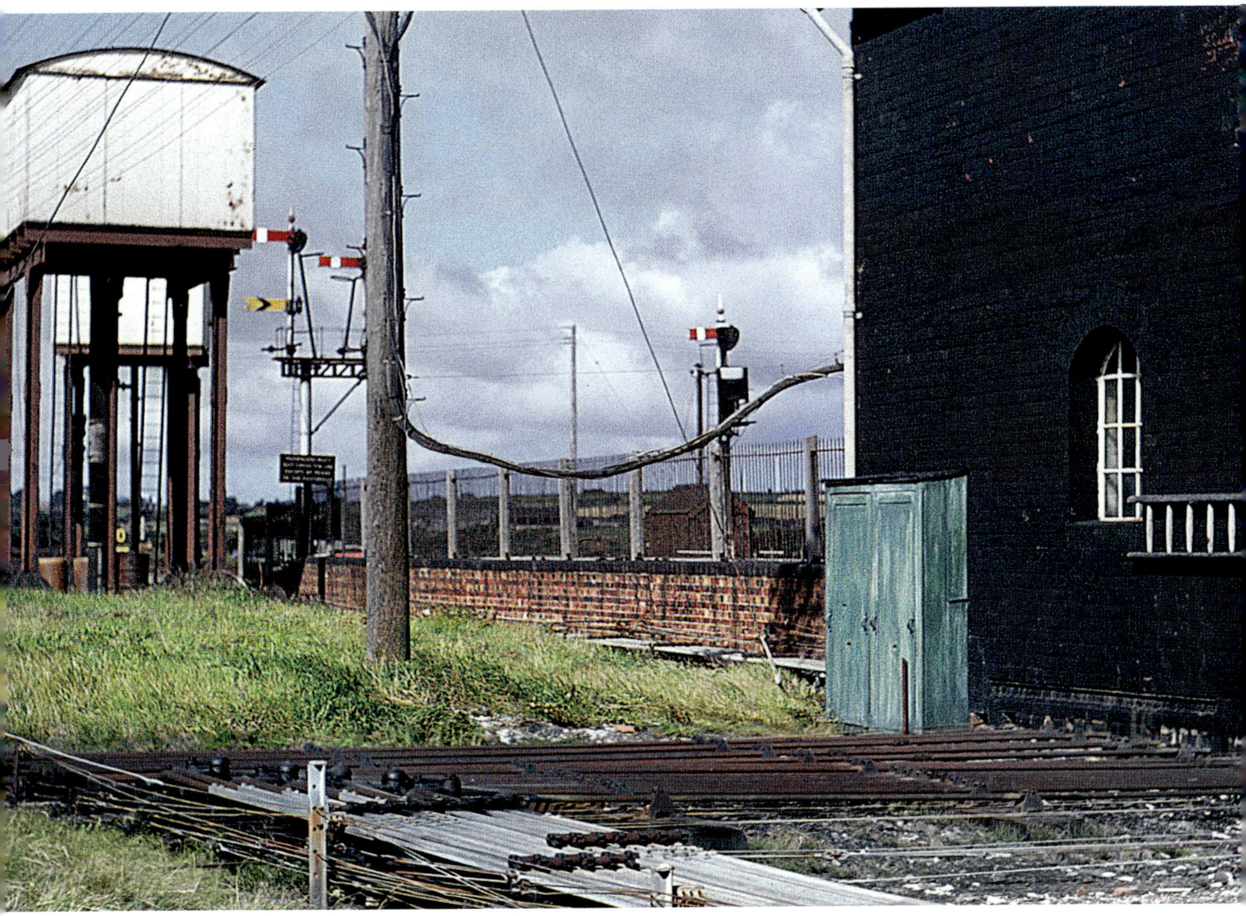

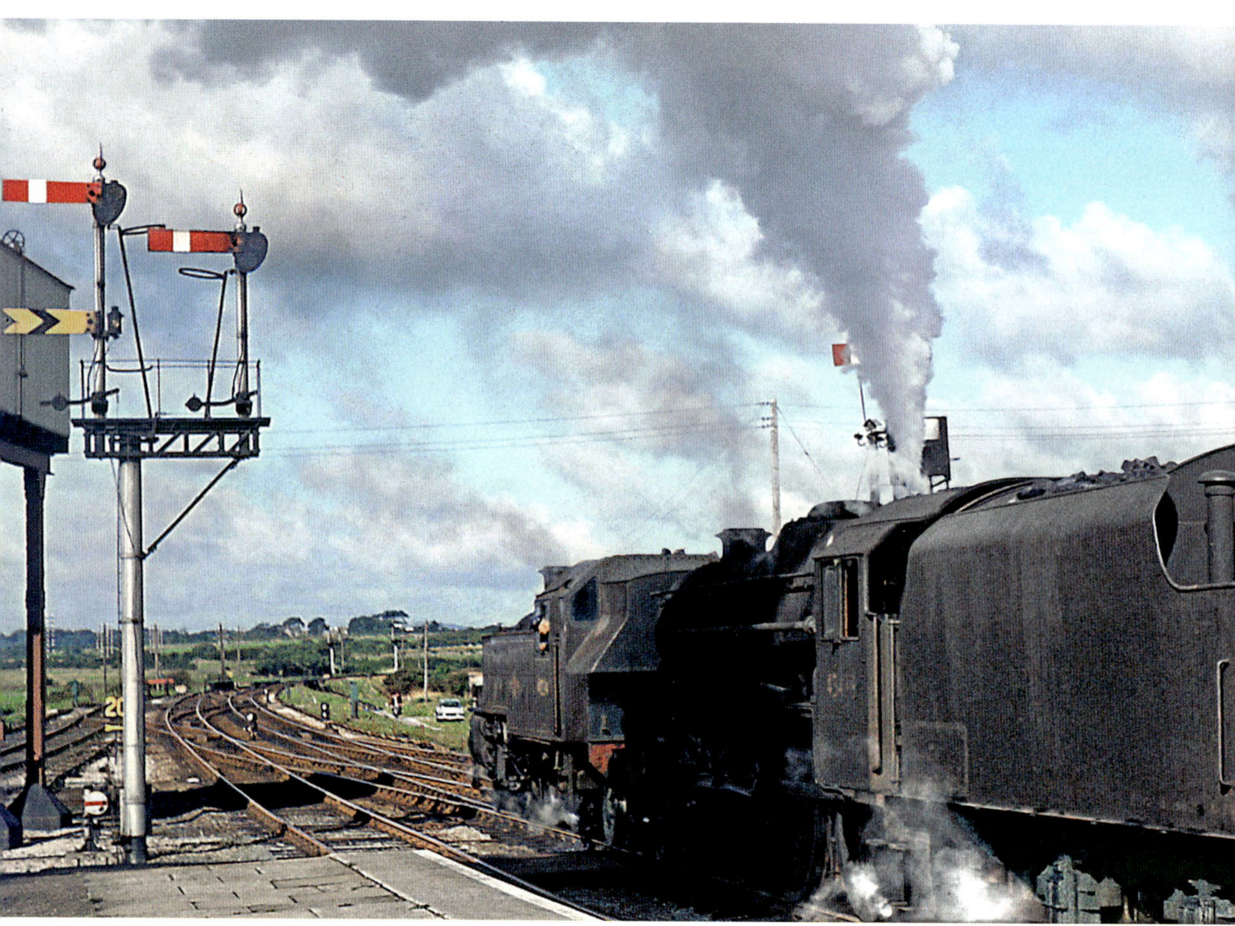

The October 1961 issue of the *Railway Observer* noted five tank engines all coupled together working over the Carnarvonshire Railway route on the morning of 5 August. They were bound for here at Afon Wen to deal with returning holiday traffic, such as that from the Butlin's Holiday Camp. The five were immediately followed by two 2-6-4Ts with a train of empty stock. In this final 'Superslide' taken on an August 1964 Saturday, a holidaymaker working to the north via the Carnarvonshire line will soon depart from Afon Wen. The locomotives concerned are Chester-allocated 'Black 5' No. 45438 with Ivatt 2-6-2T No. 41234 from Bangor depot acting as a pilot.

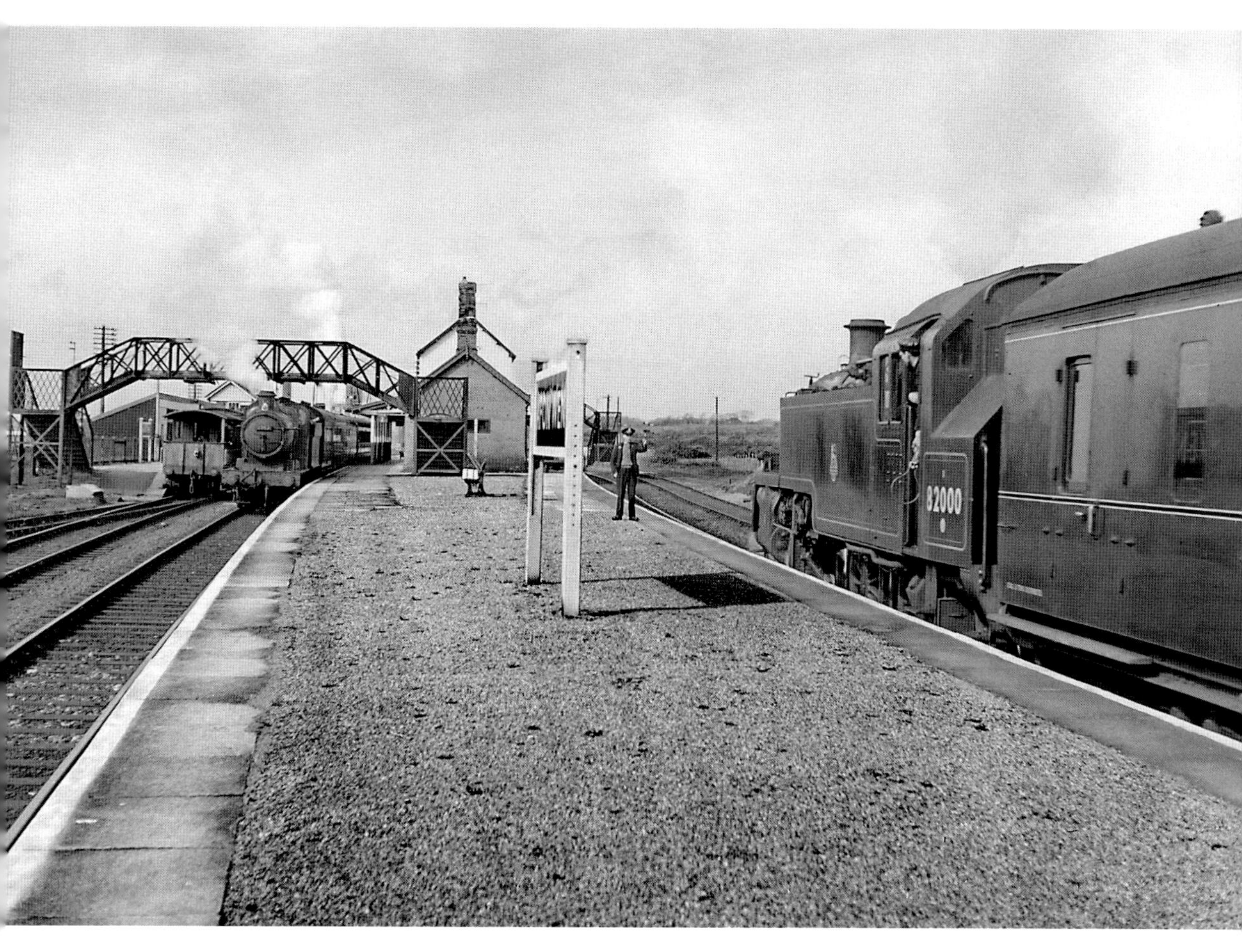

The Cambrian Railways had a number of junctions that grew up not near population centres but in isolated locations where the lines just happened to come together. In addition to Afon Wen, the CR became famous for this type of remote junction in Wales and had others at Barmouth Junction (renamed Morfa Mawddach in 1960), Dovey Junction, Moat Lane Junction, Three Cocks Junction, and Talyllyn Junction (Bala Junction also fell into this category but was not CR). This is the final photograph at Afon Wen, taken on 7 April 1961 at the east end of the station. There were three platforms, two of them served from a central island and all occupied on this day. On the right, class leader No. 82000 arrives on the 8.20 a.m. from Dovey Junction and its token is about to be handed over at this bidirectional platform. Facing us is No. 2287 with the 10.25 a.m. Pwllheli to Machynlleth, and on the left is a freight service to Pwllheli headed by No. 82009. Afon Wen station closed in December 1964 when the line to Caernarvon closed; however, Afon Wen signal box remained in use until the spring of 1967 on the Cambrian coast line from Machynlleth to Pwllheli that is still open today.

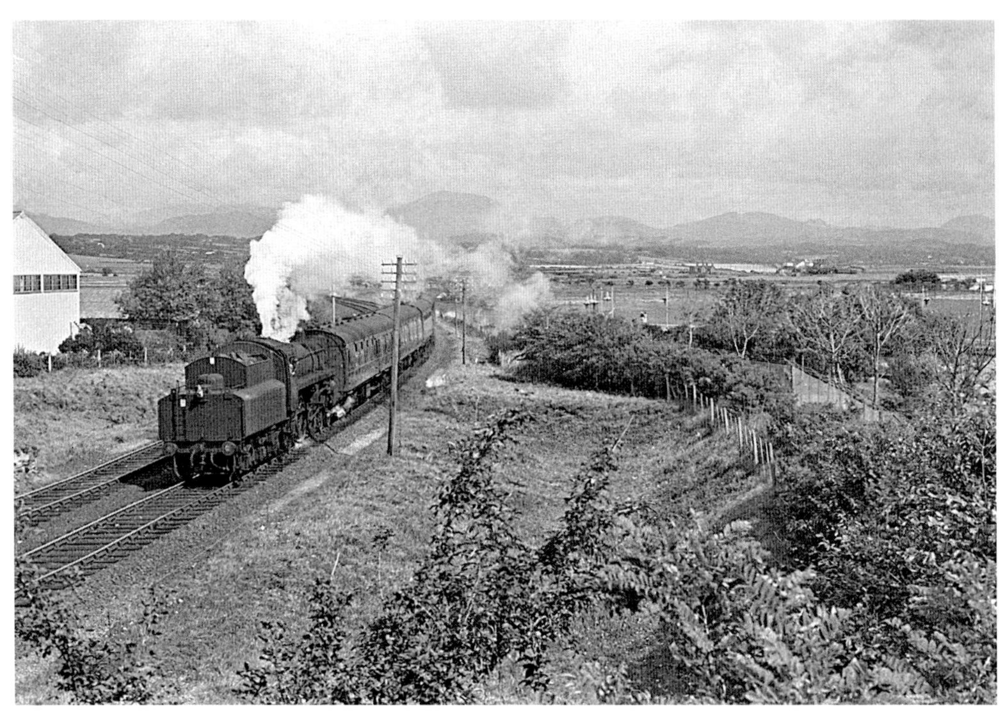

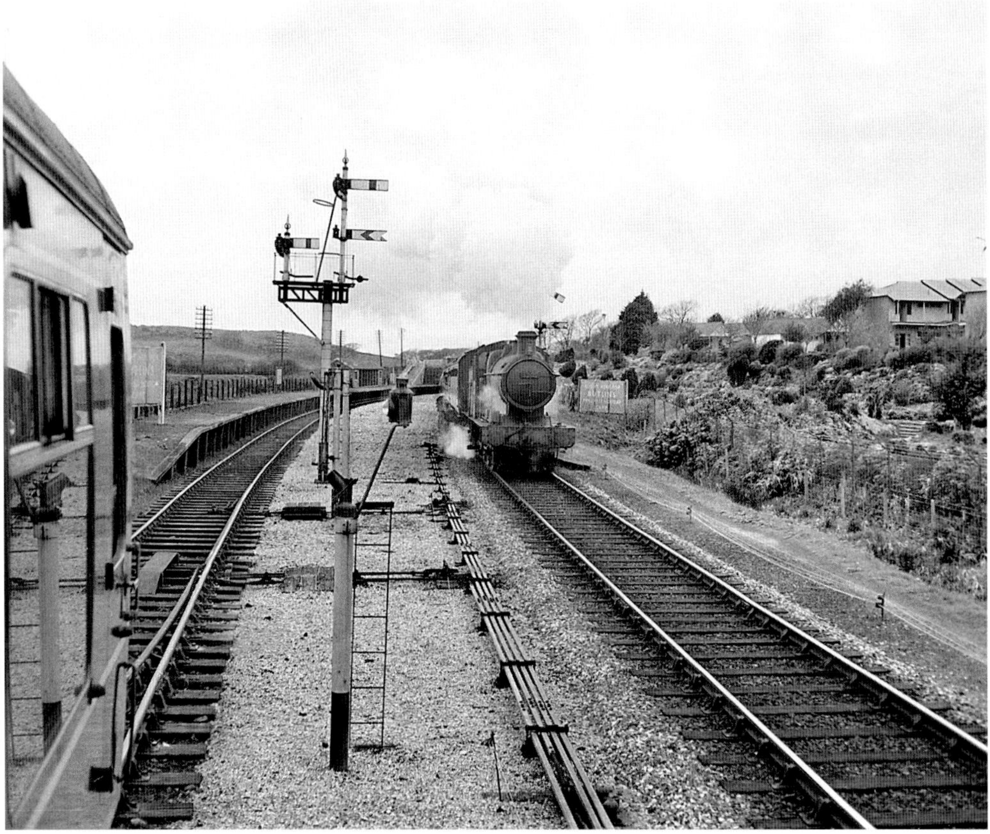

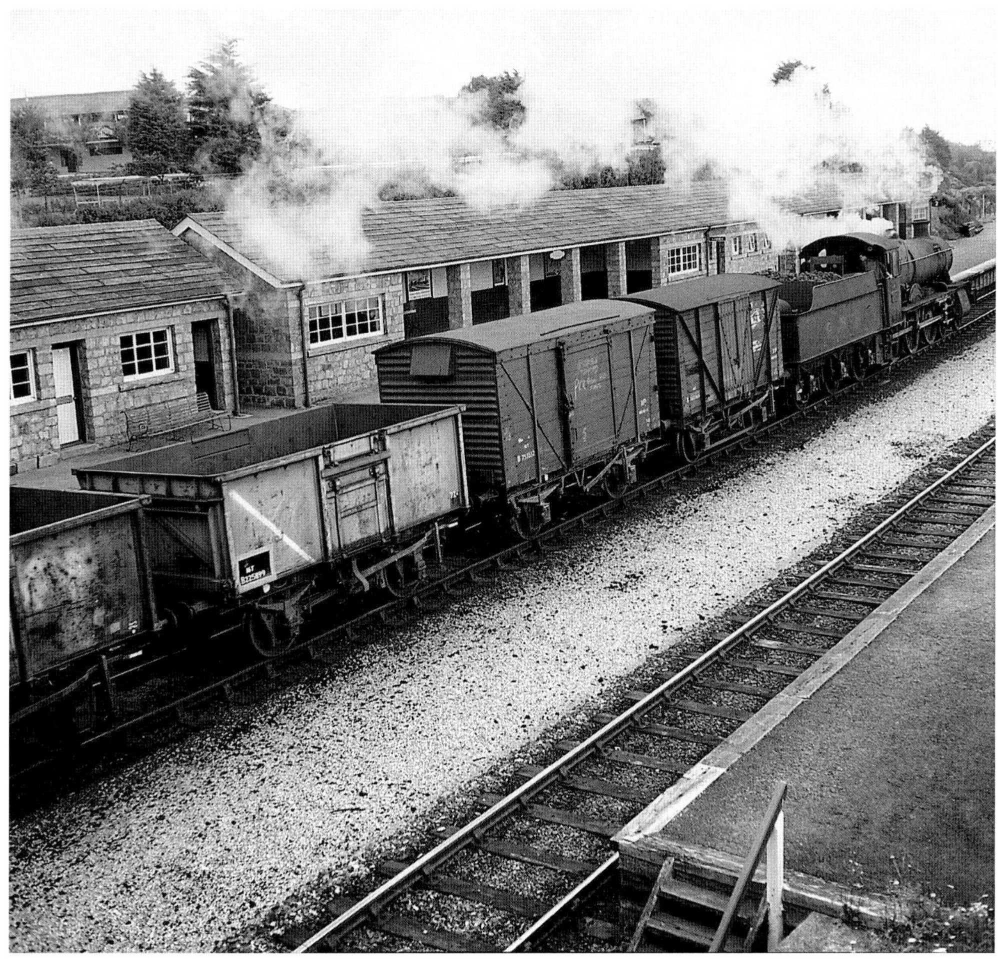

Above and opposite page: The track between Afon Wen and the Butlin's Holiday Camp destination of Penychain had been doubled in 1947; it had opened as Penychain Halt in 1933 and was upgraded to station status in 1947. The double track is seen in the first photograph and what appears to be a 75xxx 4-6-0 is running backwards towards Penychain through part of the camp complex on an unknown date. The second shows activity at Penychain's east end and is taken from an approaching DMU on 7 April 1961; just departing is No. 3209 with the 5.30 p.m. Pwllheli to Barmouth. Note there are up direction signals here on both tracks allowing bidirectional running. The third photograph dates from 26 August 1964 as a 'Manor' passes through with an eastbound freight. Ellis has listed the locomotive as No. 7814 *Fringford Manor* but the author has serious doubts about this. The Engine History card for No. 7814 shows that in the spring of 1964, this locomotive's tender was changed; from then, it ran with a visibly different larger tender from the one in this photograph. In the author's book *The Last Years Of Steam Around Central Wales*, there is a photograph of No. 7814 with this larger tender on page 112 at Tregaron on 11 June 1964, just before its transfer out of Wales to Gloucester later that month.

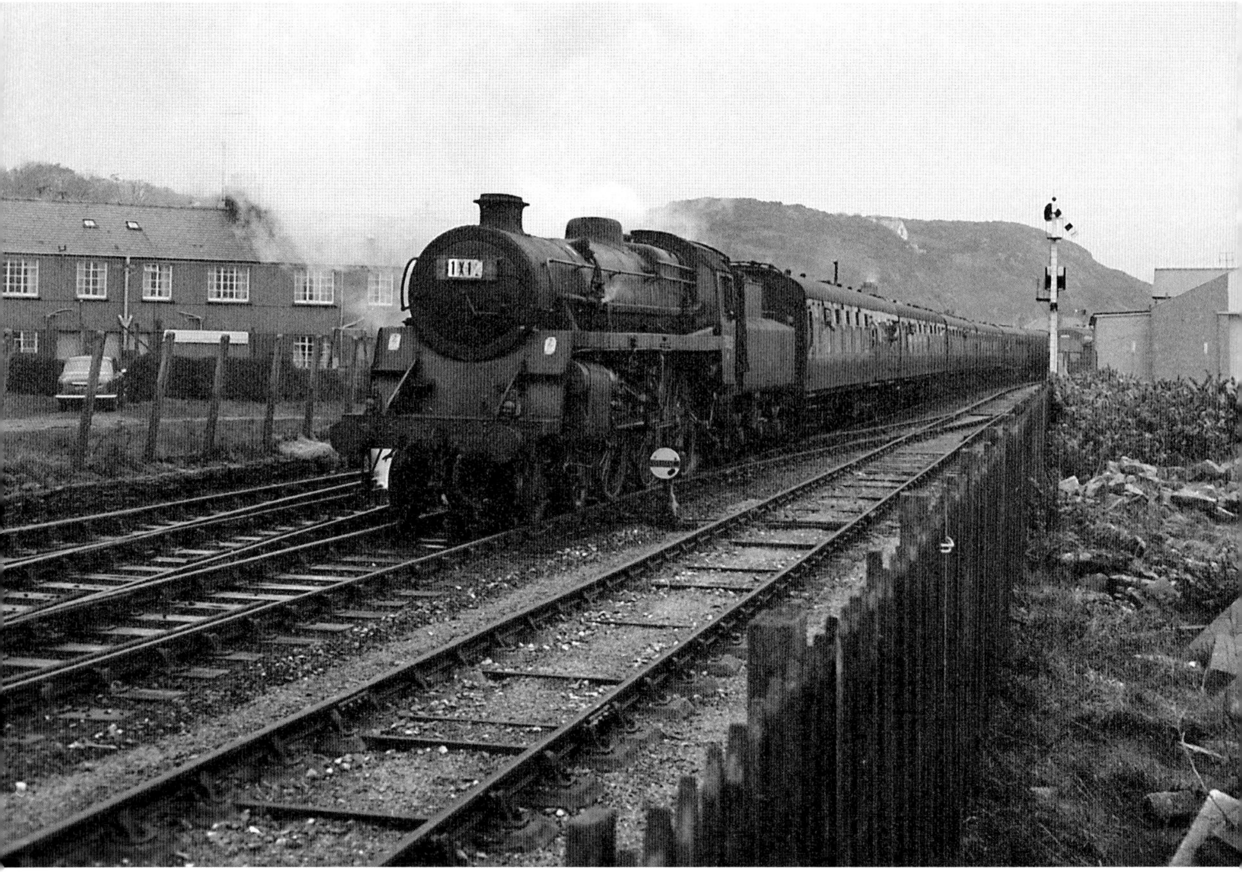

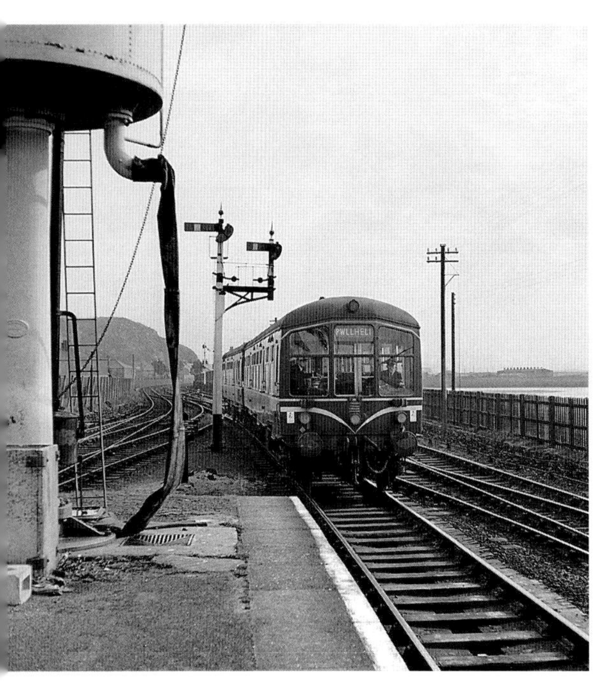

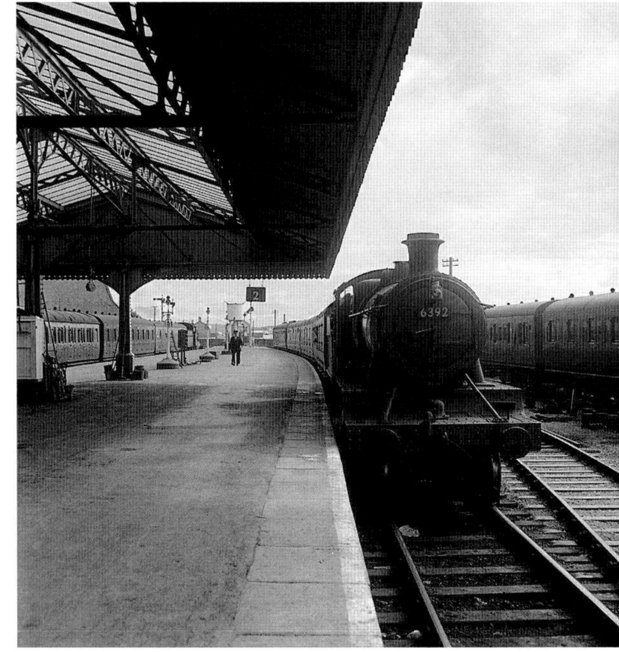

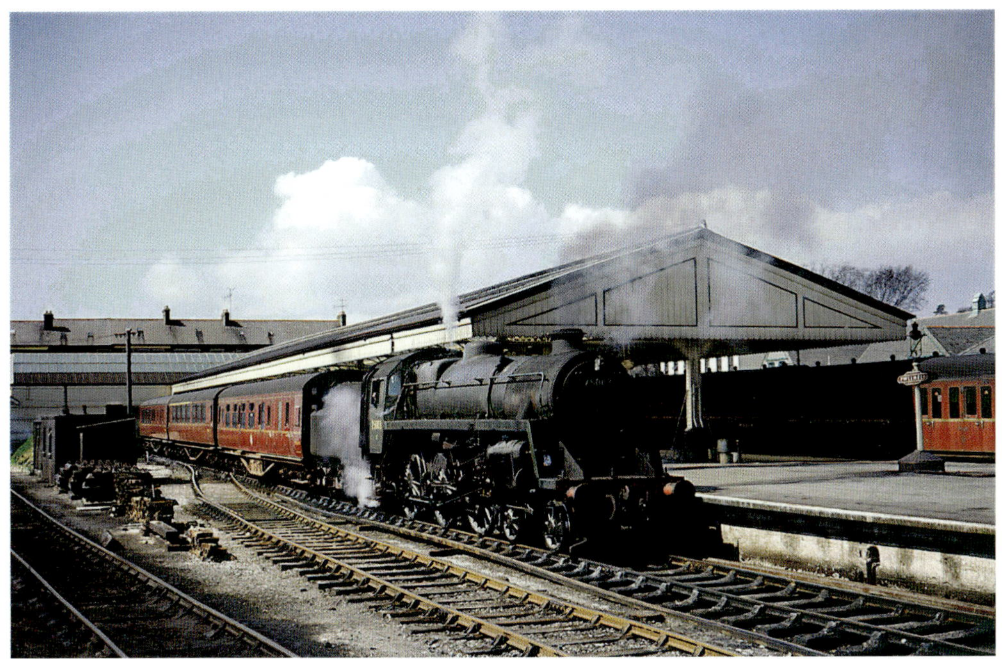

The original Cambrian Railways station at Pwllheli opened in 1867, but a half-mile extension westwards (on an embankment constructed by Pwllheli Corporation for harbour works) was opened to this station nearer to the town centre in July 1909. Taken on Kodachrome II film and showing a manufacturer's date stamp of July 1963, No. 75003 is about to depart from Pwllheli with a three-coach local over the Cambrian route. The BR Standard Class 4 4-6-0 came about because of a requirement by the Western Region (WR) for a longer range than the 2-6-4 tank engine, but still with a restricted axle loading—something similar to the GWR 'Manor' class. The former Cambrian lines were very much in the minds of authority where the BR Standard Class 5 4-6-0 was precluded by being too heavy. No. 75003 was built at Swindon and entered service at Shrewsbury during August 1951. Twenty were initially allocated to the WR and authority was obtained to apply BR-lined Brunswick green livery to them; No. 75029 was the first to emerge in May 1957 with No. 75003 following in May 1959. The lined green livery is still visible, just, under the grime; No. 75003 finished its days at Worcester and was withdrawn from there in October 1965.

Opposite page: Now, three arrivals at Pwllheli showing slightly different locations spread over a period of about six years. The first shows No. 75020 on the forty-two-chain-long double track section from Pwllheli East signal box (by the engine shed) to Pwllheli West signal box (just visible in the third photograph) opened in connection with the National Eisteddfod held here in 1925. No. 75020 has charge of the Warwickshire Railway Society's 'Cambrian' rail tour that ran in poor weather on 16 April 1966 in the 'newest' of all the photographs in this entire book. No. 75020 has a double chimney but will shortly be seen again on page 55 with its original single chimney, this change happening in 1962. The DMU arriving in the second photograph is that Ellis will use for his journey to Bangor on 7 April 1961. The scheduled arrival time was 10.20 a.m., and in the background to the right of the DMU is the outline of Pwllheli engine shed. The final view dates from 8 August 1960, and No. 6392 is preparing to back out of the terminus after arriving at Pwllheli with the 6.40 a.m. from Machynlleth; just visible behind the water tower is Pwllheli West signal box.

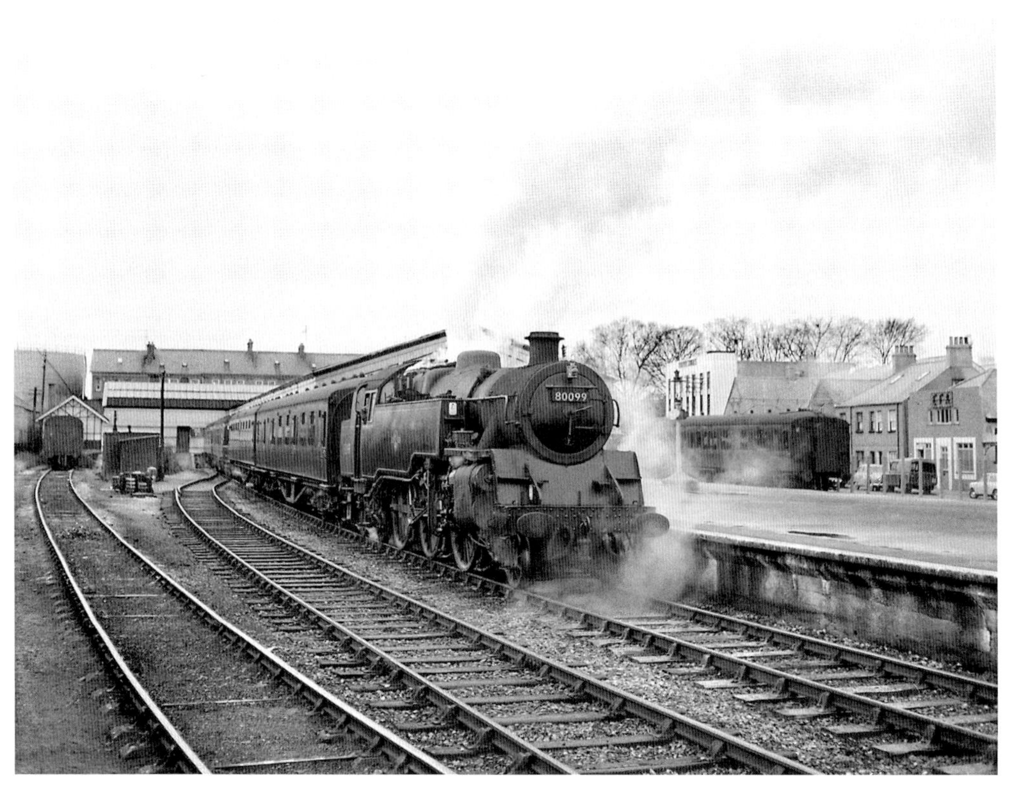

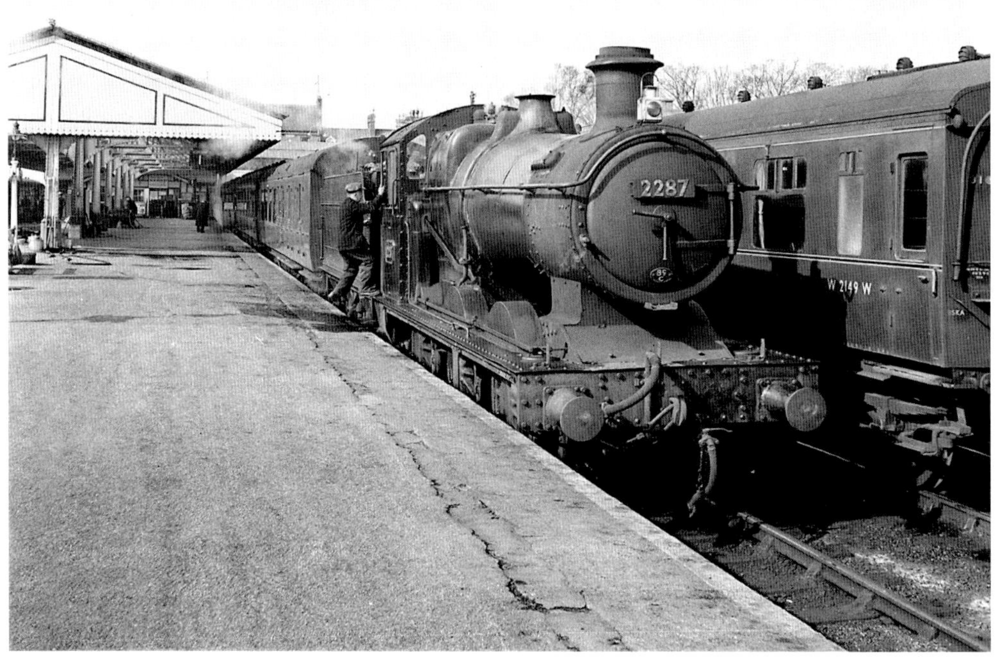

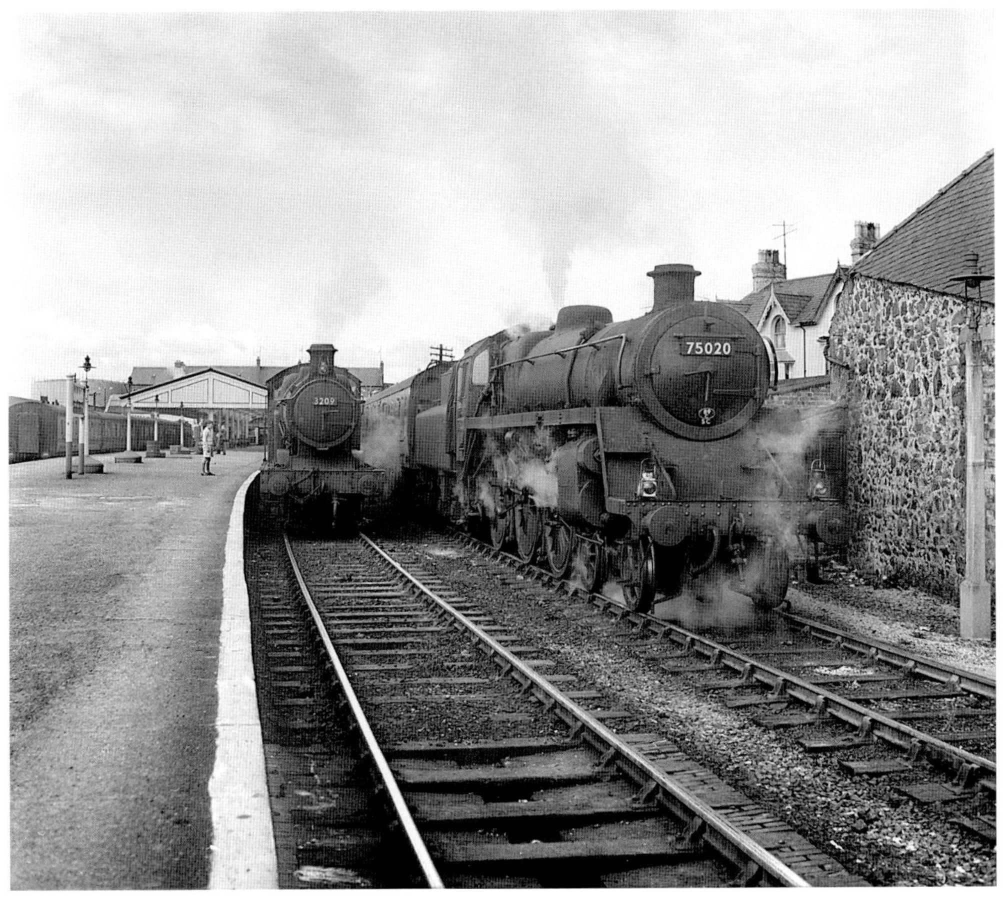

An enduring Victorian ambition was the extension of the railway to Porth Dinllaen, but this never happened and Pwllheli remained a terminus (although a horse-drawn tramway did once operate further west to Llanbedrog). Pwllheli station had a semi-island platform with two faces and can be seen in the following three photographs. Firstly, No. 80099 stands ready with what is believed to be the 1.55 p.m. to Portmadoc on New Year's Day 1964; at the rear is a two-car DMU. The second photograph dates from 7 April 1961, when No. 2287 has charge of the 10.25 a.m. stopping service to Machynlleth. There were stops or request stops at every station and halt along the route, and it would take two hours and fifty-six minutes for No. 2287 to cover the 57.75 miles. The final photograph was taken on Monday, 8 August 1960, and on the left, No. 3209 has charge of the 10.25 a.m. to Machynlleth. On the right and displaying an express lamp code is No. 75020 (still with a single chimney) coupled to stock for the 'North Wales Radio Land Cruise'; there was no platform on this track. Introduced in 1951 and equipped with loudspeakers for a running commentary, these summertime scenic specials provided popular round trips across North Wales through places such as Barmouth, Dolgellau, Corwen, Denbigh, Rhyl, Bangor, and Caernarvon.

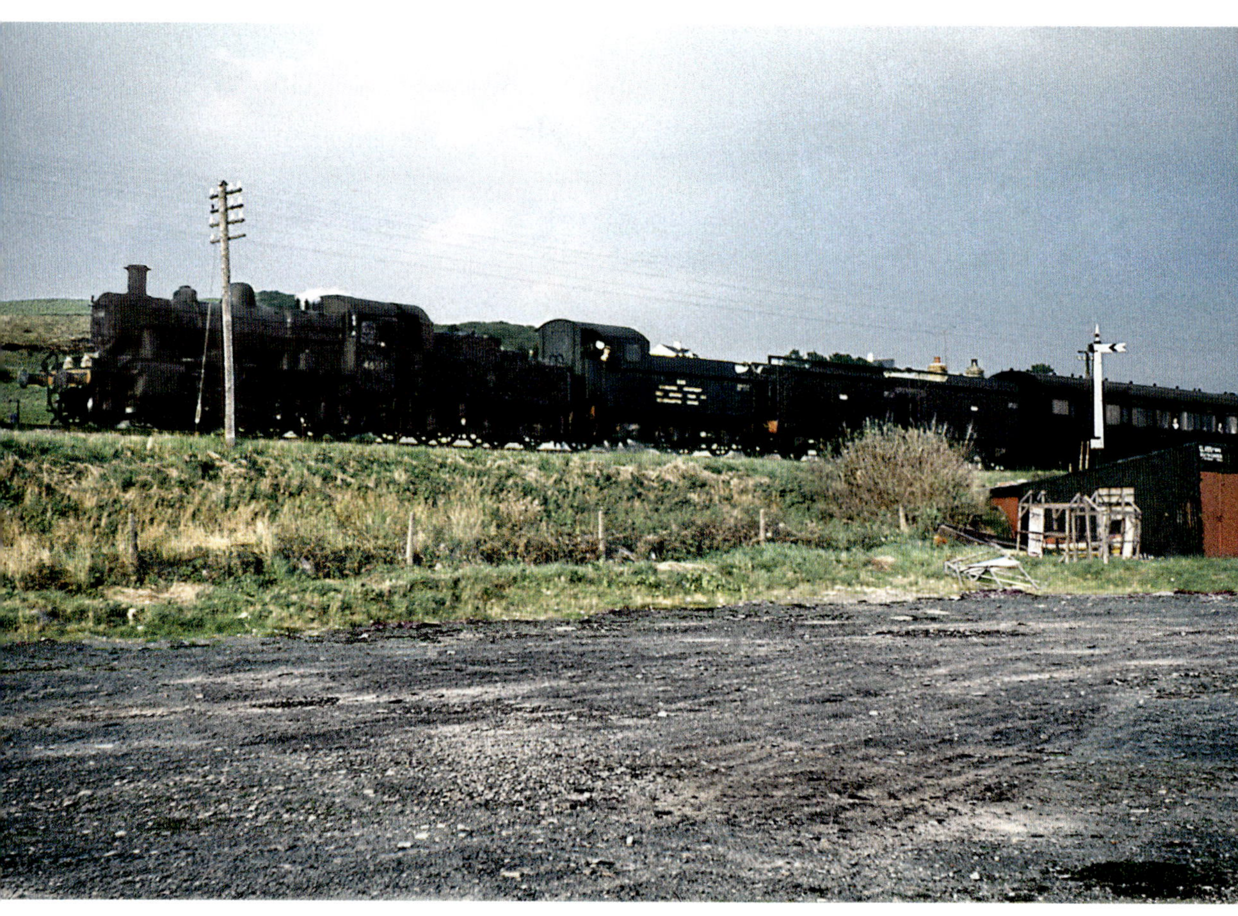

Ellis has left no details at all with this photograph, and while not of the best quality, it is of a somewhat rare type of train. The locomotive is an Ivatt Class 2 2-6-0 and, despite being of LMS design, is probably one of those built at the ex-GWR Swindon works in the early 1950s. The number is very difficult to decipher, but it could be No. 46515 that was allocated to Oswestry from the late 1950s until the early 1960s. This is a weed-killing train and is composed of old GWR tenders plus staff accommodation. The location was a puzzle for the author, but a possible site is east of Criccieth station with the photograph taken behind the Esplanade and including Criccieth's down fixed distant signal.

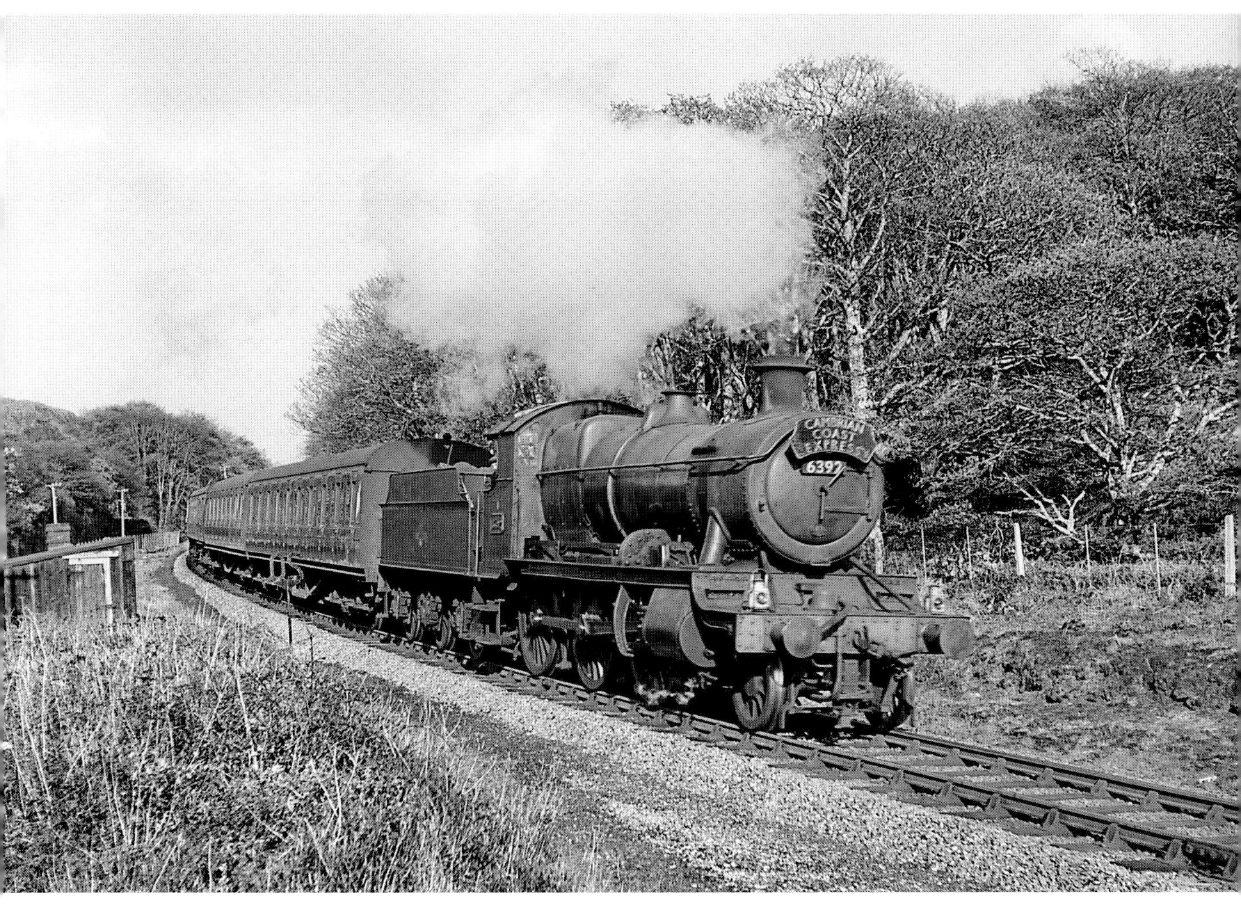

This was found very 'out-of-sequence', and the author can find no record of it at all in Ellis's normally excellent notebooks that list his black and white photographs. This location is about 1 mile west of Portmadoc and close to the site of the one-time Wern Siding. No. 6392, withdrawn in October 1961, has charge of the route's premier down service, the 'Cambrian Coast Express'. This title was first used in 1921 and applied to various summer expresses between Paddington and the Cambrian Coast. It was not until June 1954 that the WR introduced a through restaurant car (to Aberystwyth) train for the first time ever, serving Montgomeryshire and resorts along Cardigan Bay throughout the year; the restaurant car surviving until 1961 Although the name has seen some use since, the last steam-hauled 'Cambrian Coast Express' (to Aberystwyth) ran on Saturday, 4 March 1967.

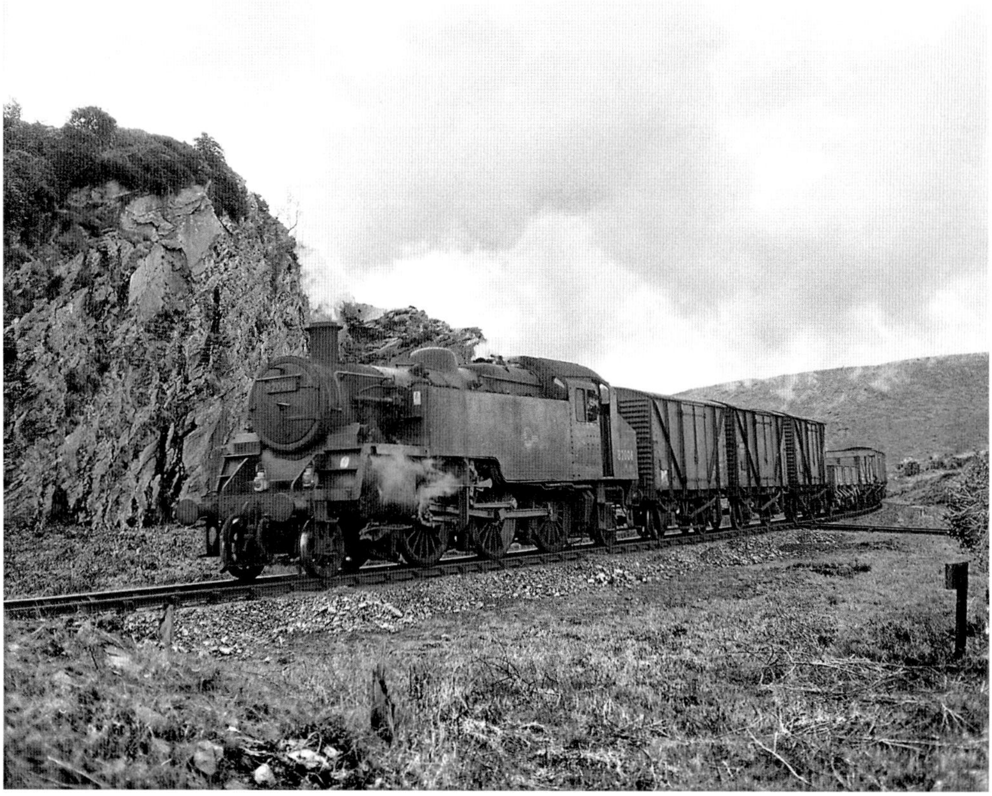

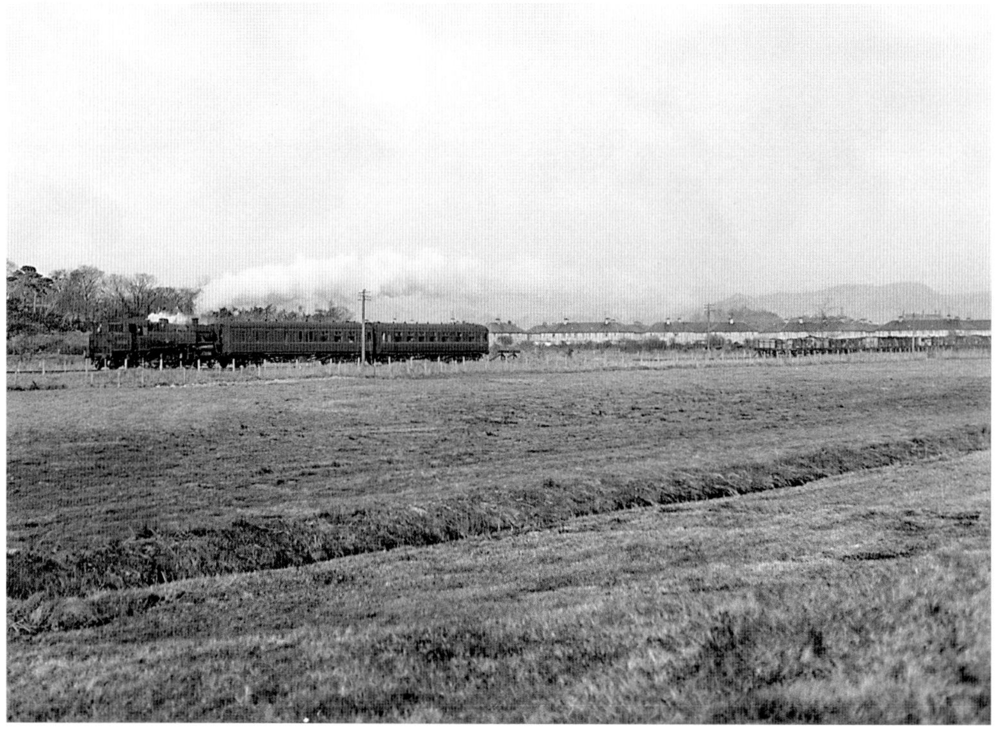

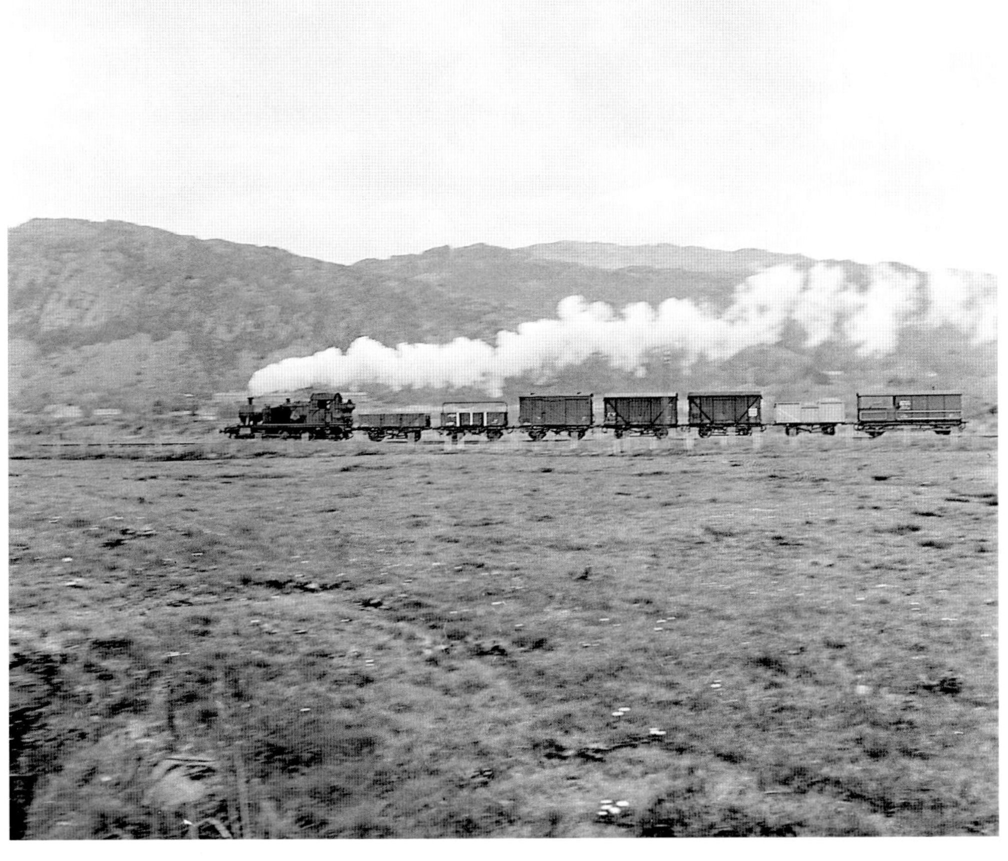

Although there were no details from Ellis to go with the previous photograph close to Portmadoc, there are for all of these next three. First, taken on FP3 film with settings of 250/5.6 on 11 April 1964 at about 12.45 p.m., this is again by the site of Wern Siding. About to descend the 1 in 50 grade to Portmadoc is No. 82006 with a partially fitted freight train. Secondly, taken the day previously, the 6.00 p.m. Barmouth to Pwllheli just after leaving Portmadoc with one of the BR Standard Class 4 2-6-4Ts, possibly No. 80098. Before the BR Standard tank engines arrived and replaced them, the GWR 45xx and 55xx 2-6-2Ts were often seen, there were fifteen allocated to Machynlleth by 1947. An unidentified member with the larger water tanks fitted from No. 4575 travels onwards nears Portmadoc in April 1960.

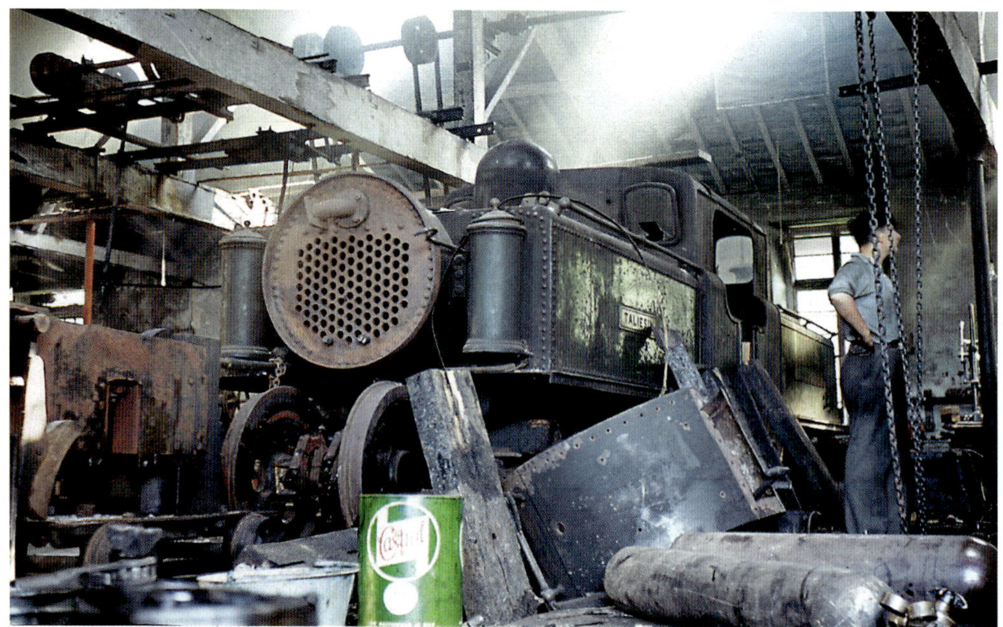

Above: This and the next three photographs are all taken at the narrow-gauge Festiniog Railway's Boston Lodge works; however, none of them have any details such as date or content. After much research, the author has come to the conclusion that it is more likely all were taken in the summer of 1955; the earliest colour photographs in Ellis's entire collection that can be precisely dated are from 1955. This is *Taliesin*, a Double Fairlie 0-4-4-0T that entered traffic on the FR in 1886. When built, this locomotive's name was *Livingston Thompson* (an early director of the FR), becoming *Taliesin* in 1931. In 1939, the engine was put in the erecting shop for repairs, but due to the pressures of the Second World War, the work was still unfinished when employees from the old FR were paid off in 1946. Following the rebirth of the FR in 1954, the first public passenger services ran in July 1955, work finally started on *Taliesin*, and it entered service in September 1956.

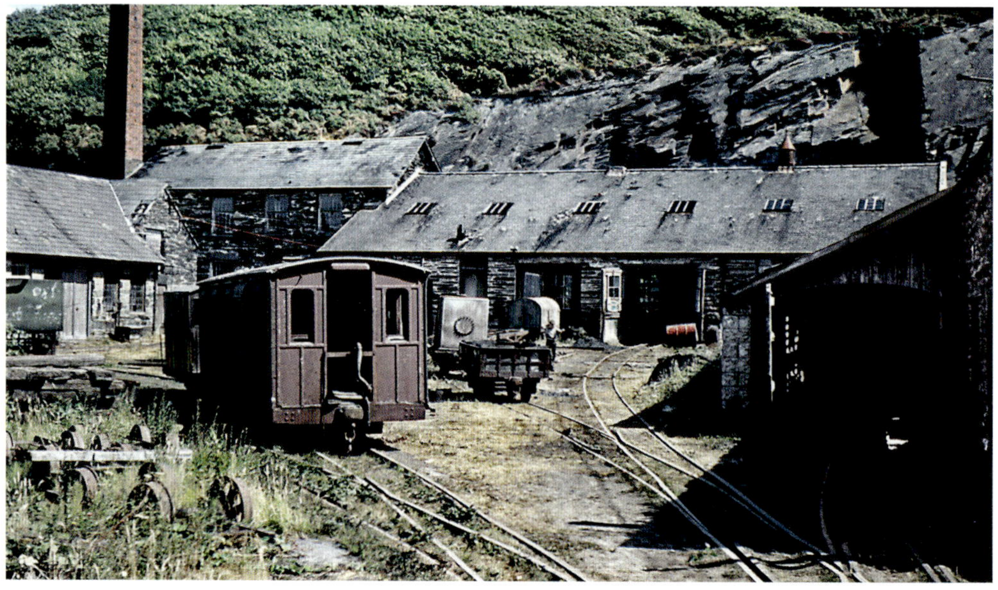

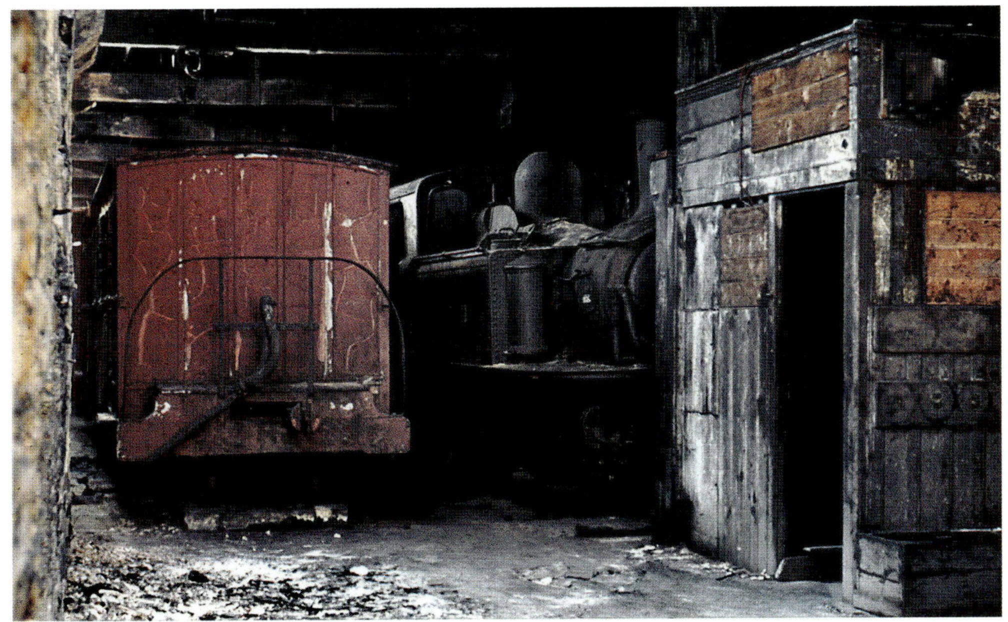

Above, below, and opposite below: Three more photographs at the FR's Boston Lodge works that are all believed to date from the summer of 1955. First, a general view of the Bottom or West Yard with tracks fanning out, left of centre is the machine shop, to its right the erecting shop, and on the extreme right is the paint shop. The last two working locomotives on the FR were *Princess* and *Merddin Emrys* when things came to an end at the beginning of August 1946. Inside the locomotive shed in the second photograph is *Merddin Emrys*; it had been left in 'last day' condition still with water in the tanks and coal in the bunker. Finally, this rusting hulk is *Palmerston*; it had last worked in 1937. In 1940, *Palmerston* had been fitted up in this position as a stationary boiler to work a steam hammer in connection with a lease of part of the works and machinery.

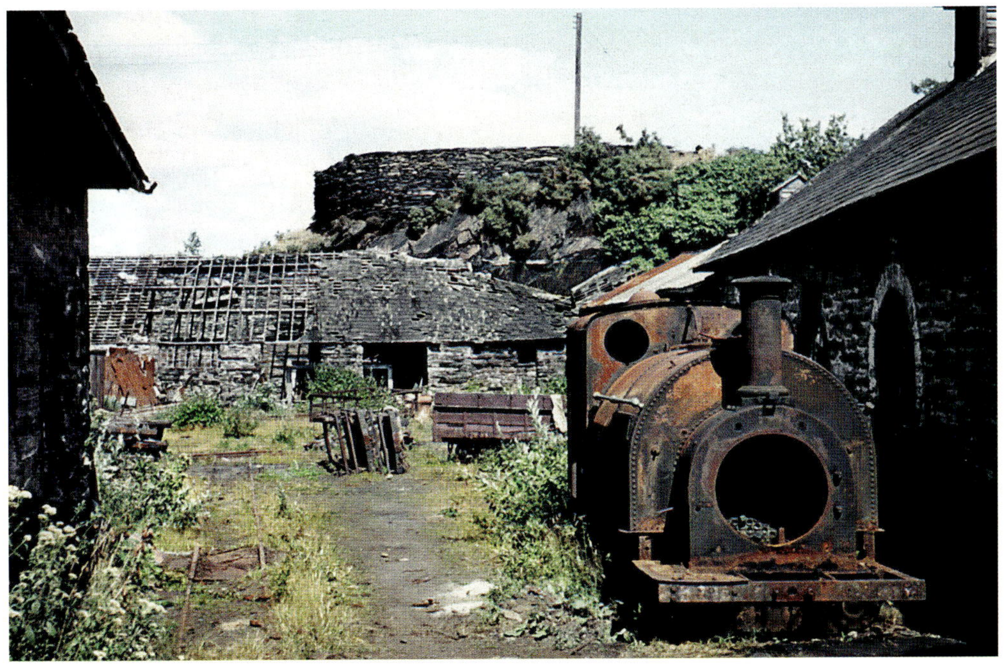

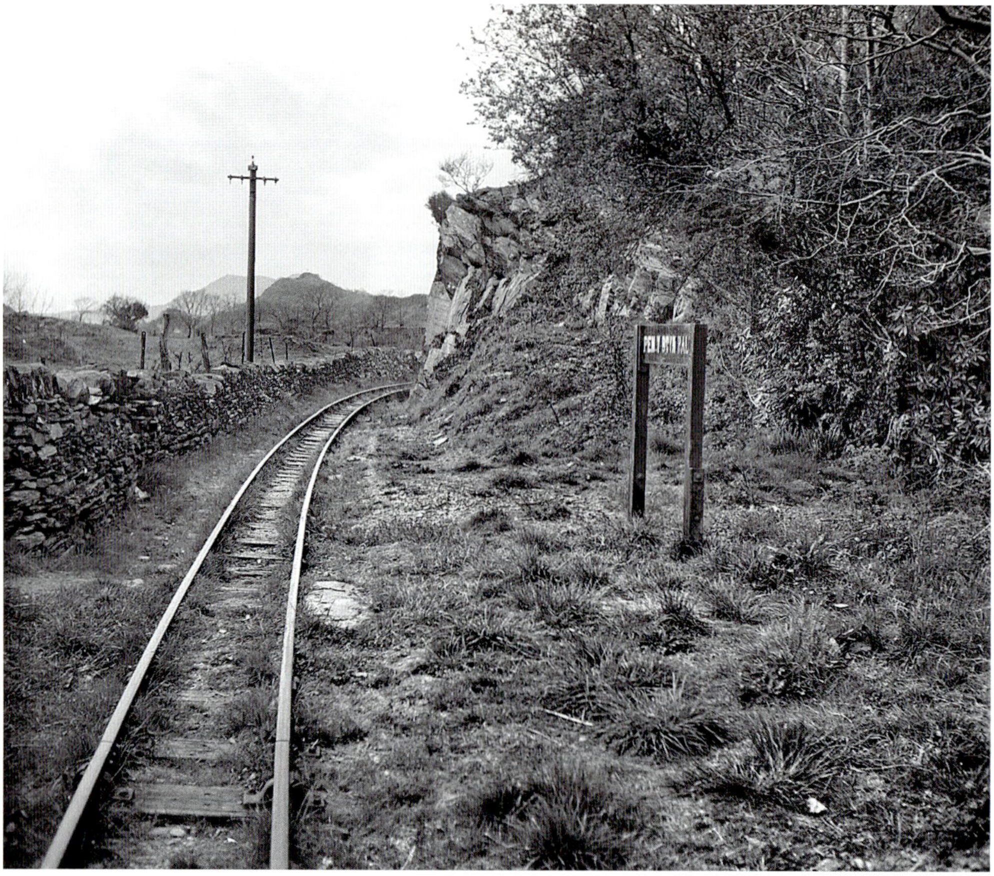

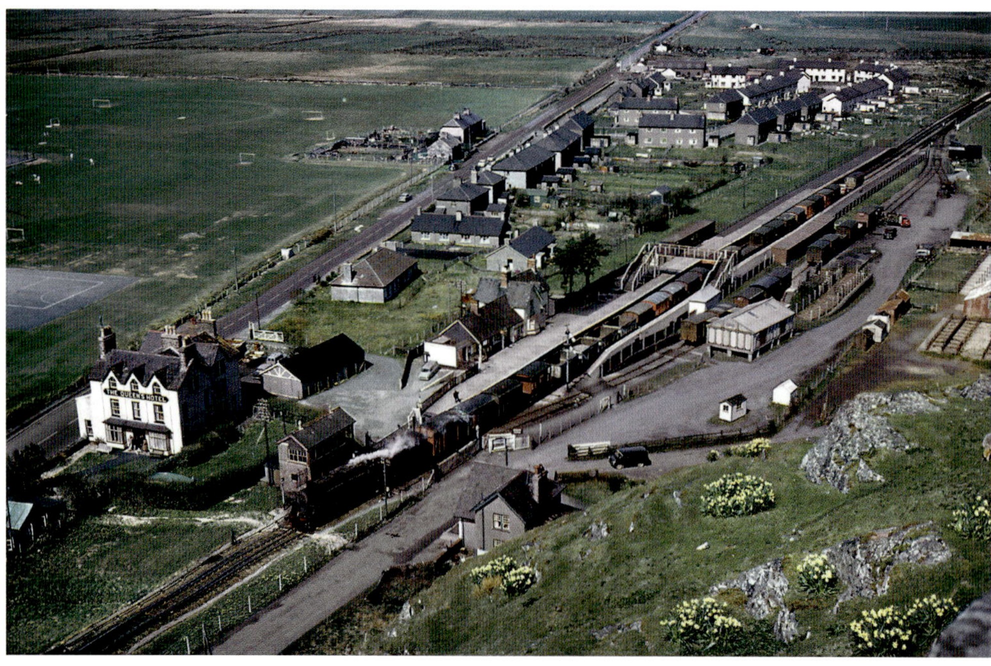
PEN Y BRYN HALT

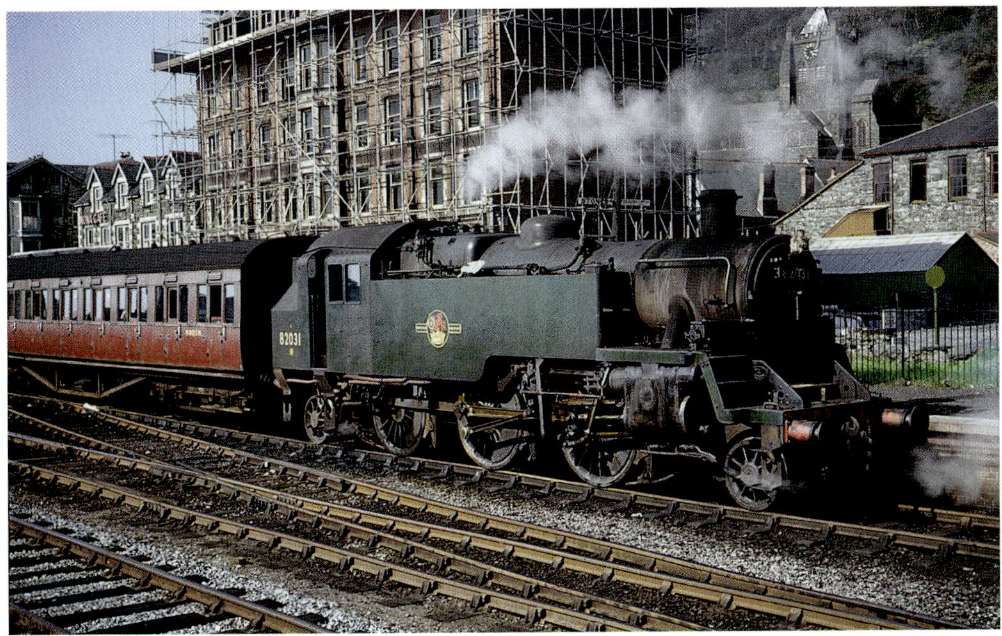

Above: We move further south to Barmouth with a series of photographs over the next few pages taken on the afternoon of Friday, 26 April 1963. No. 82031 stands waiting for custom at the up bay platform opened by the GWR in 1923, just to the south of the main station and level crossing (the main platforms at Barmouth were extended at the same time). The time according to the clock face on St John's Church in the background looks to be 4.14 p.m. Ellis has not listed the service that No. 82031 will work, but it is possibly a local to Dolgellau. The author has always thought these 82xxx tank engines an attractive class, particularly so in green livery—lined green livery would have been even better. All were built at Swindon, and No. 82031 entered service in December 1954 at Barry. It arrived locally at Machynlleth in January 1960. No. 82031 received a light intermediate repair at Eastleigh works in the summer of 1964, and although not withdrawn until December 1966 from Patricroft, Manchester, there was little suitable work available latterly. Over the twenty-five months before withdrawal, No. 82031 spent over seventeen of them in storage.

Opposite above: Robert Ellis James-Robertson (but always known to the author and his father as Ellis) was born on 8 July 1922 and grew up in Swansea, moving at the age of eleven with his family to Pen-y-Bryn in Edern, Pwllheli, North Wales. Perhaps that is why this photograph was taken of Pen-y-Bryn Halt on the FR during April 1960, one of this railway's lesser-known stops. The halt was between Minffordd and Penrhyndeudraeth where this view is looking towards Portmadoc. It had only opened in 1957 when that season's services began on 20 April; in 1956, Minffordd had been the terminus. Pen-y-Bryn Halt was closed on 5 November 1967.

Opposite below: A view of Harlech station plus its environs taken from Harlech Castle and dating from the spring of 1963. Just pulling away is an unidentified 82xxx Class 3 2-6-2T with a long Barmouth-bound freight train that looks to be made up of two separate services each with its own brake van. It is difficult to be 100 per cent certain at this distance, but it does appear that the lamp code on the locomotive indicates this is a partially fitted freight service, in the middle of which are gunpowder vans from Cooke's Explosives works at Penrhyndeudraeth. When opened in 1867, there was a passing loop at Harlech but with only one platform on the down side; after the grouping, the GWR built a second on the up side. The playing fields to the left are those of Ysgol Ardudwy, a secondary school that even today generates a considerable amount of business for the railway. The open land above the playing fields is now a housing estate, and much of the goods yard area is nowadays occupied by a small industrial estate plus the Ysgol Tanycastell primary school.

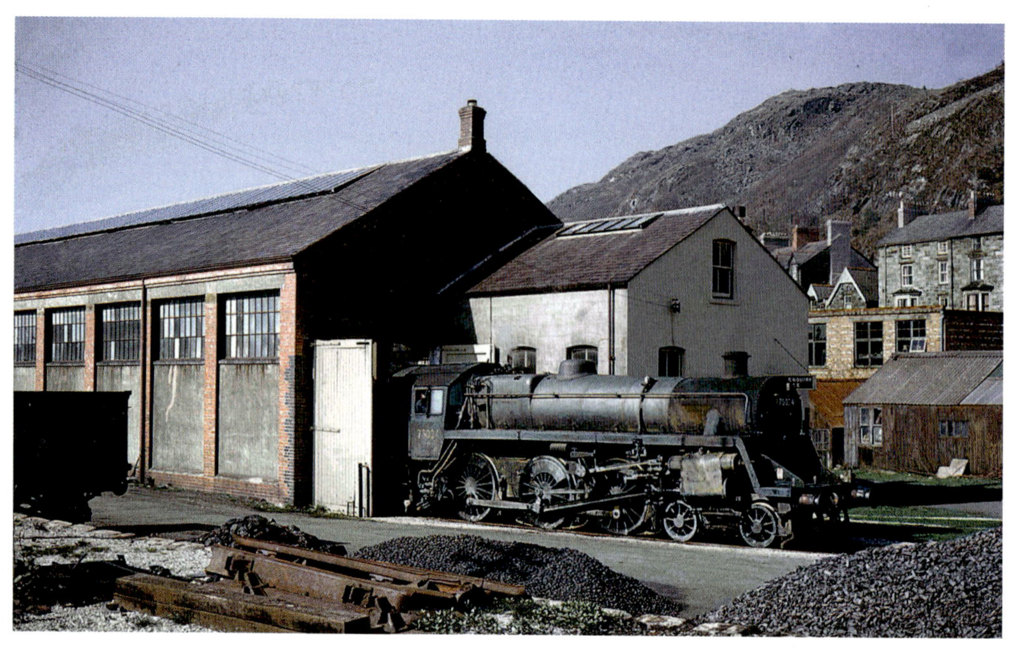

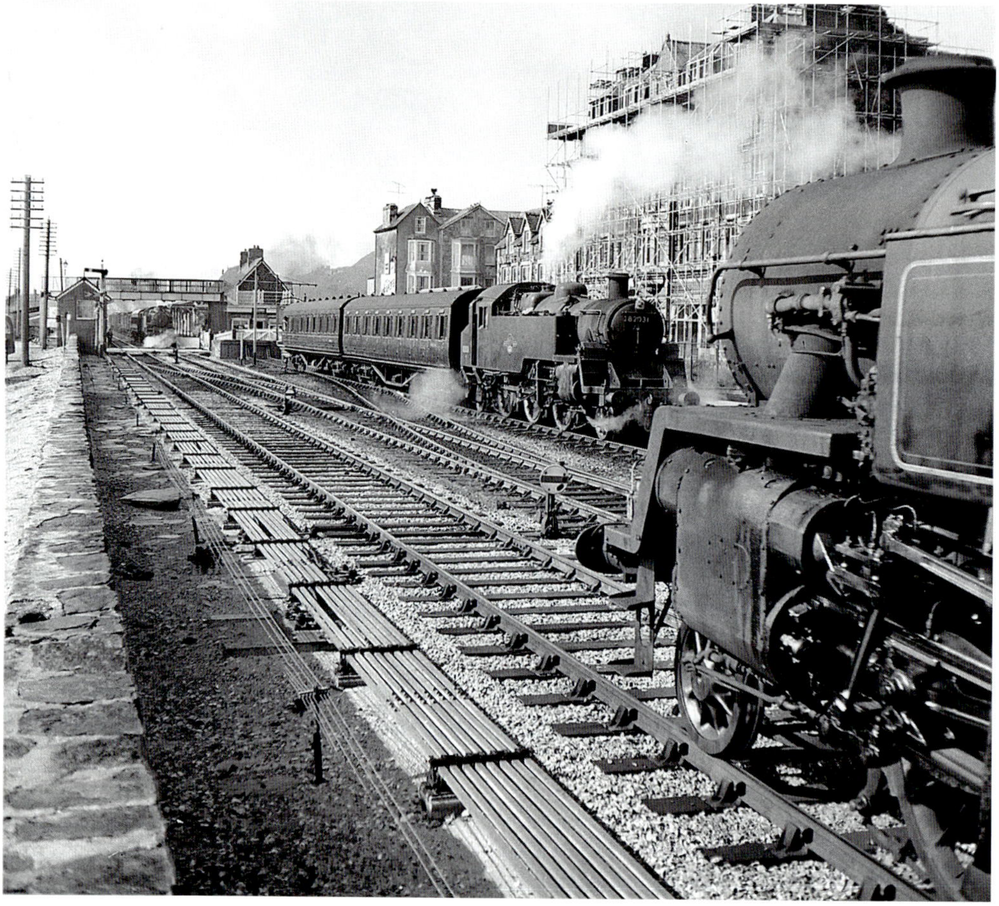

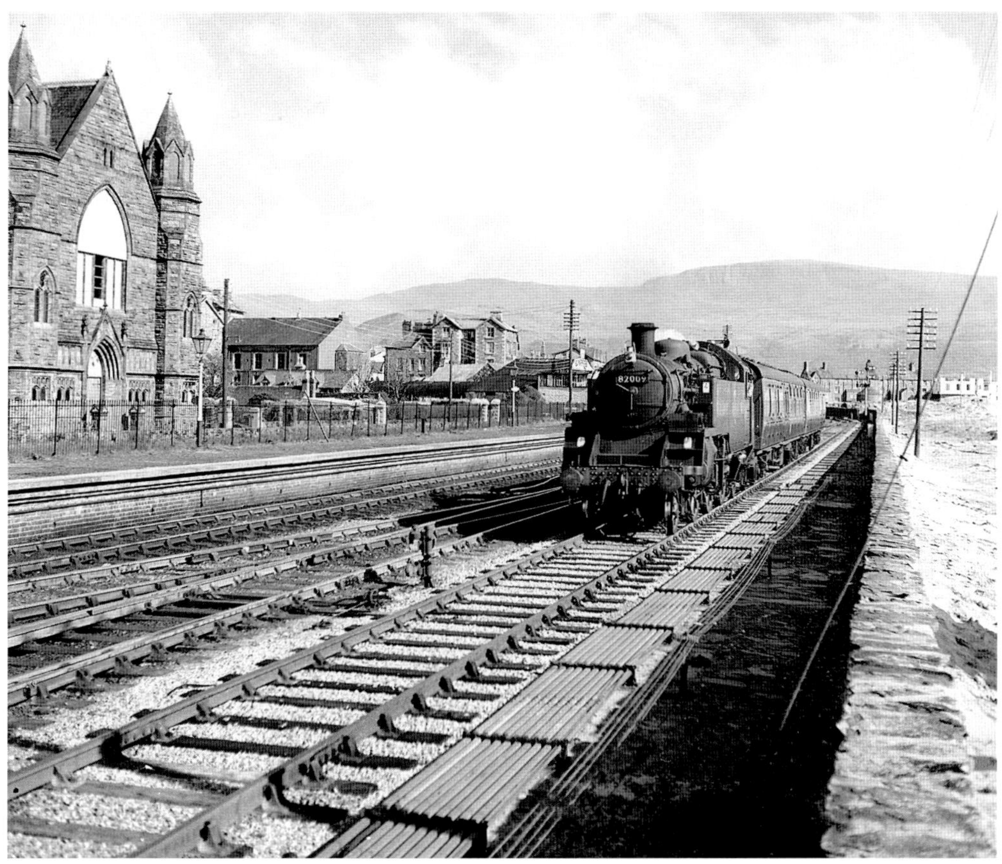

Above and opposite page: Three more photographs at Barmouth that all date from the afternoon of Friday, 26 April 1963. The goods yard was north of the station on the east side of the Cambrian coast line, and poking its head out of the goods shed is No. 75024. It was re-allocated from Tyseley, Birmingham, to Machynlleth in November 1962 and in the summer of 1965 had heavy intermediate repair a very long way from Wales—Cowlairs works, Glasgow. This repair enabled No. 75024 to survive until November 1967, latterly working from Tebay as a banking engine on Shap incline. Standard tank engine enthusiasts will enjoy the second photograph, taken at about 4.30 p.m. according to Ellis's notes. Approaching Barmouth from the south is an unidentified 2-6-4T, but both the 2-6-2Ts are known: No. 82031 in the bay on a local service and No. 82000 at the station with a Machynlleth-bound freight (both can be seen on introductory page 7). It is about 4.50 p.m. in the final photograph as No. 82009 arrives with the mid-afternoon service from Machynlleth. The large building on the left was once an English Congregational Chapel but is now the Dragon Theatre; in front of it is the up bay platform opened by the GWR in 1923.

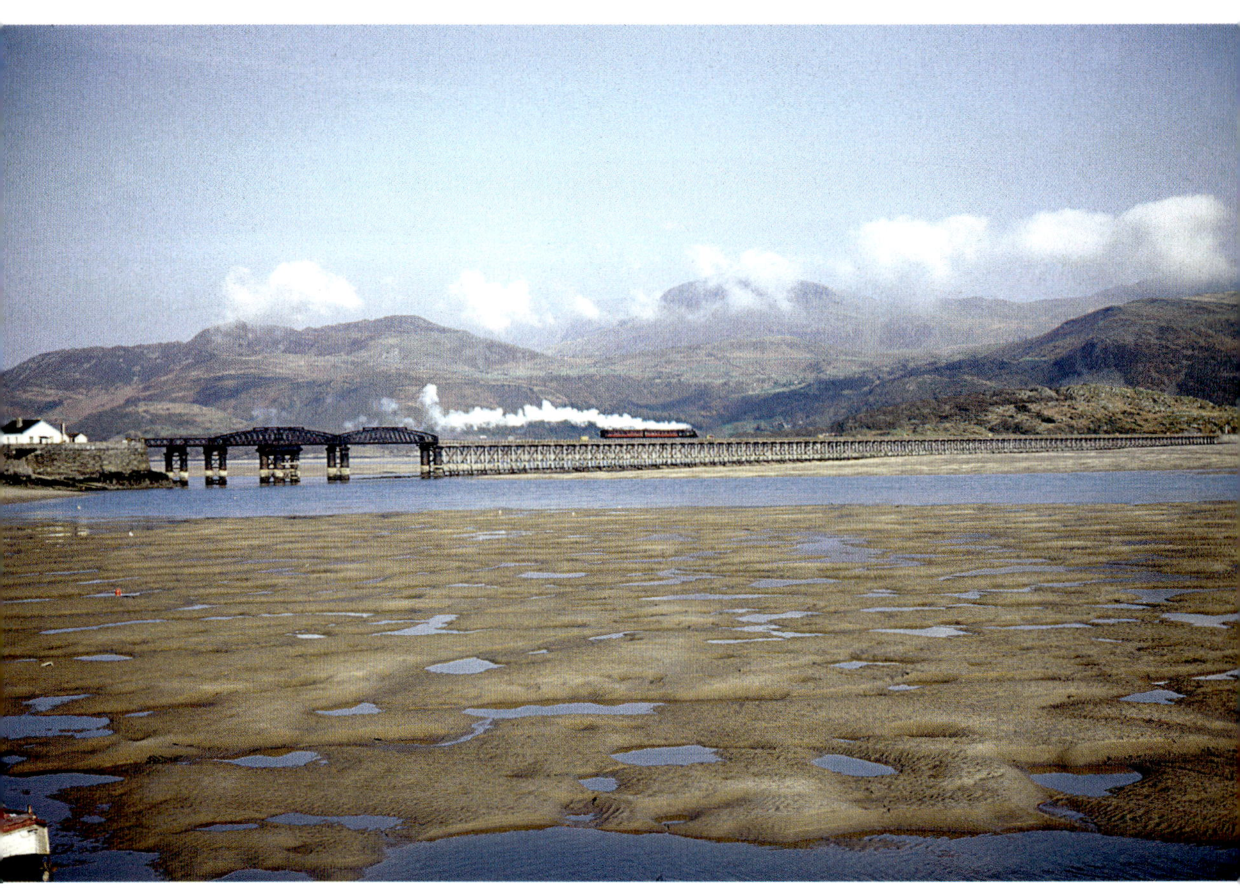

A picture-postcard view of the famous Barmouth viaduct taken on Friday, 26 April 1963. No. 82031 is heading over to Morfa Mawddach (Barmouth Junction previous to June 1960) with what could be a Dolgellau-bound local service. When built, it badly hit the trade of local ferrymen. This became even worse when a footpath was built alongside the railway over the bridge in 1879; they received compensation for loss of earnings. The large 113-foot span nearest Barmouth rotated around a central pivot to maintain the shipping channel; its foundations were sunk into rock 90 feet below high-water level. When this section had to be opened, it needed an eight-man team using crank handles on the swinging span, and it could open either clockwise or anti-clockwise; either way, the workers became marooned in the process. It was still capable of opening at the date of this photograph, but this is not the case today.

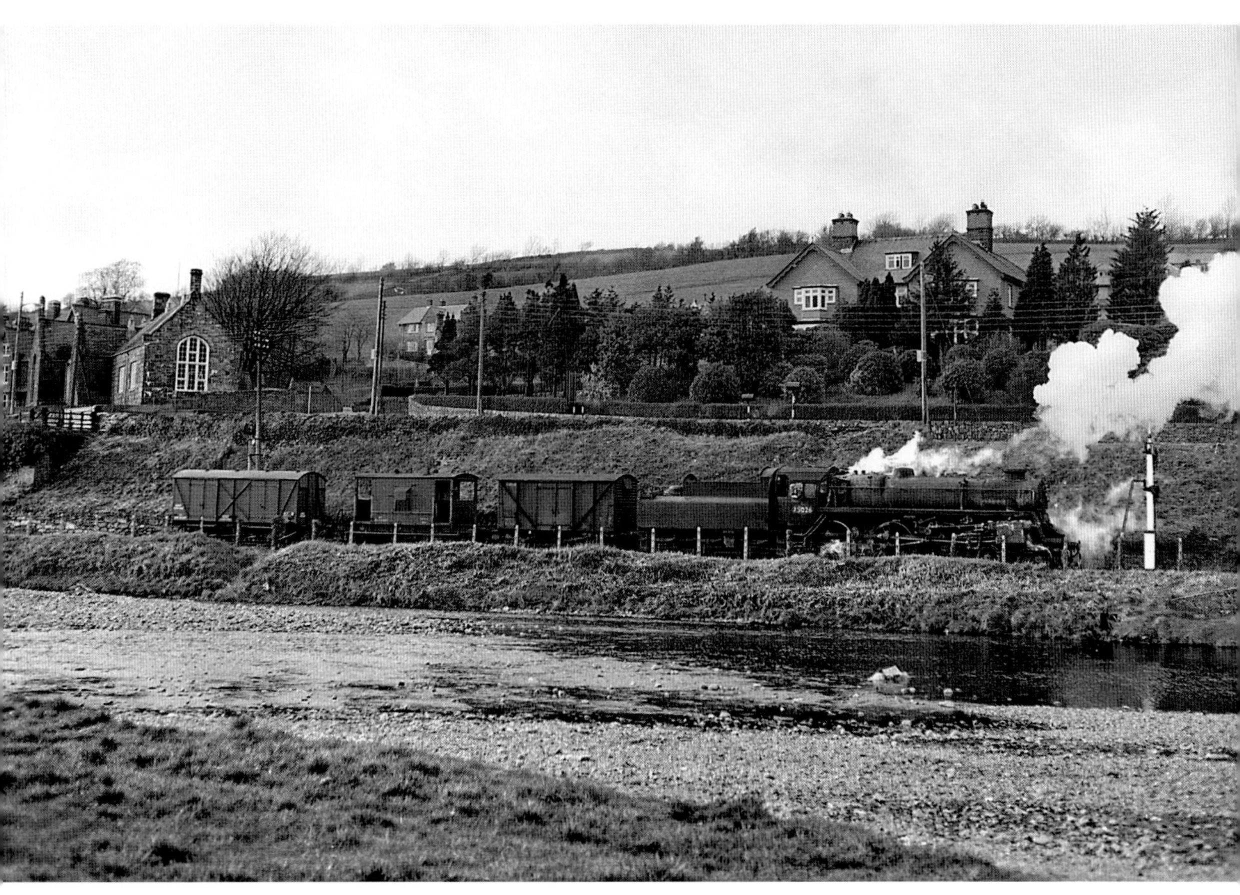

Certain Welsh place names have been spelt in different ways over the years, and a famous example is where this photograph of No. 75026 engaged in some shunting was taken. Dolgellau was the name officially adopted by the local Rural District Council in 1958, but many other variations have been used over the years, including those used by the railway. The CR arrived from the west and their original station only open for a short time in the 1860s was spelt 'Dolgelli'. The Bala & Dolgelly Railway arrived from the east, and despite the spelling of the railway company, their station was spelt 'Dolgelley'; this became the town's permanent station. In 1960, BR officially renamed the station to Dolgellau, the same as the RDC; four different spellings being used by the railway over the years. No. 75026 (fitted with a double chimney in June 1962) is just to the west of the station by the goods yard on 7 April 1964; the freight service was withdrawn less than one month later. As with classmate No. 75024 seen earlier at Barmouth, this was another locomotive that had a works visit to Scotland in 1965 and survived until the end of 1967 at Tebay banking trains up Shap incline.

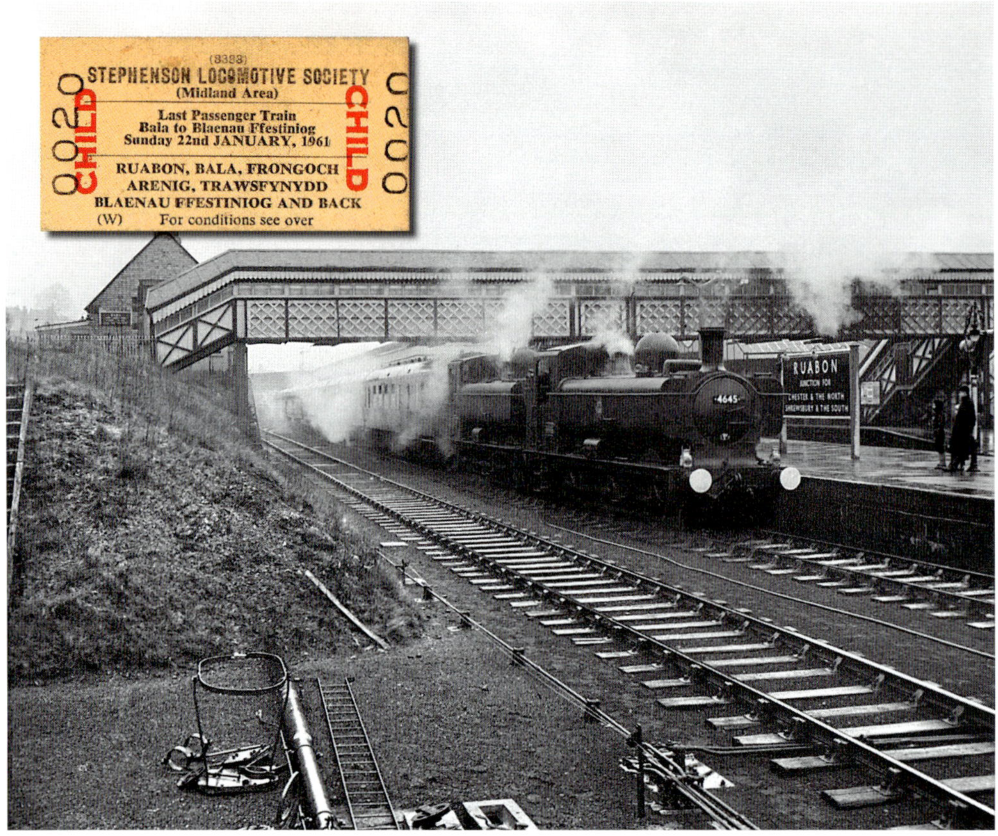

A trip the author and his father in addition to Ellis travelled on was the SLS (Midland Area) 'Last Passenger Train to Blaenau Festiniog' that ran on Sunday, 22 January 1961. The tour started from here at Ruabon with pannier tanks Nos 4645 plus 8791, and the weather was foul. Nearly 50 miles of single track and numerous signal boxes had to be specially opened for this double-headed special, and this was reflected in the cost of 17s 6d (8s 9d for the author aged nine using this ticket). Despite being a Sunday, connections were made with service trains from both the Chester and Birmingham directions. The nominally independent companies striking west of Ruabon (all worked by the GWR)—the Vale of Llangollen, the Llangollen and Corwen, the Corwen and Bala, and the Bala and Dolgelly—were able to get running powers through to Barmouth over the CR, and it was all open throughout to the coast by the summer of 1869. All four were eventually absorbed into the GWR, and it provided that company with a means of competing against the LNWR (via Bangor and Afon Wen) from Merseyside. The GWR were also able to siphon off most traffic from the coast north of Aberdovey away from the CR's Whitchurch line, and hence even more trade taken from the LNWR.

Opposite above: A very photogenic location, this is Berwyn Halt to the west of Llangollen. On the left is the River Dee and to the far right is the main A5 Holyhead road; these two, plus a minor road and the railway, were confined together in a narrow valley. No. 75020 is pulling away towards Corwen on 8 September 1963 with the 1.35 p.m. through train from Chester to Barmouth. Berwyn was demoted to 'Halt' status in 1954, and the railway closed totally at the end of 1964. Yet the line through Berwyn has been restored to working order by the heritage Llangollen Railway; they have also rebuilt the cantilevered platform extension (removed in the late 1950s) that used to be attached to the right side of the viaduct. The Llangollen Railway announced it was going into receivership on 1 March 2021.

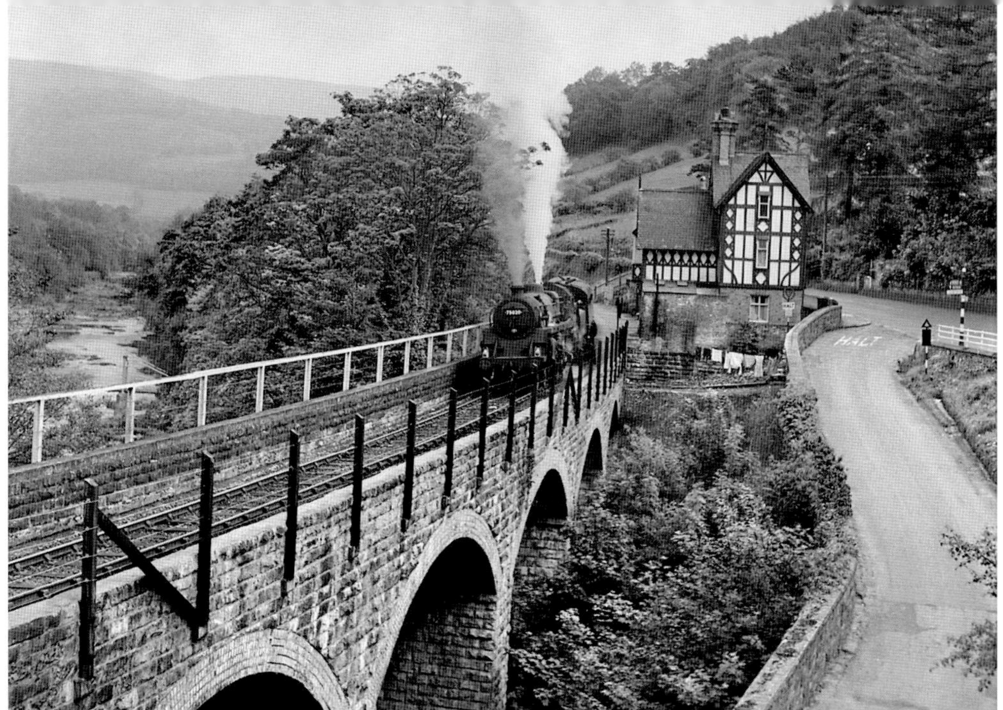

Below: It is just before 4 p.m. on 9 September 1961 and departing from Bonwm Halt is an unidentified GWR Class 74xx lightweight pannier tank with the 3.25 p.m. service from Bala to Wrexham. The timetable indicates this working had second-class accommodation only, but the first coach has two '1s' underneath the middle compartments and so does have first-class on this day. In the previous commentary, it was said the railway through Berwyn closed in December 1964; however, it was not that straightforward. The passenger service over the entire length from Ruabon to Morfa Mawddach (the one-time Barmouth Junction) was scheduled to cease on and from Monday, 18 January 1965. This was brought forward due to flooding that washed away part of the route with heavy rain falling for several days up to 12 December 1964. Through passenger services officially ceased from Ruabon to Barmouth on and from Monday, 14 December 1964, but continued (after some repairs) from Bala to the coast and also between Ruabon and Llangollen until scheduled closure the following January. The flood damage was not repaired between Bala and Llangollen. In fact, the end of 1964 and beginning of 1965 was a traumatic time for the railways of Wales, with some quite long strategic routes closing for passenger services, such as Aberystwyth to Carmarthen (56 miles), Caernarvon to Afon Wen (19 miles), Ruabon to Morfa Mawddach (53 miles), and Whitchurch to Welshpool (34 miles).

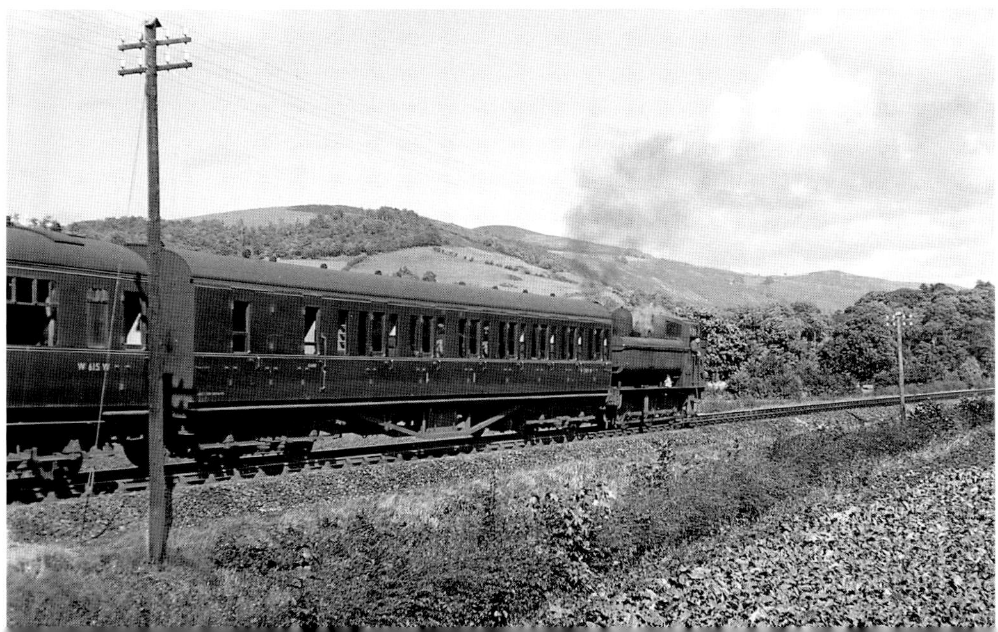

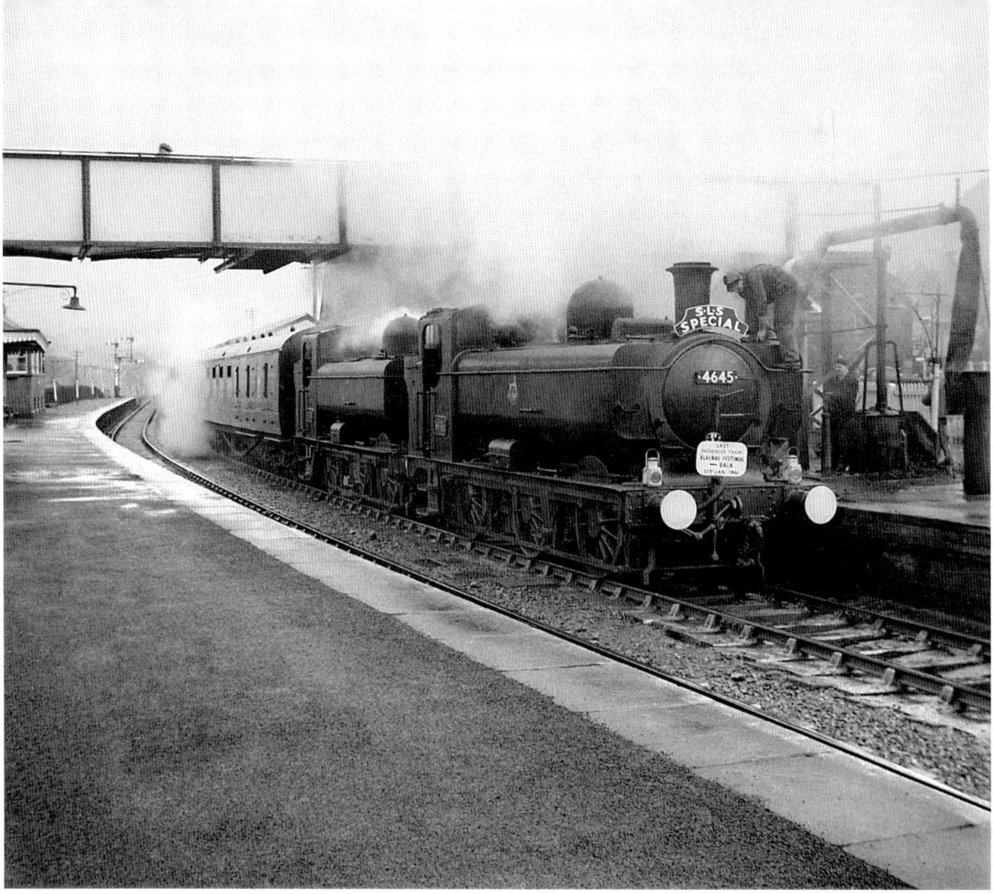

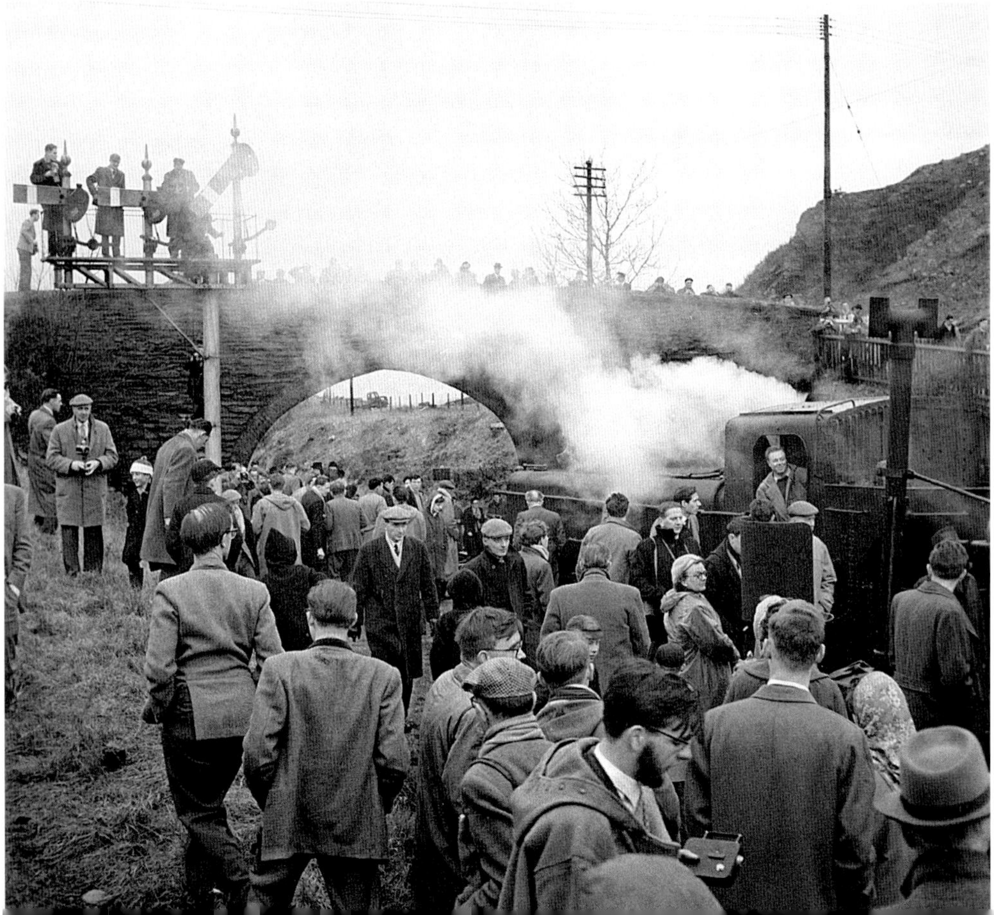

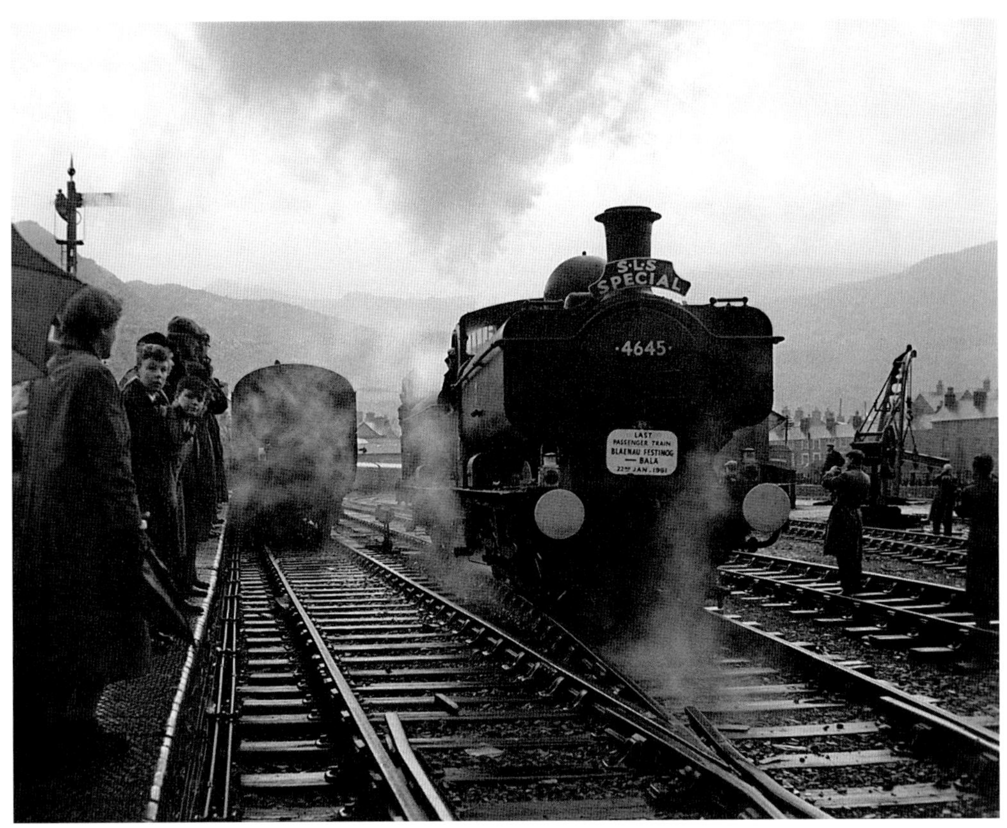

Above and opposite page: Three more photographs of the SLS 'Last Passenger Train to Blaenau Festiniog' rail tour with pannier tanks Nos 4645 and 8791 that ran in very poor weather on Sunday, 22 January 1961. It had originally been due to run one week later, but as track demolition was scheduled to start that weekend, the tour was brought forward by one week. First, during a water stop at Corwen on the outbound journey, the signals behind the special are for the two separate routes to Ruthin and Ruabon. Enthusiasts are everywhere during the outbound stop at Trawsfynydd in the second photograph. The pannier tanks have uncoupled following arrival at Blaenau Ffestiniog Central (officially spelt by the railway with two 'fs' from 1951) in the final photograph and will run back to Tan-y-Manod where there was a turntable. Note the 'fs' spelling difference between the tour headboard on No. 4645 and the tour ticket on page 68. No. 4645 was replaced by No. 9669 at Bala on the return as it had run short of coal. This special trip had elicited a record response from SLS members; some 500 travelled but over 100 had their applications refused as the train was loaded to the maximum eight coaches allowed (GW saloons obtained from Craven Arms). The tour had started from Ruabon behind time (due to a late connection) and arrived back there nearly fifty minutes late; nevertheless, the Birmingham direction connection was held. Reports of the tour even appeared in newspapers such as *The Guardian* and *Daily Express*, plus BBC TV Wales and ITV Midlands. The final goods train over the Bala to Blaenau Ffestiniog branch ran five days later; however, the section from Blaenau Ffestiniog Central towards Trawsfynydd was retained. This was to be used for traffic from Trawsfynydd nuclear power station over a newly-built link at Blaenau Ffestiniog connecting with the ex-LNWR branch to Llandudno Junction. The roughly 7 miles of track from Blaenau Ffestiniog to the power station transfer facility is still in place today, but now disused.

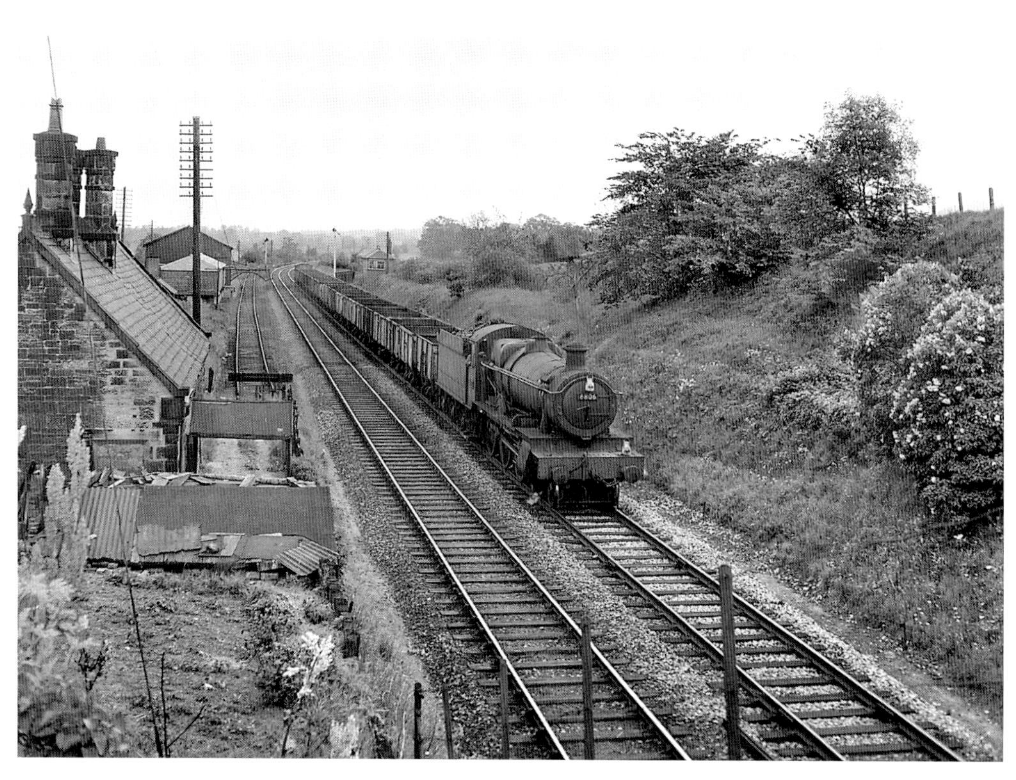

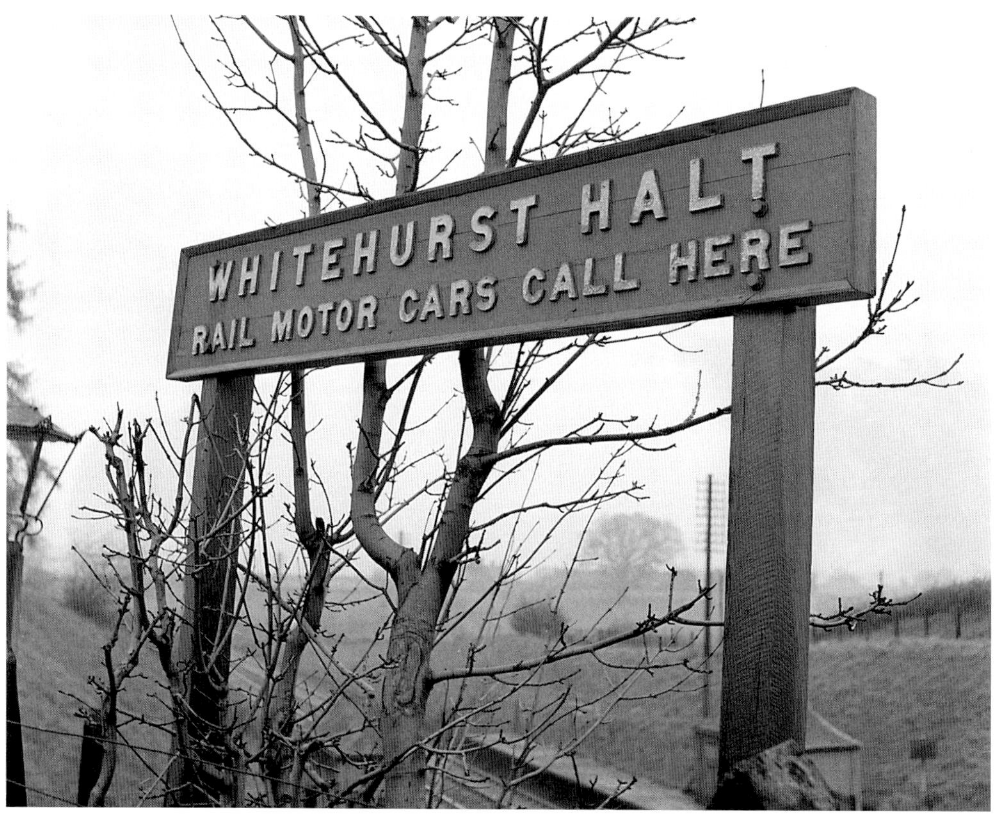
WHITEHURST HALT
RAIL MOTOR CARS CALL HERE

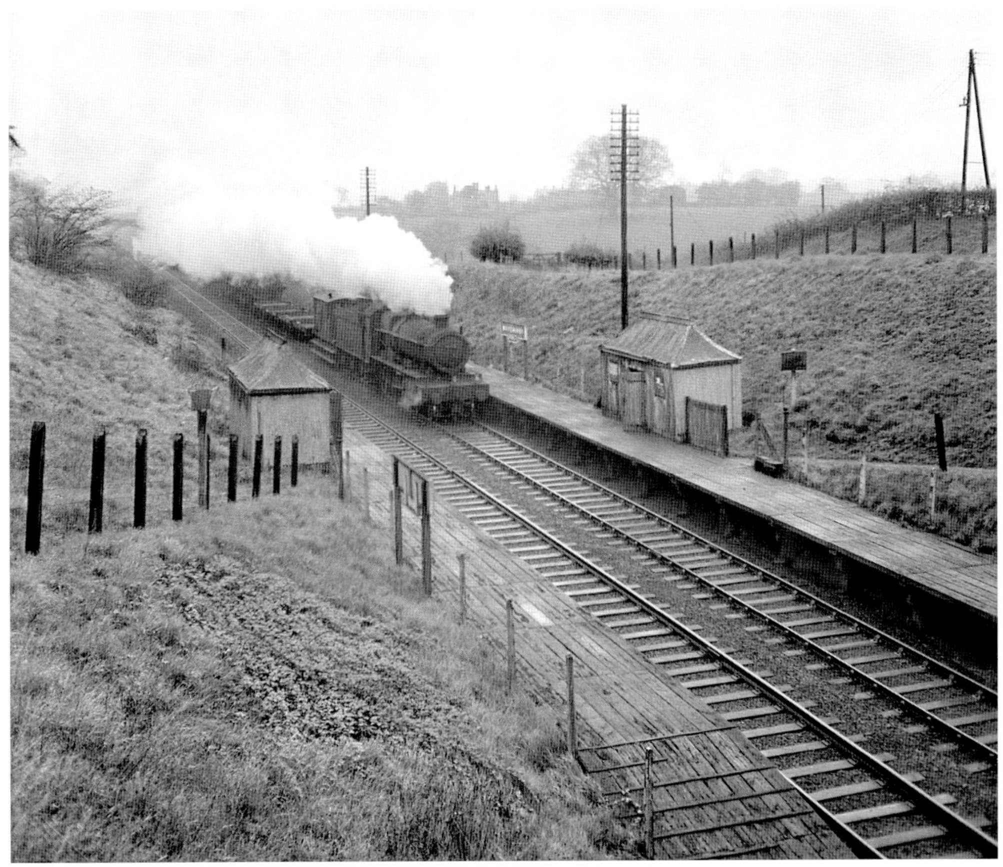

Above and opposite page: The Shrewsbury & Chester Railway wished to provide a railhead for Llangollen and opened the station in the first photograph during October 1848; it was over 5 miles from the town and named Llangollen Road. By 1862, the line from Ruabon to Llangollen itself was open; there was now little need for Llangollen Road, and the station closed that same year, although it continued to deal with freight. Worcester-allocated No. 6806 *Blackwell Grange* passes the site of Llangollen Road station on 8 September 1963 hauling a northbound freight with Whitehurst signal box in the distance, the photograph taken from the A5 road bridge. The May 1960 SLS house magazine noted the goods yard here 'seemed very busy'. In the early twentieth century, the GWR felt the area still had passenger potential and opened a station on the other side of the A5 road bridge in 1905. Initially, this was called Llangollen Road Halt but changed to Whitehurst Halt in 1906; the platforms were built of timber with pagoda-type shelters. Both photographs here date from July 1961 as a southbound freight train passes through, although Whitehurst Halt had closed in September 1960.

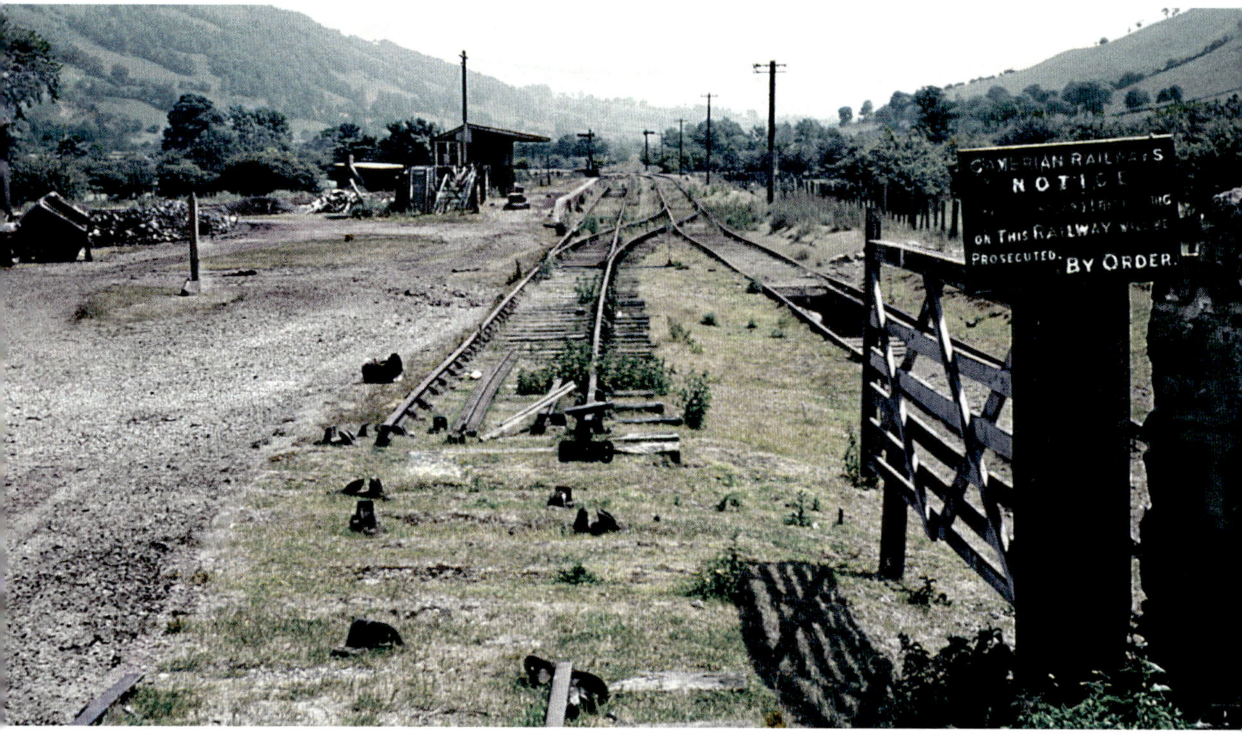

CAMBRIAN RAILWAYS
NOTICE
ON THIS RAILWAY
PROSECUTED.   BY ORDER.

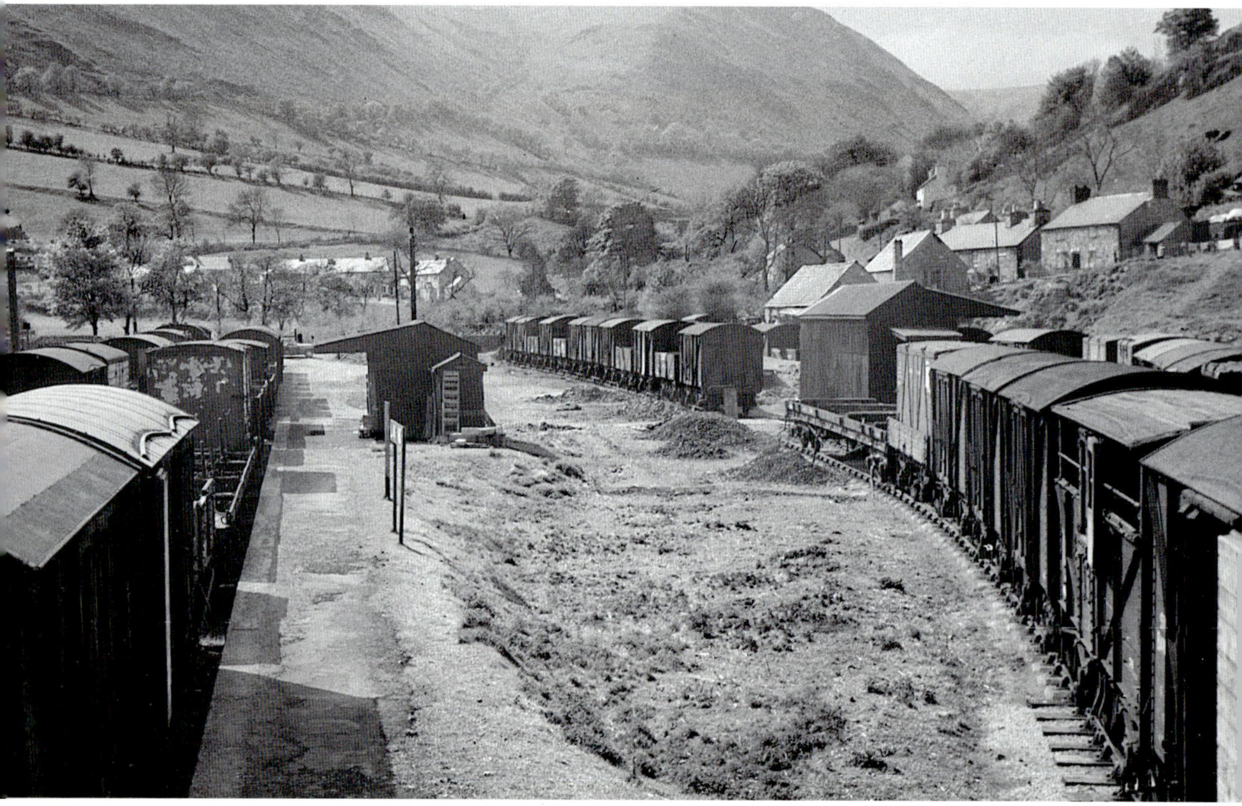

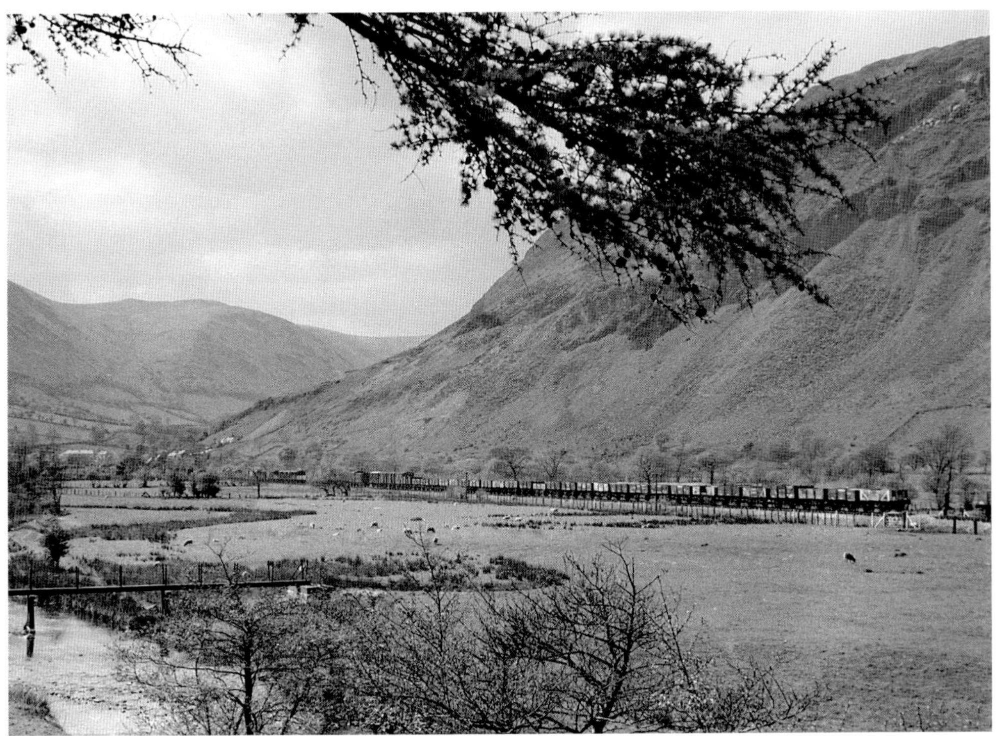

Above and opposite page: The earliest of various schemes for a railway up the Tanat valley was suggested in the 'Railway Mania' period of the mid-1840s, but this and subsequent ones all came to nothing. By late Victorian times, there was a growing belief that where the expense of a fully equipped railway could not be justified, a railway built and operated to a more modest standard could provide an economic alternative. It was the Light Railways Act of 1896 that provided the way forward, and an order was obtained in 1899 for a 15-mile-long line to the lead-mining village of Llangynog at the head of the Tanat from existing CR tracks at Porthywaen. The Tanat Valley Light Railway opened in 1904, but traffic never came near the figures hoped for by its promoters. Passenger services ceased at Llangynog on and from 15 January 1951, freight on 1 July 1952, and the track was lifted back to Llanrhaiadr Mochnant commencing in January 1958; freight continuing to the latter until December 1960. All three photographs are at or close to Llangynog but sadly none are dated. In the colour photograph (no earlier than 1955), the track once continued behind Ellis over the road to a granite exchange yard, to the right is an inspection pit where the engine shed used to be. For several years after closure, the line was used for wagon storage.

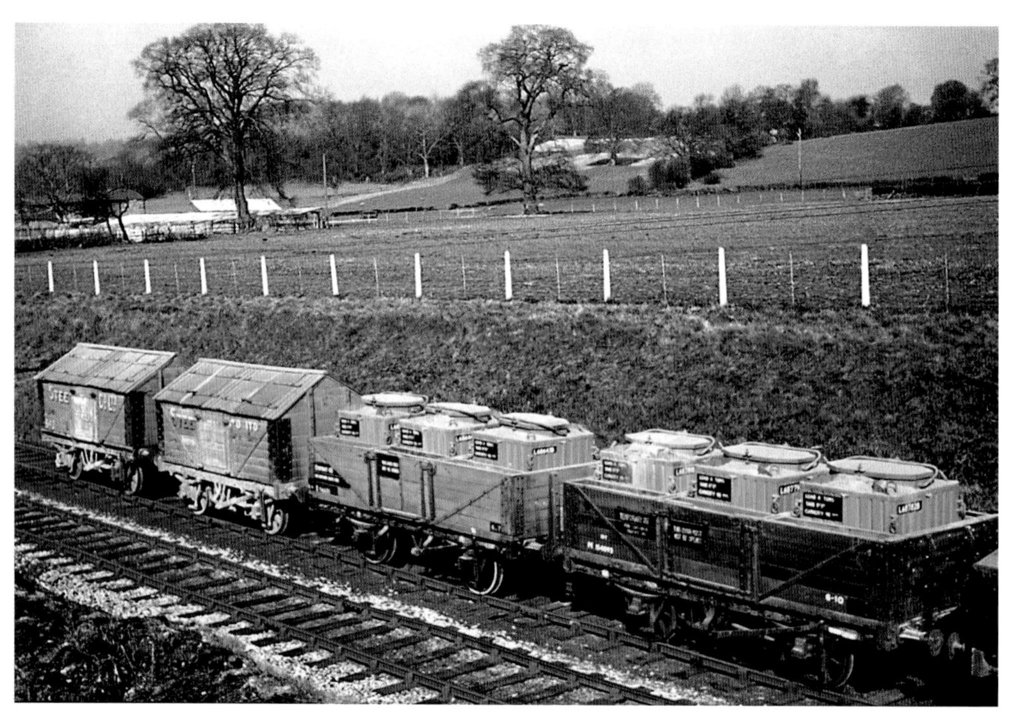

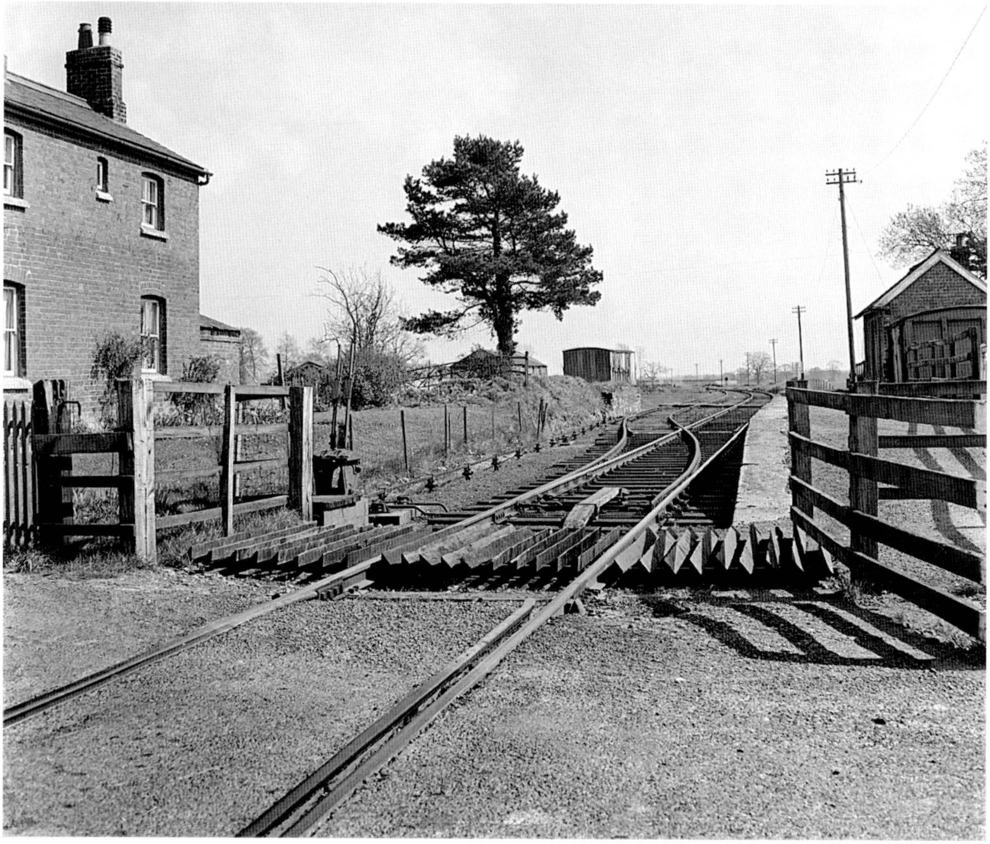

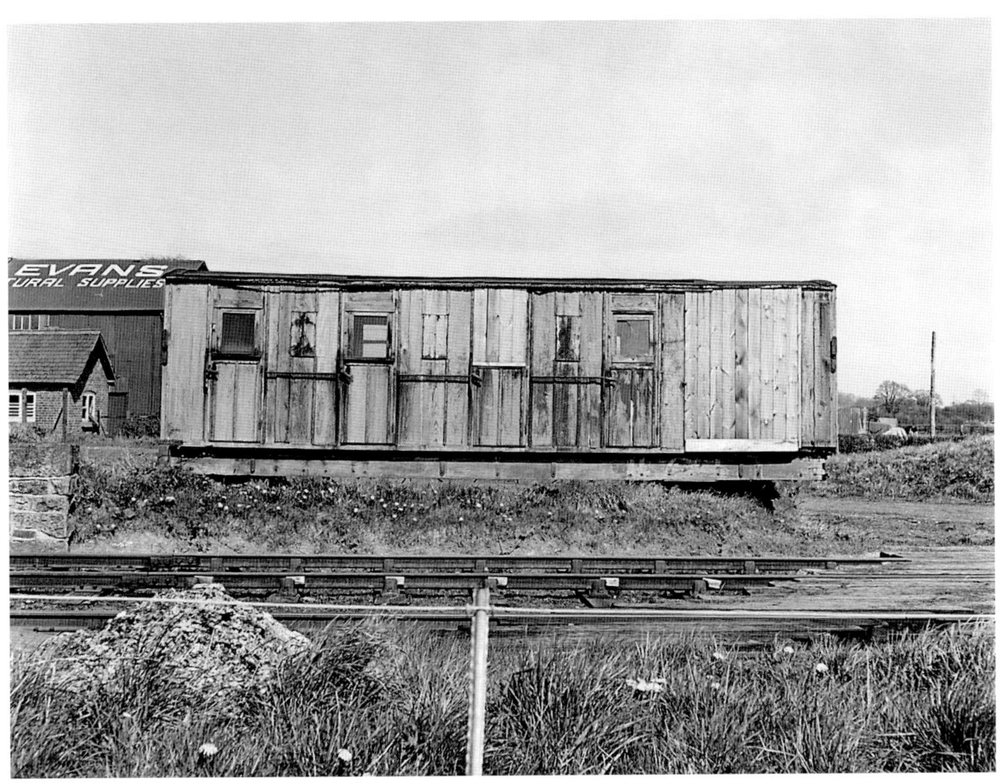

Above and opposite page: The undated colour photograph was taken between Porthywaen and Llynclys Junction (on the CR main line from Oswestry to Welshpool), an area rich with quarries. At the rear are covered (cottage top) 10-ton lime wagons belonging to Steetley Co. Ltd. The containers in front are also probably connected with Steetley's limestone business; the author saw similar containers at Trevor (between Ruabon and Llangollen) in January 1964. Paul Bartlett has given the author advice over these wagons and thinks a likely date is late 1955 or early 1956. The black and white photographs date from the spring of 1960 and are at Nesscliff & Pentre on what became the Shropshire & Montgomeryshire Light Railway. This line had been shut down by the Board of Trade in 1880 and remained derelict for decades, very rare for railways in Victorian times. It reopened in 1911 and during the Second World War was taken over by the military who built numerous ammunition depots along the line; it closed in 1960. The first view is looking towards Shrewsbury with the stationmaster's house on the left; the passenger service had ceased in 1933. The coach body on one end of the goods loading dock and, visible in both photographs, was reputedly acquired for the line's opening in 1866, it later finding this new use. There were many similar examples of recycling along the line, the company having a reputation for seemingly never throwing anything away that might have a potential future use of some kind.

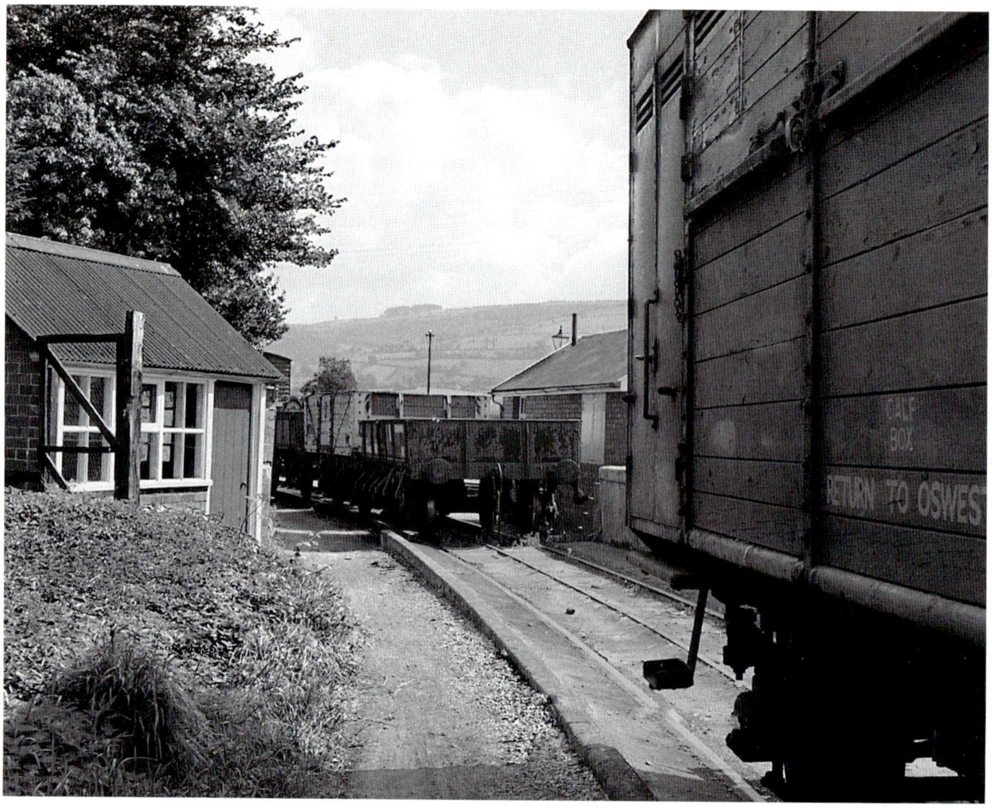

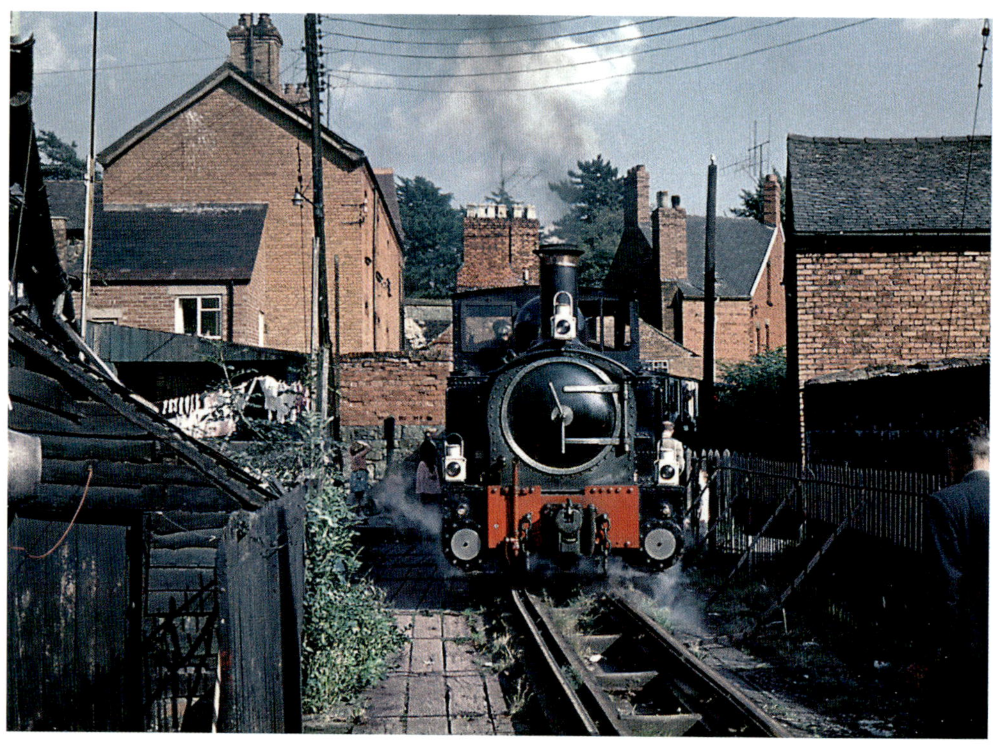

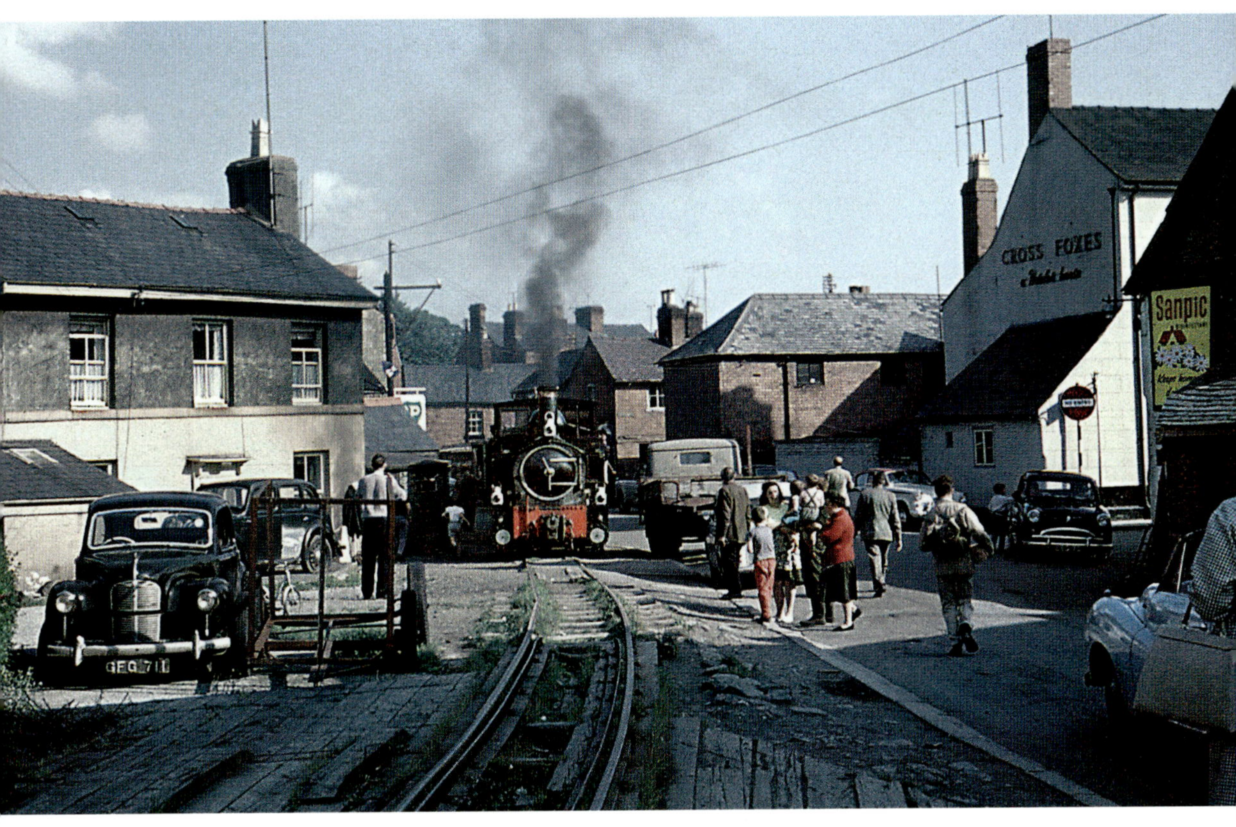

Above and opposite page: Another railway that came about as a result of the Light Railways Act of 1896 was the narrow-gauge Welshpool & Llanfair Light Railway; their Light Railway Order was obtained in September 1899. The gauge chosen was 2 feet 6 inches, a gauge that had not been widely used. The more common 1 foot 11.5 inches was considered too narrow, and the usual wider gauge of 3 feet was excessive. The W&LLR opened for goods traffic in March 1909, and passenger services started that April. A condition of the original 1899 LRO was that the narrow-gauge line must be worked by an existing company, thus creating a ninety-nine-year agreement with the CR, which changed to the GWR following the grouping, and then BR, who closed the line on and from 5 November 1956. Even before the last trains ran, there had been thoughts of a preservation scheme, and on 23 November 1956, the Welshpool and Llanfair Preservation Society was set up in London. These photographs at Welshpool are all believed to have been taken on 17 August 1963, the last day services officially worked over the town section. First, mixed-gauge track by this cattle dock that still exists today. The colour photographs are, just after crossing over Church Street and then by the side of the Cross Foxes Inn, both feature No. 823 *The Countess* (the GWR shortened this locomotive's name to *Countess*, but the preservation society had already restored it to *The Countess* by then).

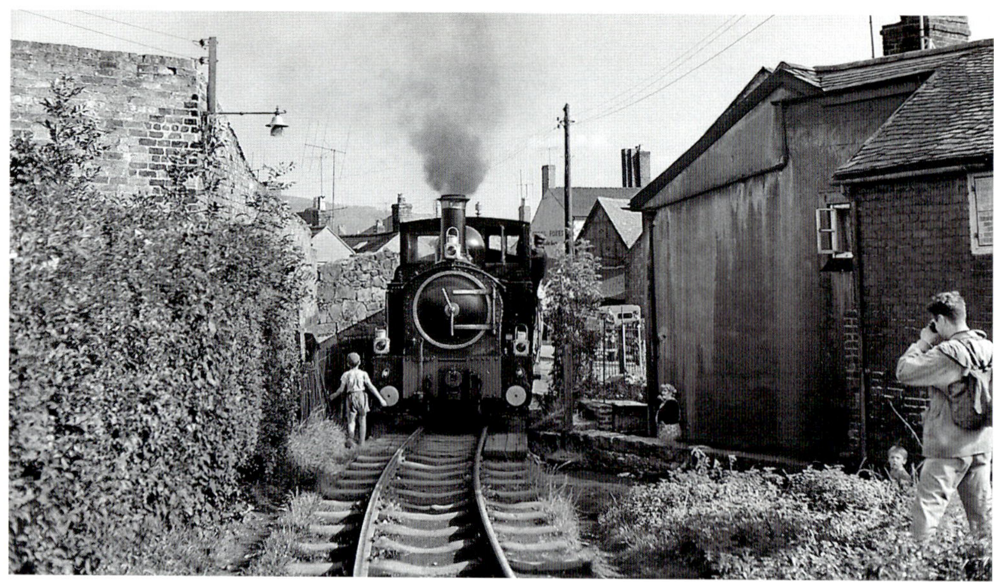

Above, below, and opposite above: The success of the Preservation Company was marred by the overwhelming desire of Welshpool Borough Council to prevent the re-opening of the roughly 1-mile-long town section between Raven Square and the narrow-gauge terminus. Much of the town section followed the course of an earlier horse-drawn tramway—the Welsh Pool Rail Road—that connected to the Montgomeryshire Canal but was abandoned by 1854. The council were particularly determined not to allow trains along the section with very narrow confines and dangerous clearances. This can also be seen in the previous set of photographs, where the railway was carried over the Sylfaen (Lledan) Brook on a continuous bridge with washing hanging almost within touching distance of the train. The track was laid on longitudinal beams with inside protective steel plates over the brook. This set of photographs at Welshpool is again thought to have been taken on 17 August 1963, the last day services officially worked over the town section. First, with the Cross Foxes Inn just visible in the background, then past houses on Bronybuckly, and finally approaching Raven Square. Both of the line's original locomotives— No. 822 *The Earl* and No. 823 *The Countess*—were in use on this day.

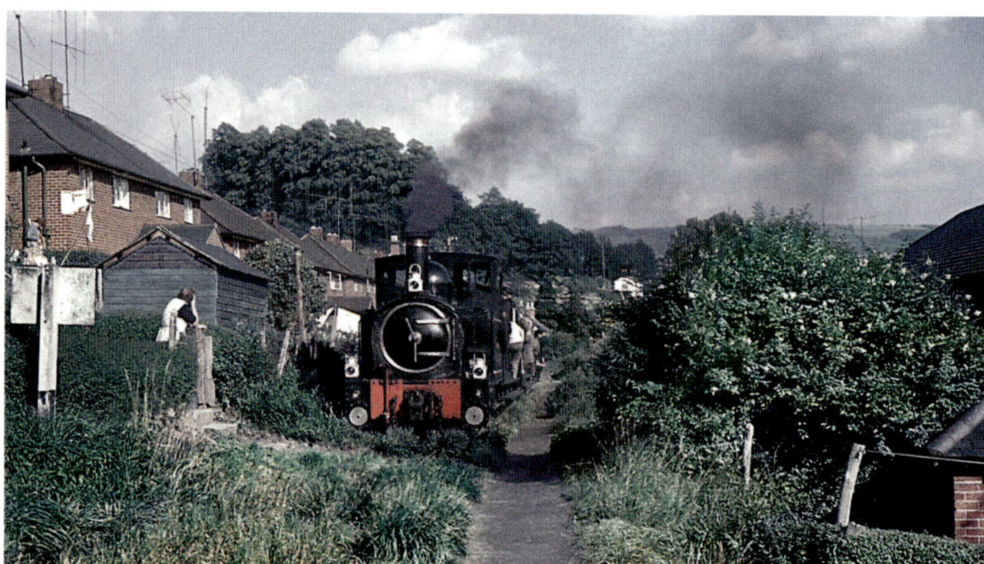

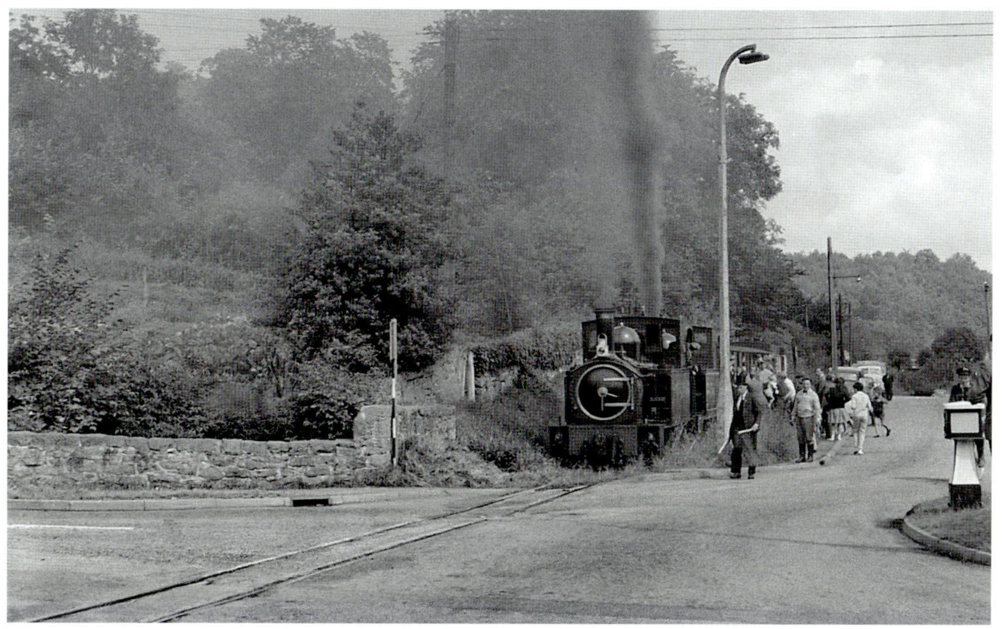

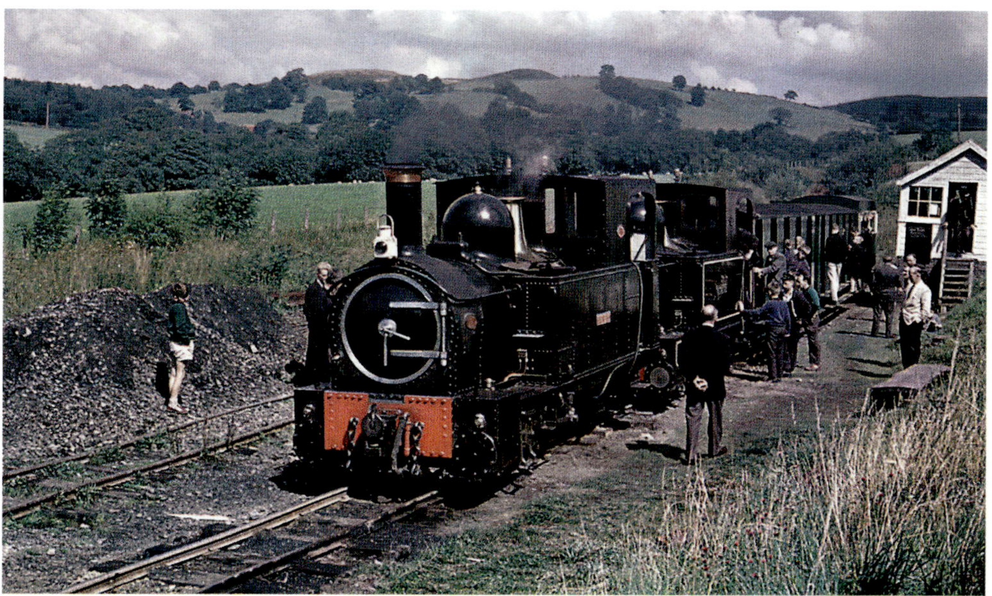

After the closure of the line in 1956, the railway's two locomotives were stored at Oswestry works. *The Earl* (in front) arrived back in July 1961 and *The Countess* (behind) in October 1962; both are seen at Castle Caereinion with another photograph understood to date from 17 August 1963. An informal passenger service had been run at times since the return of the first steam locomotive. A formal re-opening took place on 6 April 1963 when the earl of Powis (after whose predecessor *The Earl* was named) officially declared the section open between Llanfair Caereinion and Castle Caereinon. With the loss of the original terminus at Welshpool, the railway's headquarters became based at Llanfair Caereinion, where they still are today, and from where the services operate. The first public timetabled services over the entire length of the line to the new terminus at Raven Square, Welshpool, ran in July 1981.

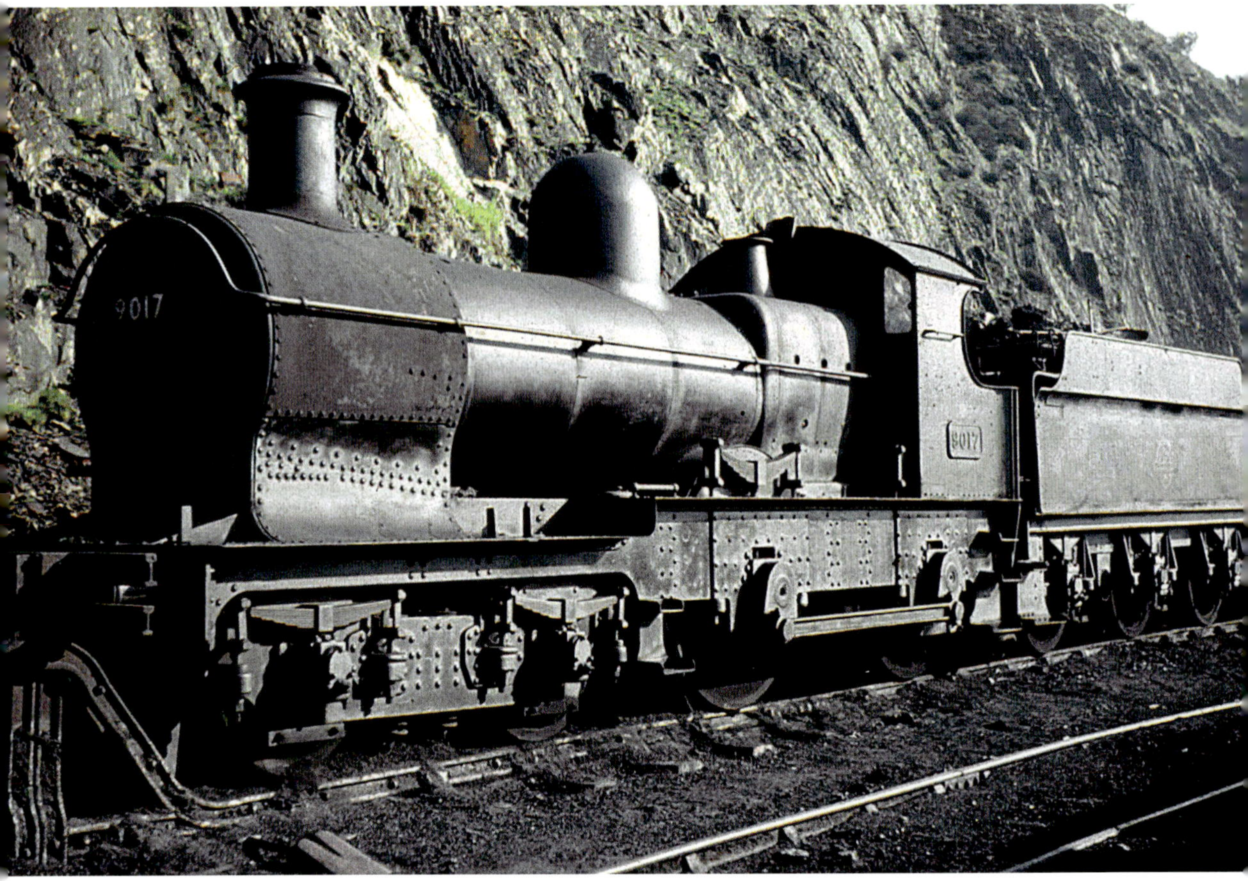

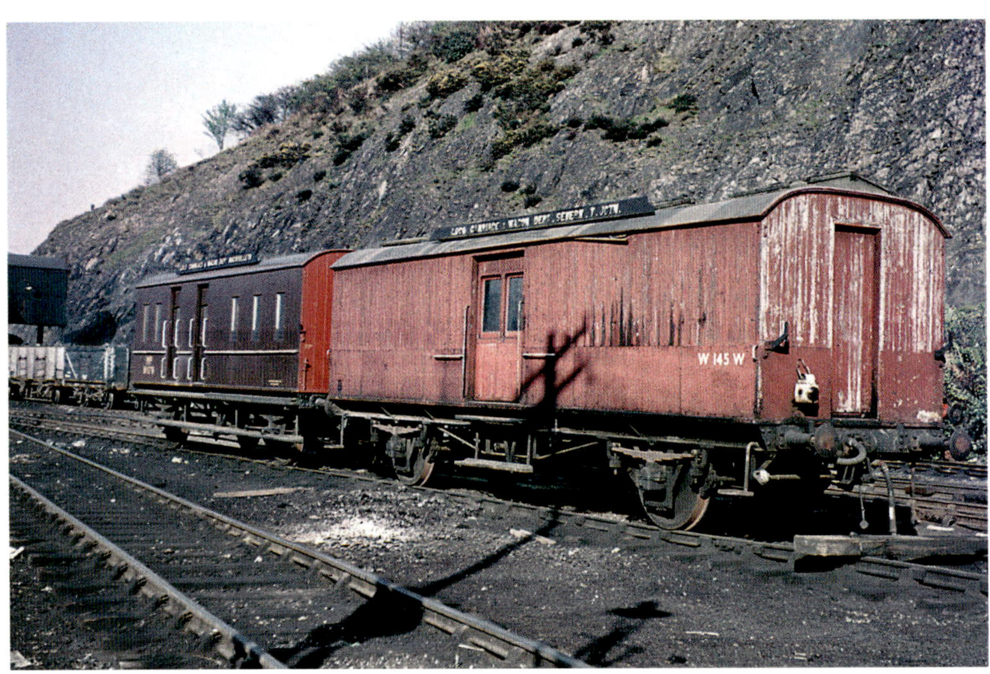

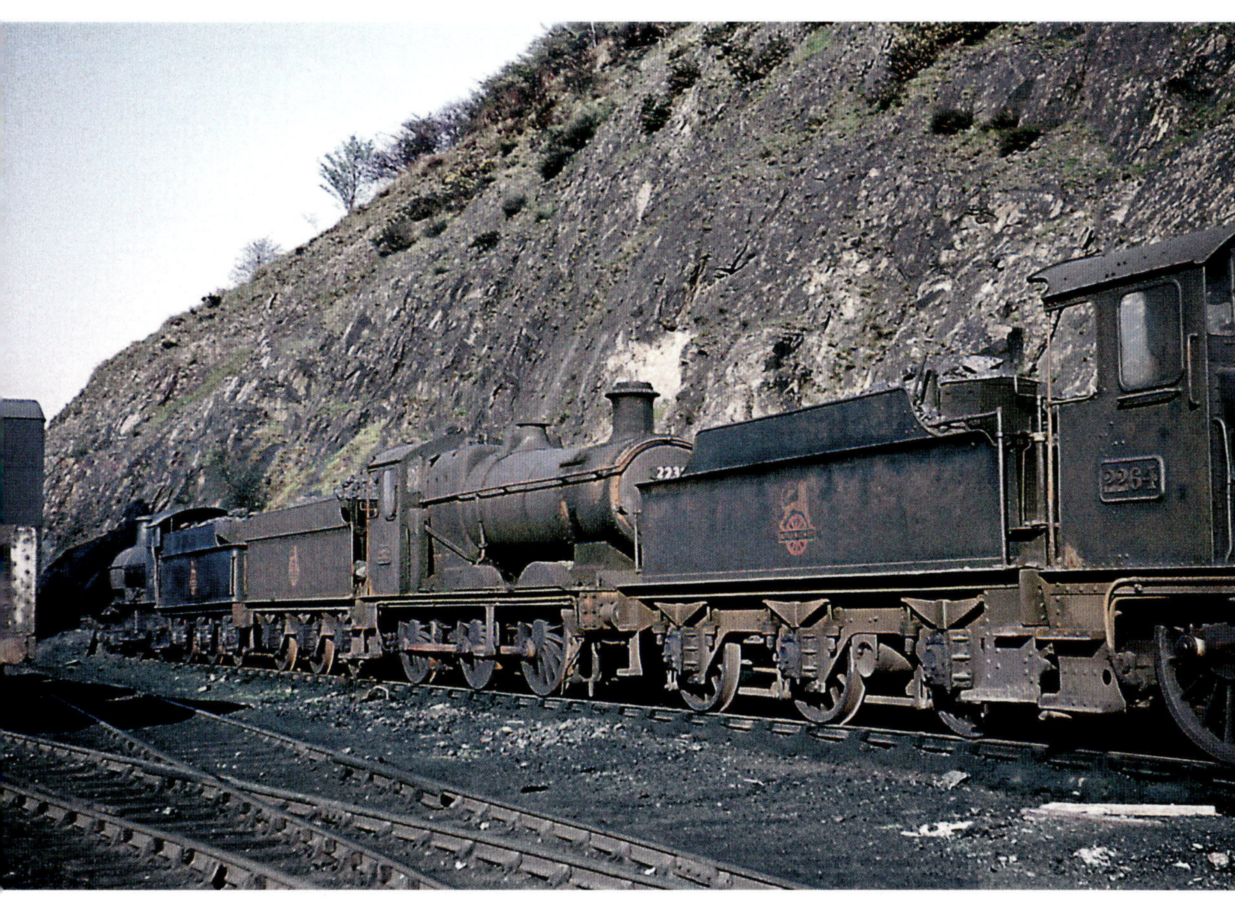

Above and opposite page: Ellis visited Machynlleth engine shed during April 1960, when these photographs plus two others in the introduction on pages 8 and 9 were taken. At the beginning of the year, only five of the 'Dukedogs' in the first photograph were left in service. The strange name arose because they were rebuilds in the 1930s using existing Duke-class boilers and Bulldog-class frames. Of those nominally in service, many were in fact in store as here with No. 9017, their main use latterly as pilots on heavy summer services. No. 9017 survived until October, then finding a new home on the Bluebell Railway, the only class member preserved. Two vehicles from the 'Loco, Carriage & Wagon Dept.' are in the shed yard. Red W145W was from Severn Tunnel Junction, but W117W behind was locally based. More stored locomotives are in the final photograph. No. 2264 had been based at Machynlleth since 1956 but would be withdrawn in June 1960. Behind is classmate No. 2232 that again had been based here since 1956, but it would be transferred away in 1961 and finally withdrawn from Worcester in September 1964. No. 9017 is at the end of the row.

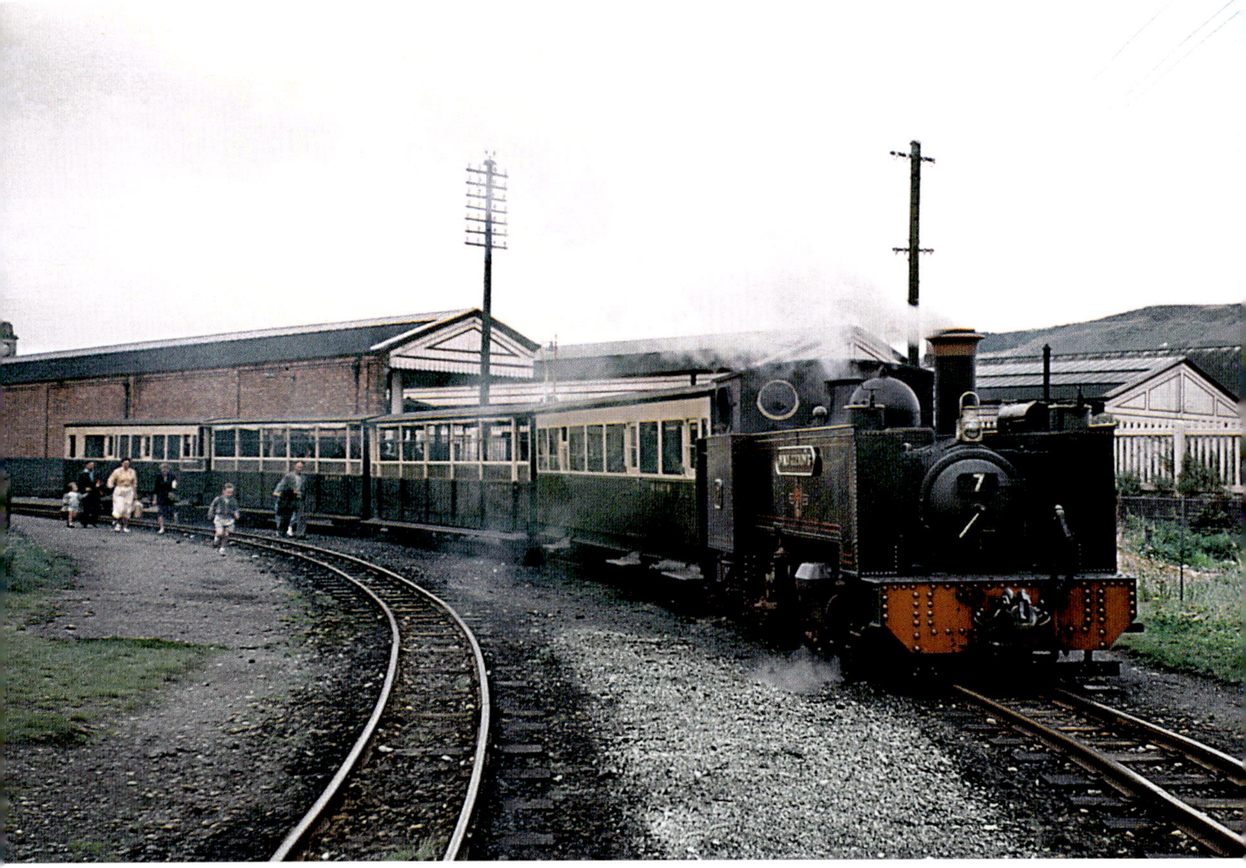

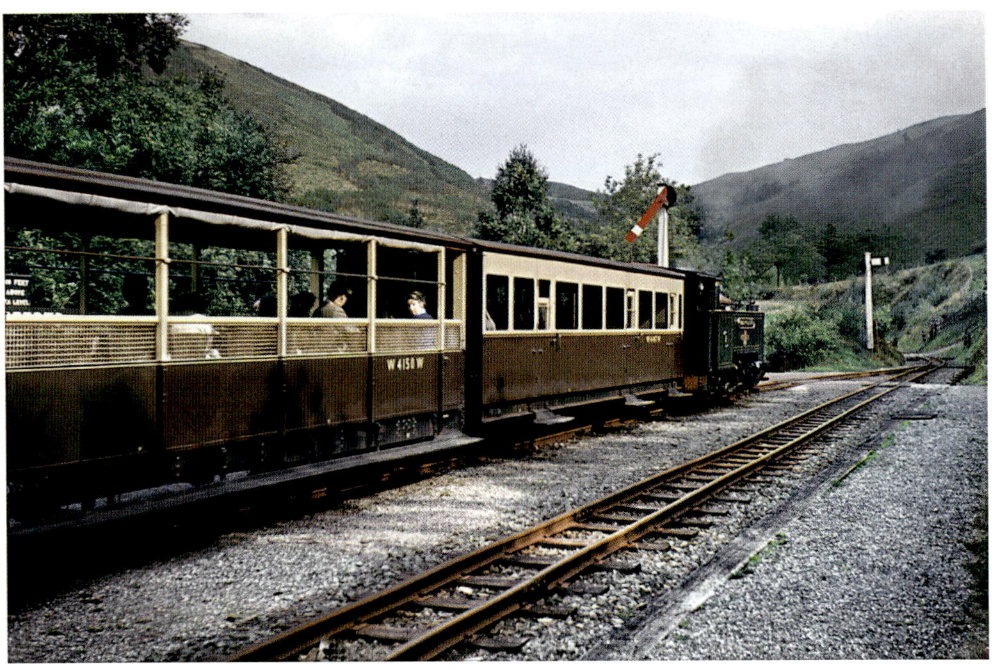

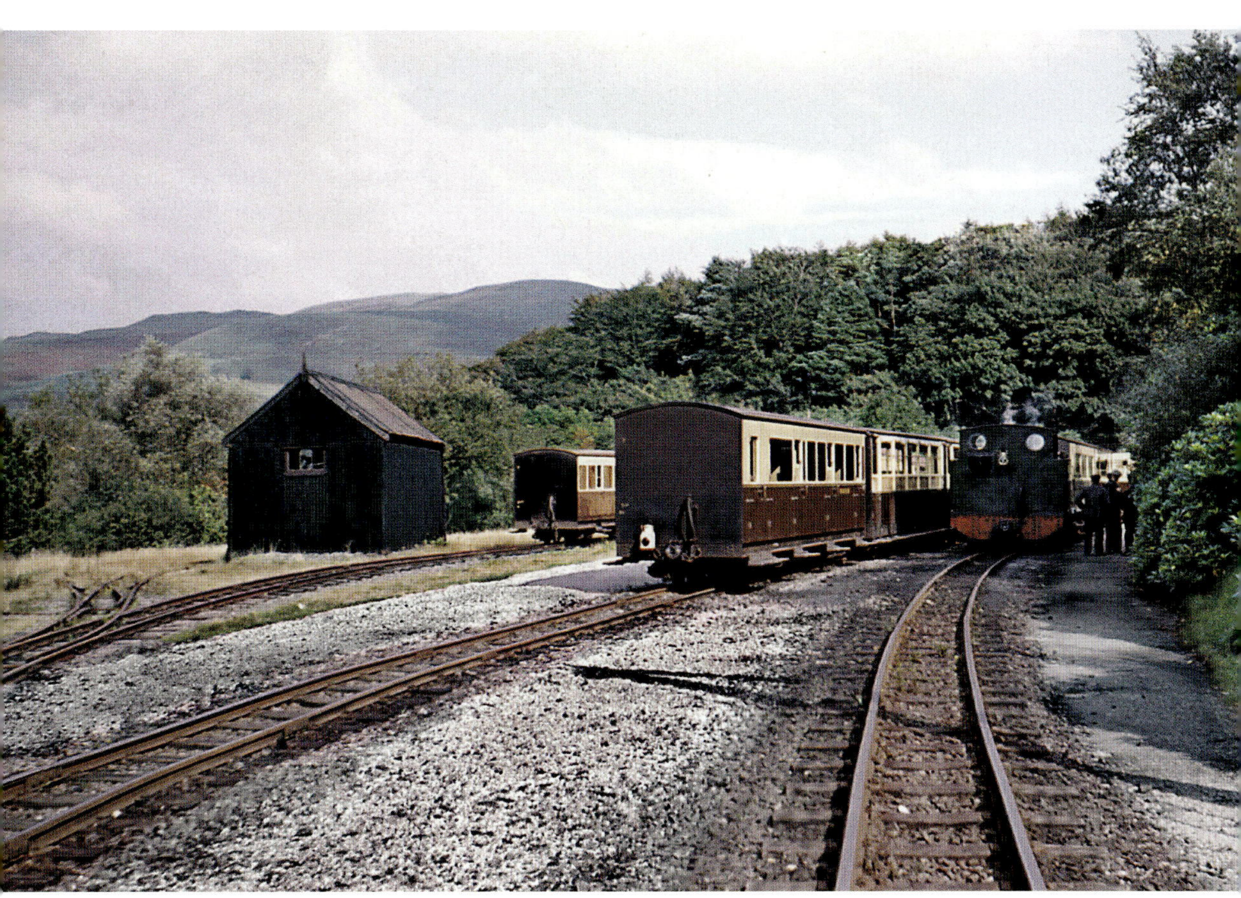

Above and opposite page: More undated colour slides from Ellis's collection, these on the Vale of Rheidol Railway are all thought to date from the late 1950s. A line that has always intrigued the author is the legendary Manchester & Milford Railway; a section of it was built to Llangurig but never used, and one of the reasons put forward for the line's failure was the American Civil War. Another scheme of the M&MR was a branch from Devil's Bridge to Aberystwyth; it came to nothing, but when the Vale of Rheidol narrow-gauge line opened in 1902 from Aberystwyth to Devil's Bridge, it closely followed the original M&MR route. Two main sources were seen as providing income for the narrow-gauge company—mining and tourism. The line came under CR control, then the GWR, and finally BR. The terminus by the side of Aberystwyth's standard-gauge station in the first photograph opened in 1925. This was at the end of a seven-chain-long extension from the original narrow-gauge terminus; No. 7 *Owain Glyndwr* awaits custom. At 7.75 miles from Aberystwyth in the second photograph was Aberffrwd, where there was a passing loop plus water facilities. The final view is of the eastern terminus at Devil's Bridge, a beauty spot famous for its triple bridge and waterfalls. In 1968, the Vale of Rheidol line became BR's only steam operation following the demise of BR main line steam; today, it is run by a charitable trust.

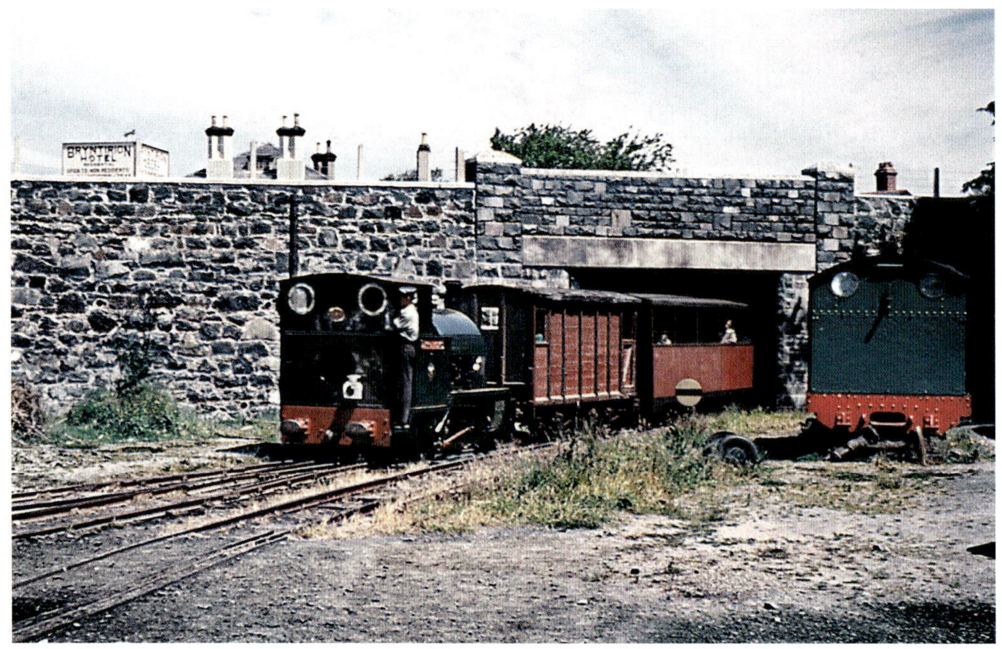

Above and below: Although undated, it is possible to close in a little on the date of these two photographs illustrating the Talyllyn Railway. The locomotive in the first view is No. 4 *Edward Thomas* (named after a former TR manager) and is approaching Towyn Wharf terminus. Built in 1921 by Kerr, Stuart & Co. of Stoke-on-Trent for the Corris Railway, it came to the TR in 1951. No. 4 is still without its 1958-fitted Giesl ejector chimney; also, the locomotive on the right is *Russell*, this was at Towyn from August 1955. Presumed taken on the same day is this view looking north-east at Towyn Pendre, location of the TR's locomotive and carriage sheds plus engineering workshops.

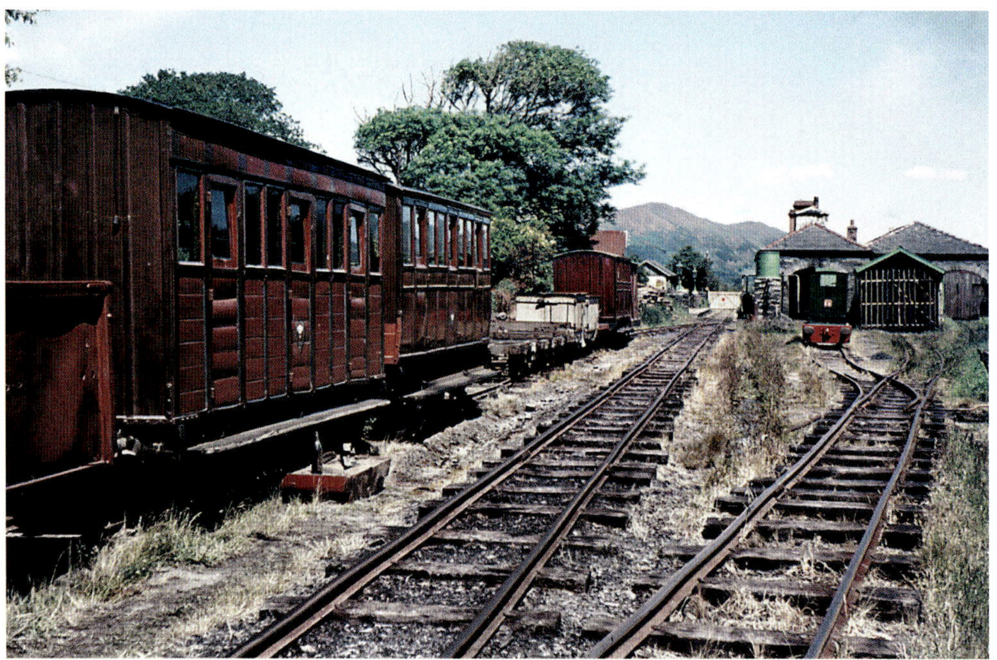

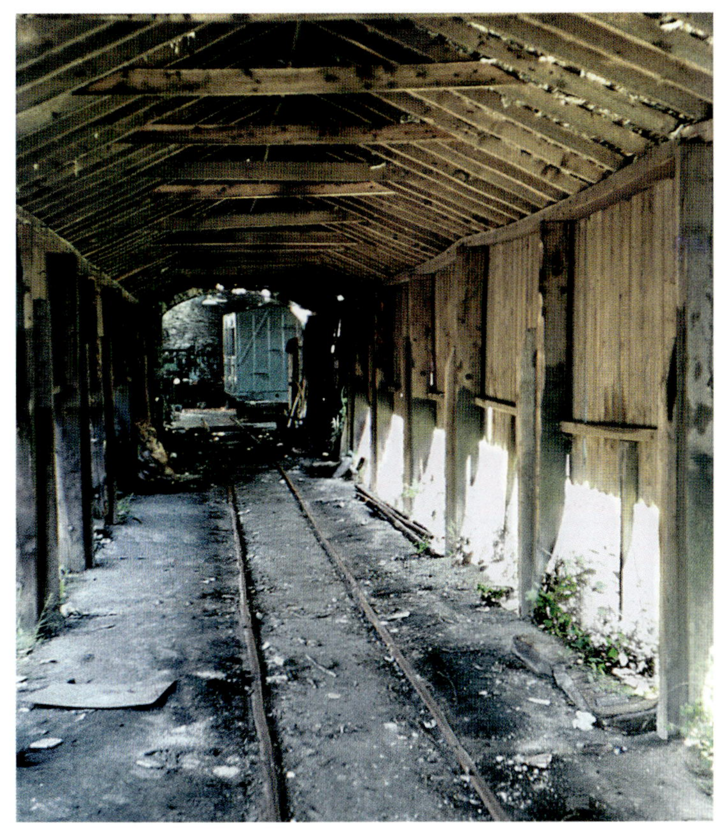

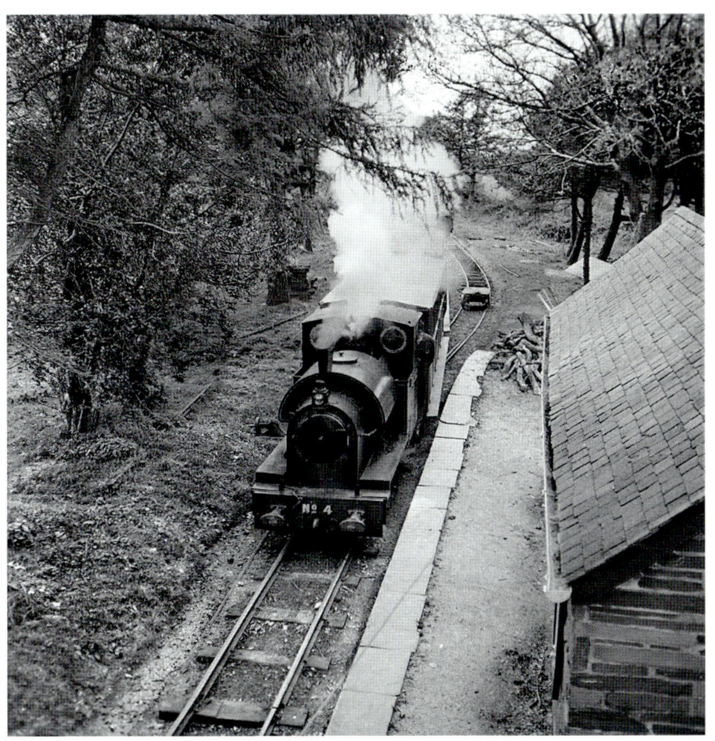

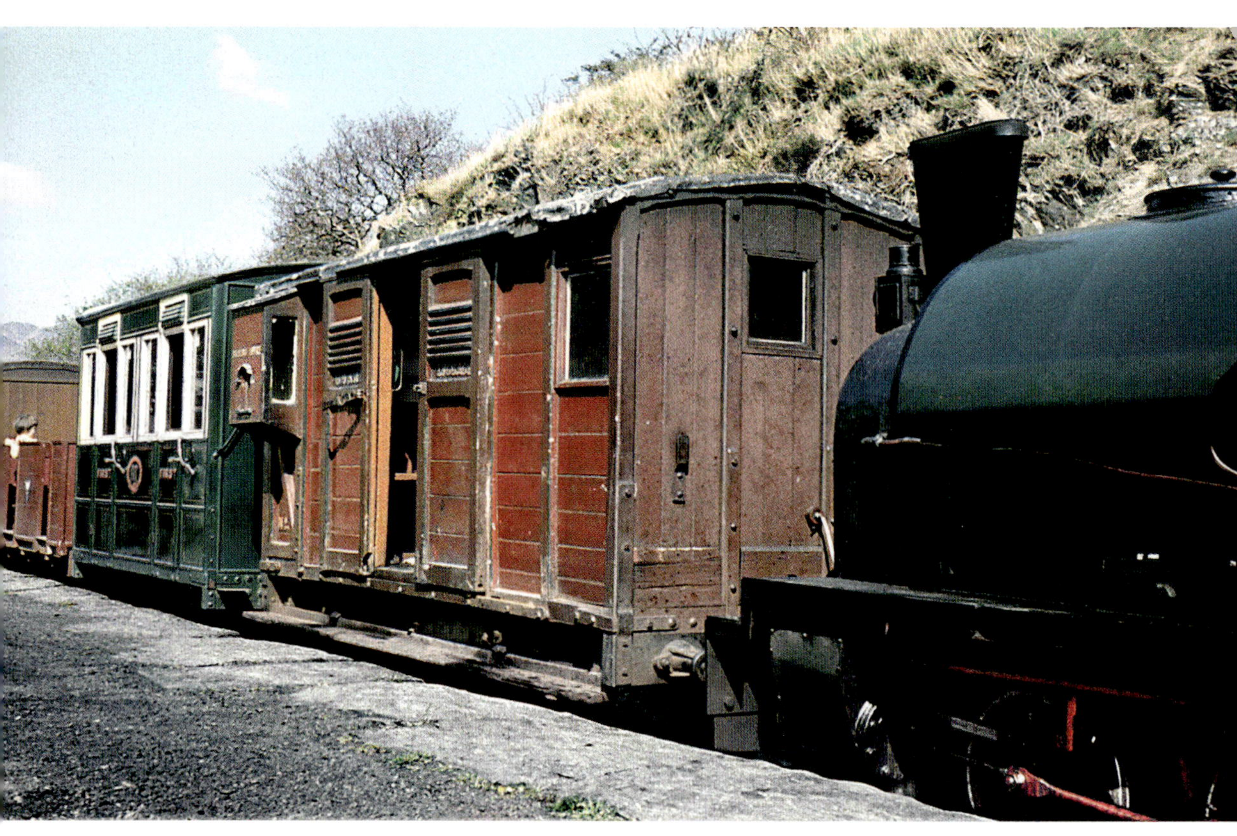

Page 87 and above: Thought to date from the second half of the 1950s, the first view is inside the old carriage shed at Towyn Pendre on the south side of the line; a replacement structure was built on the north side during the early 1960s. The next two photographs date from April 1960, the monochrome at Rhydyronen and the colour at Abergynolwyn. The intermediate station of Rhydyronen had opened in 1867, No. 4 *Edward Thomas* heads past on its way towards Abergynolwyn, by now fitted with its new chimney. At Abergynolwyn, the first vehicle is notable for the booking office window on its side, allowing the guard to sell tickets at unstaffed intermediate stations. The second is one of two coaches from the Glyn Valley Tramway, which closed in 1935; they arrived on the TR in the late 1950s. The third 'coach' came from Penrhyn Quarry and had seen service in the Penrhyn Quarry Workmen's Train. The passenger is one of Ellis's daughters; luckily, she did not fall out of this open-sided and poor-riding vehicle (see page 96).

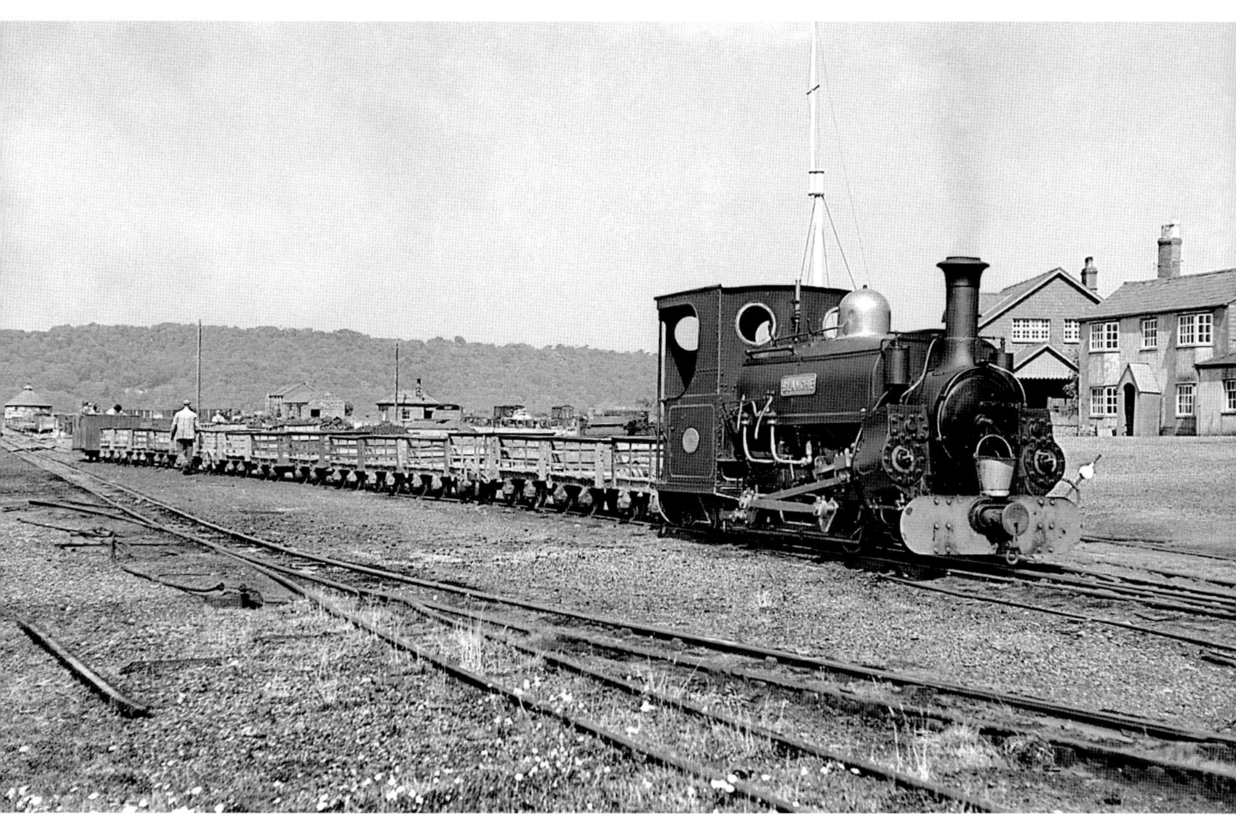

Slate extraction on what was to become the Penrhyn Estate is recorded as early as the fifteenth century, with tenants working on sites they rented. In 1782, Richard Pennant (1st Baron Penrhyn) decided to work the ground himself and set about actively buying out the about 3,000 leases. Until 1785, transport to the Menai Strait was by packhorses with panniers, for onward shipment by sea. Then a good road was built to the quarry (and beyond) to accommodate horse-drawn wagons, later forming part of Telford's London to Holyhead road. By 1793, over 10,000 tons annually was brought down from Penrhyn Quarry, about four times the amount of the next highest (Dinorwic) and around half of the entire North Wales seaborne trade in slate. This photograph is taken at what came to be called Port Penrhyn; it is at the mouth of the Cegin, and the land visible in the background is part of Anglesey on the other side of the Menai Strait. Despite continual expansion of the port over the decades, it struggled to cope. *Blanche* has a load of empty slate wagons to take back up to the quarry on 1 September 1961. Close examination will reveal the rear vehicle to be one of the 'coaches' used in the Penrhyn Quarry Workmen's Train, and similar to that already seen on the Talyllyn Railway in the previous photograph. Even further behind, the round building is a toilet for use of slate loaders and, according to Boyd, allowed thirteen men 'to engage in conversation' simultaneously; a listed building, it still exists today.

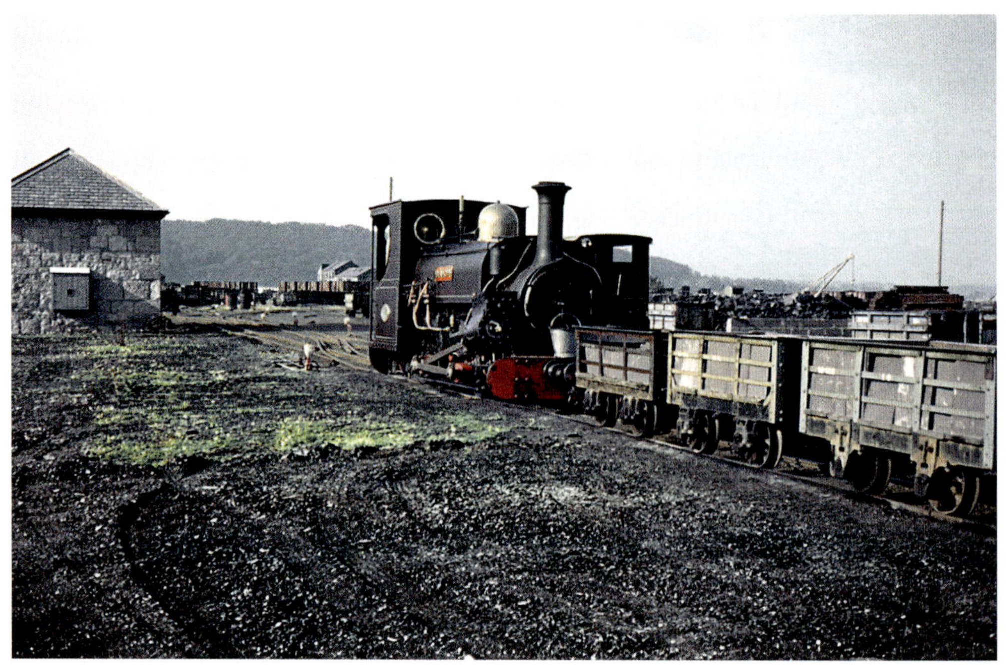

Above and below: Two more photographs at Port Penrhyn taken on 1 September 1961, first a loaded slate train arrives behind *Blanche*, and then preparing for departure with empties. Behind the loaded wagons is a pile of coal (also page 11); this was transported in specially constructed wagons to Coed-y-Parc, some only recently built. The coal was delivered by sea, often from Point of Ayr colliery, and had seen a multitude of uses, including for bunkering the quarry's steamships, locomotives, the main workshops, the five blacksmith's shops, domestic use, and steam-pumping boilers. In earlier times, Saturdays were largely given over to the transport of coal, potatoes, grain, lime, and timber—in fact, all the staples of everyday life for the quarry community.

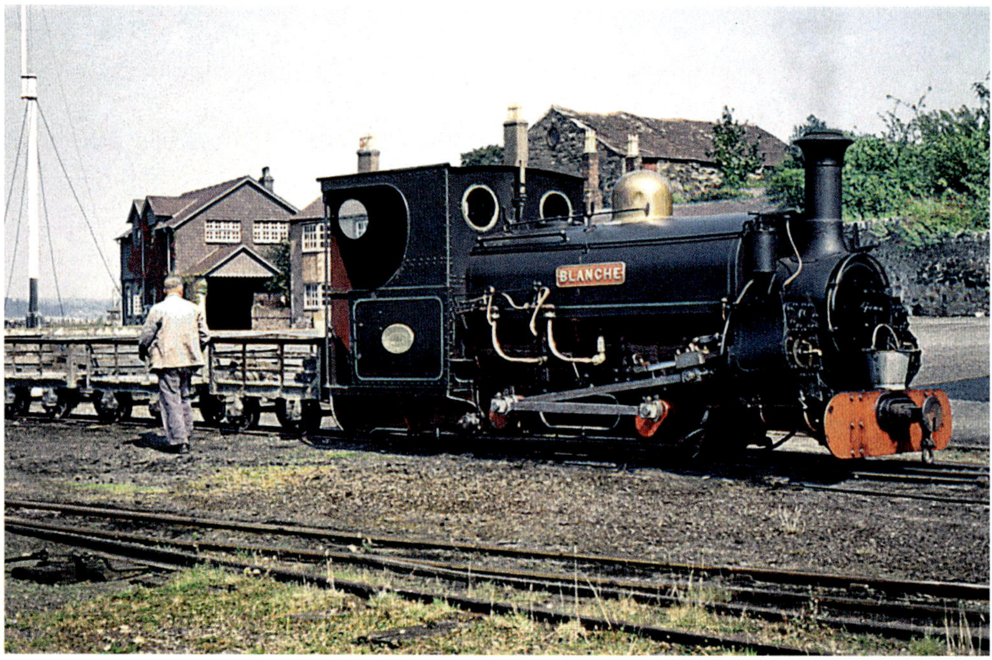

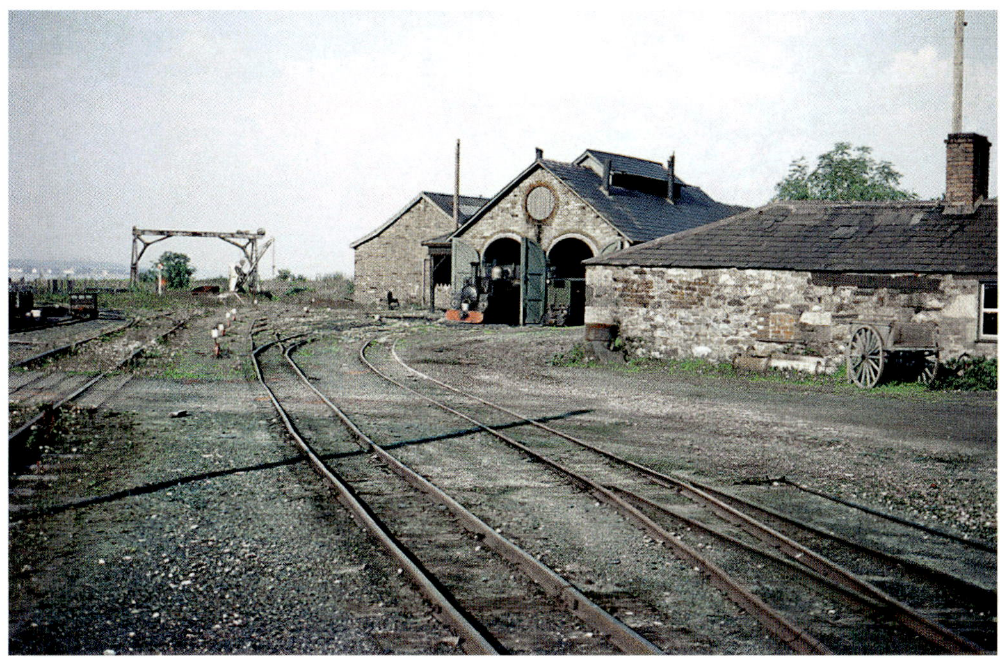

Above and below: First, *Blanche* is at the engine shed; to its right is diesel No. 24, and further to the right, a one-time smithy. To the left are the old carriage shed and 1934-built fitting shop. Further to the left is the 1891-erected overhead gantry crane across the interchange between the standard- and narrow-gauge tracks. Secondly, *Blanche* is by the 1833-built Port House, the administrative centre; distances were measured from its steps. A notable feature on *Blanche* was the cylinders were raised and inclined to permit the connecting rods to be inside the side rods; this allows the cylinders to be closer together, reducing locomotive width. Both photographs date from 1 September 1961 and are at Port Penrhyn.

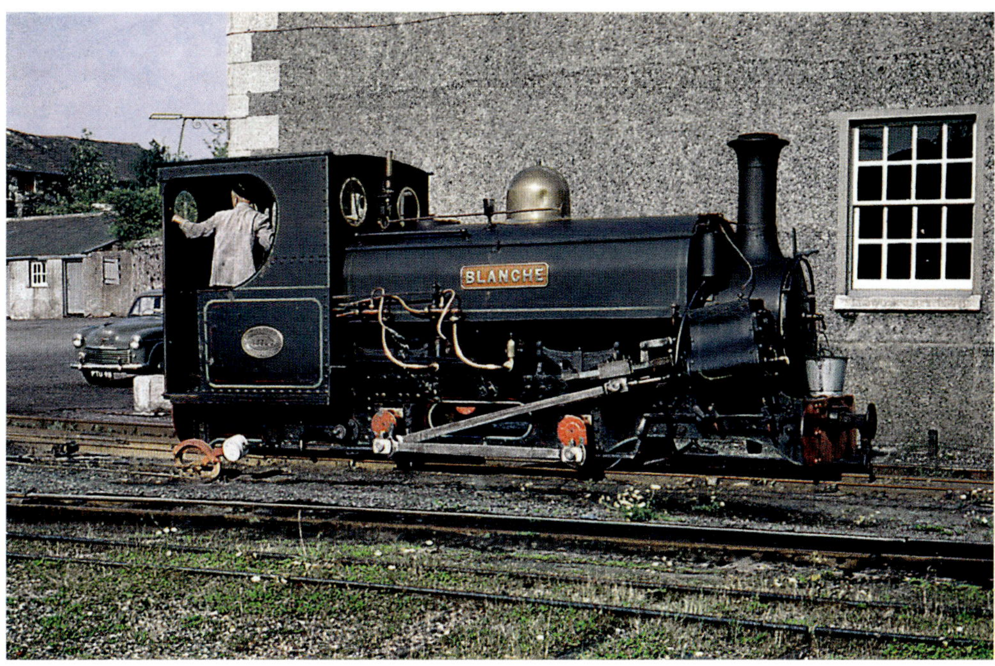

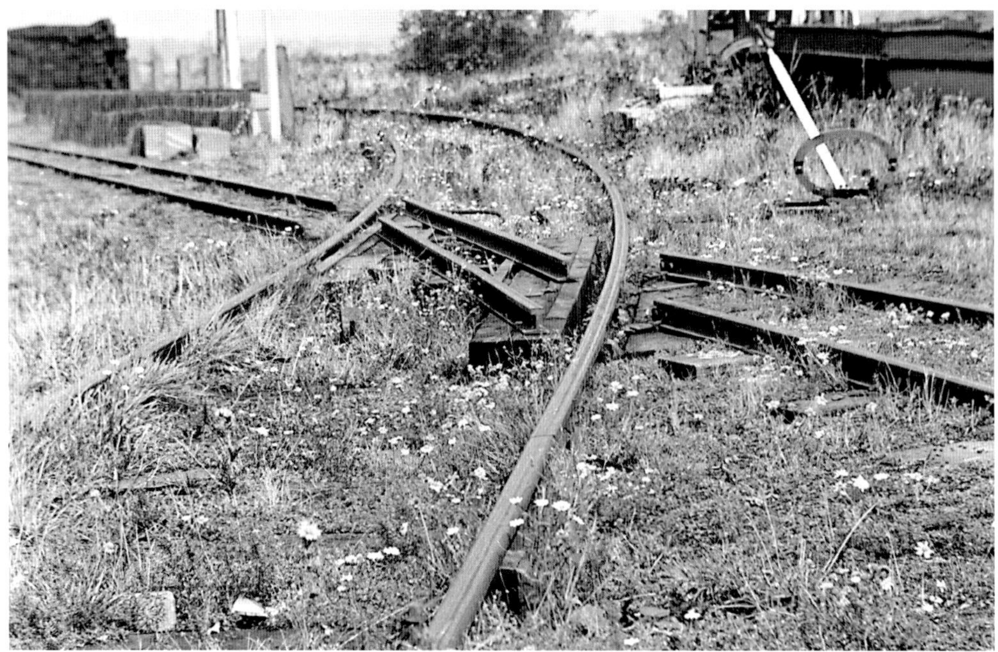

Above and below: The date of these two photographs of trackwork at Port Penrhyn is unknown. The first shows a moveable angle crossing of the narrow gauge (1 foot 11 inches inside rails) over the standard gauge. The narrow gauge has its bottom flanges bolted to iron straps to form a complete unit; this is mounted on timbers laid across the sleepers of the standard gauge. The narrow-gauge section is pivoted in the centre and can be swung inside the standard-gauge track, creating an unobstructed path for standard-gauge vehicles. The crossing is operated by a hand lever. Before 1924, any water scoop on standard-gauge locomotives would foul these crossings; the narrow gauge was lowered to give more clearance. The second shows a wheel stop.

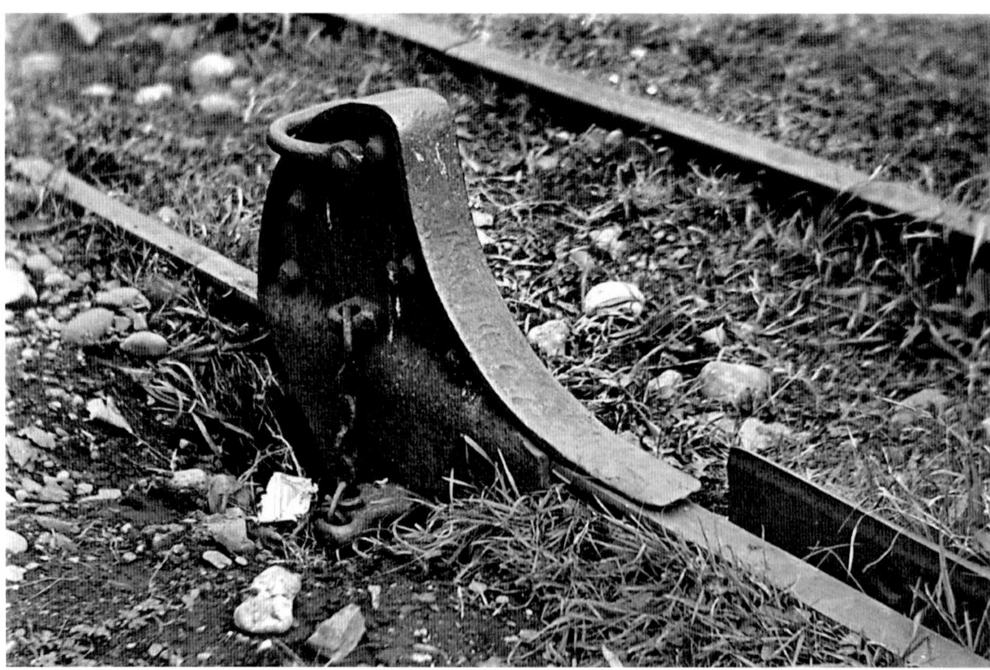

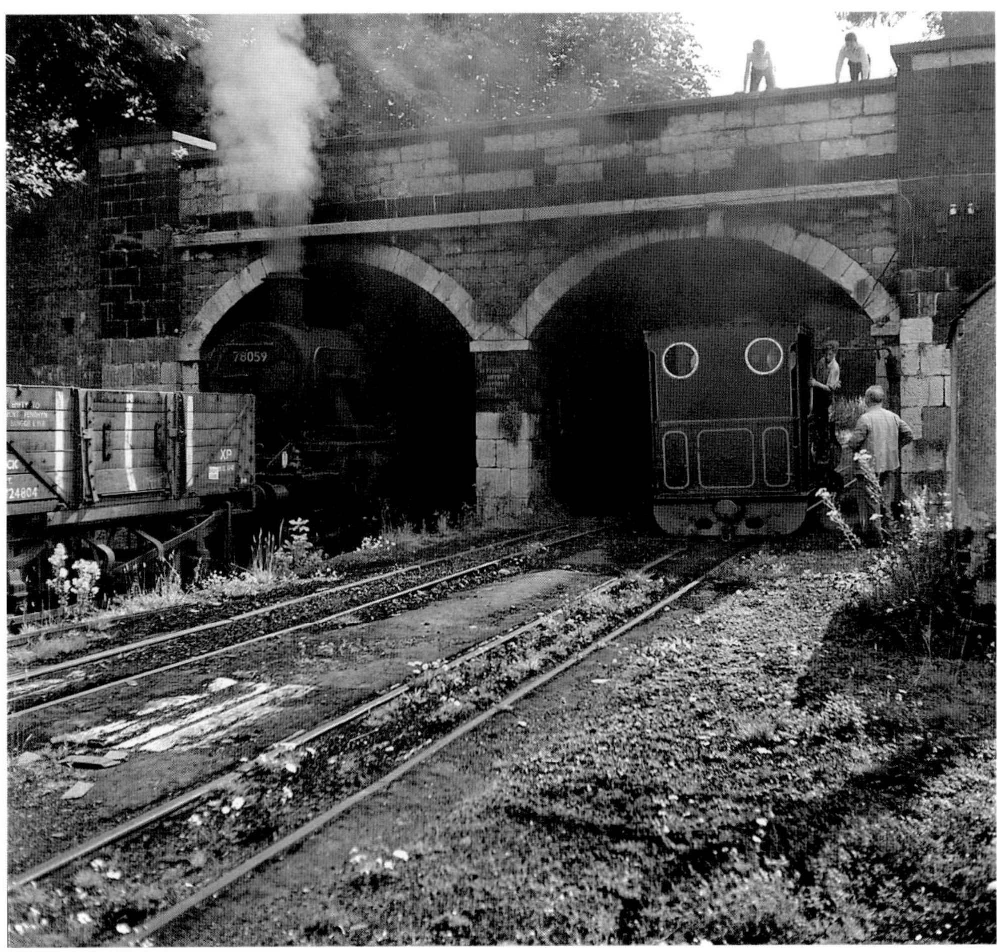

A standard-gauge branch to Port Penrhyn from the Chester & Holyhead Railway was opened in early 1852. It was built over the Penrhyn Estate as single track but some provision was made for double. The branch was 1.5 miles long and fell to the port at grades of mainly 1 in 50 and 1 in 64. Standard-gauge freight trains were propelled down-grade with the brakes pinned down; the guard would ride on the leading wagon carrying a lamp or flag. It had been classed as a siding since August 1954 and was last worked in early March 1963. Official closure came in June 1965, and the track was all lifted over the next year or so. Ellis has listed this photograph as taken on 1 September 1961 with No. 78059 in charge of the standard-gauge service; wording on the wagon says 'Empty To Port Penrhyn LMR' and also 'Shunt With Care'. Even in mid-Victorian times, the standard gauge at the port took almost one-third of quarry production. This view is at the south end of the Port Penrhyn complex where the now double track Penrhyn line plus the standard gauge were side-by-side and passed underneath this Regency-style over-bridge. On the narrow-gauge side of the bridge was a watering point, being used by *Blanche*. One of the two signals along the narrow gauge was in front of the central arch on the opposite side of this bridge, and also wooden gates, normally closed save during working hours (see page 11).

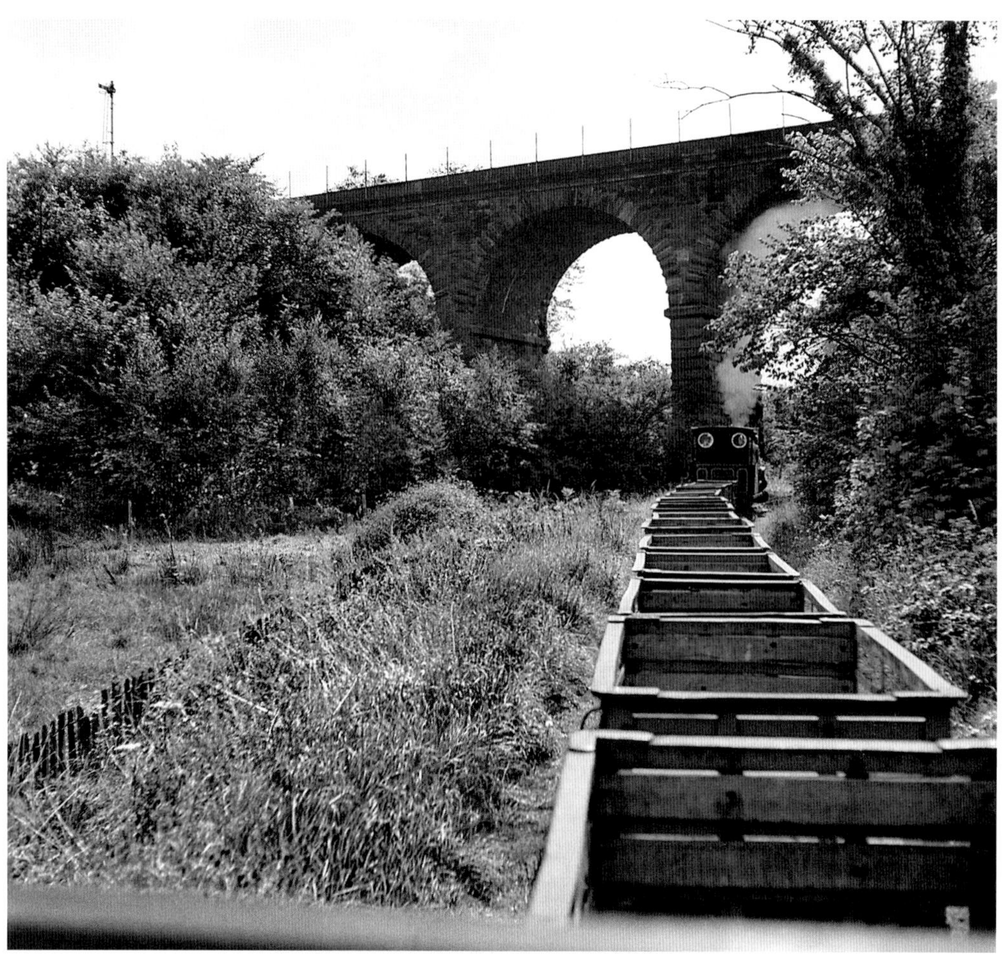

Taken during a southbound journey up the Penrhyn Railway from Port Penrhyn to the Coed-y-Parc complex on 1 September 1961, *Blanche* is hauling a trainload entirely of empties (no loaded coal wagons) plus one 'coach'. Dominating the view is the Chester & Holyhead Railway's Cegin Viaduct. The viaduct has seven semi-circular arches each of 35-foot span; it has masonry piers, although the stone arches are faced with brick. The Penrhyn Railway and the Cegin pass through adjacent arches and are now about 70 feet above sea level. Just beyond the viaduct when the narrow-gauge line was built, the river was diverted; a consequence was the municipal boundary crossed over the railway and back again (this boundary follows the original course of the Cegin).

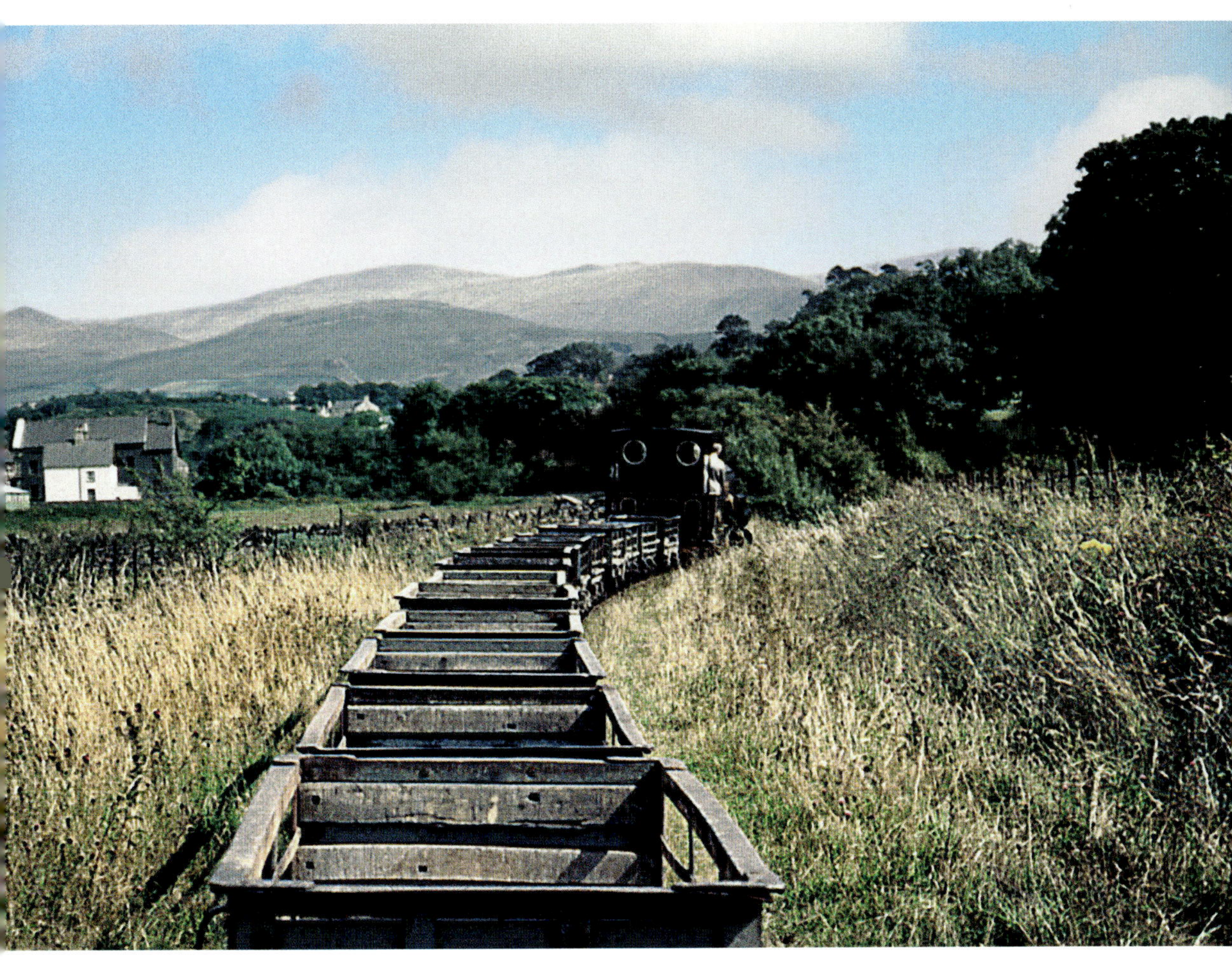

Initially, the author thought this was just a general scenic view taken on the same southbound journey from Port Penrhyn as the previous photograph. It is in fact the location of the Pandy (Tregarth) loop. The roughly 250-yard-long loop is to the right, and its impression can just be made out through the undergrowth; to the left on the north side was a long siding. Services passed each other on the right, and the loop was used until 1928 when, following a reduction in trade, there was no need to have two trains running at the same time. The loop had no signalling, and there was a water tank here for up services if required. Another distinctive feature at the loop, again only just visible, is that instead of the normal fencing created from slabs stuck in the ground; here, the fence is made from iron railings. All stock ran on double-flanged wheels until 1878. Thereafter, all wagons for the new Penrhyn Railway were single-flanged. Most stock used just in the actual quarry remained double-flanged, running loose on their axles; gauge precision was not essential and very useful in the quarry that included lightweight portable crude track. In 1891, some conventional pointwork (i.e. not for double-flanged stock) was installed at this loop, the first place it was encountered on a journey to the port; derailment would be inevitable here with any double-flanged stock sent down from Coed-y-Parc. The Penrhyn Railway was open throughout by 1879; however, a number of alternative routes were considered. One of them would have gone straight ahead at this location towards the white building in the distance on the left. This building still exists today, but now in natural stone instead of bright white, the owners offer B&B accommodation.

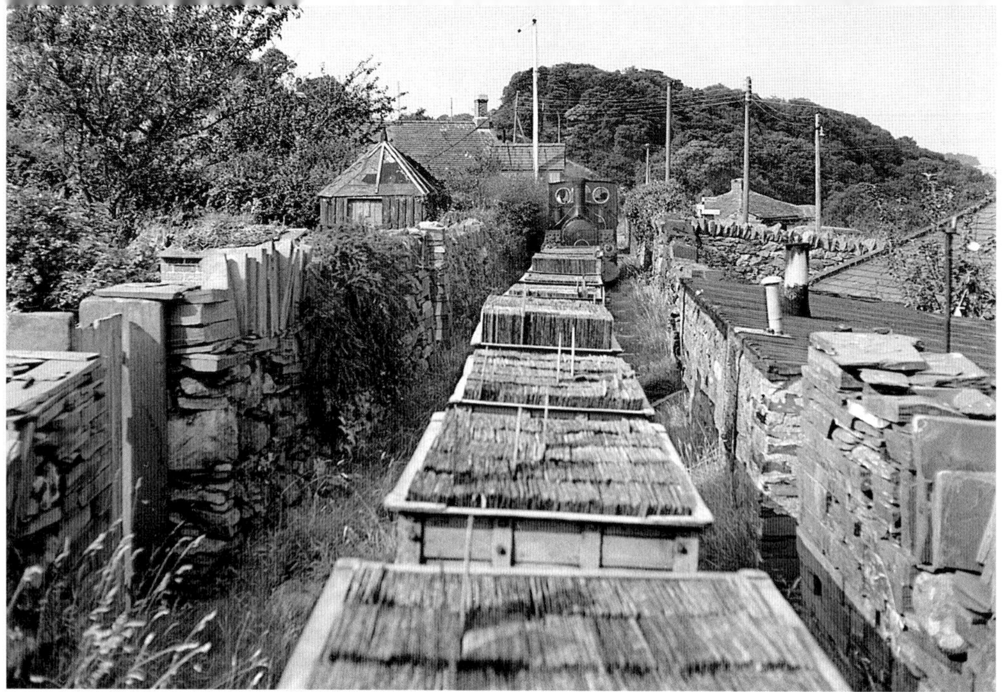

Above: The loaded down journey to Port Penrhyn on 1 September 1961 with *Blanche* at the head is on a tightly confined section with the back gardens of houses on Bron Ogwen to the right. *Blanche* has just descended the Penrhyn Railway's steepest intended grade of 1 in 36 (an unintended section of 1 in 33 existed near the port) and is approaching the Hen–Durnpike crossing—a somewhat risky location for road users. The old Penrhyn Railroad (see below and opposite below) and new Penrhyn Railway both used the same alignment here. Straight ahead can be seen one of the railway's two signals on a very tall post (the other was at the port). The signal posts were painted white, and by this time, the signal face was white save for a wide black stripe vertically down it in a similar position as with conventional main line signals. The signal pointed westwards from the post, and unlike that at the port, it was painted identically on both faces.

As explained on page 89, initially, horses with panniers transported the slate before a new road was built used by horse-drawn wagons; the latter needed about 400 horses hired from farms on the Penrhyn estate. The imposition of a 'Horse Tax' at the end of the eighteenth century (to help pay for increased military costs) substantially raised expenses, and countrywide thought was given to reducing the need for horses. Serious consideration was given to a canal, and a survey was made, but it was not an economic proposition; instead, a railway was seen as the way forward. The Penrhyn Railroad (today we would think of it as a horse-drawn tramway) opened in 1801 and made part-use of the existing 1798-opened 1-mile-long Llandegai Tramway from the port.

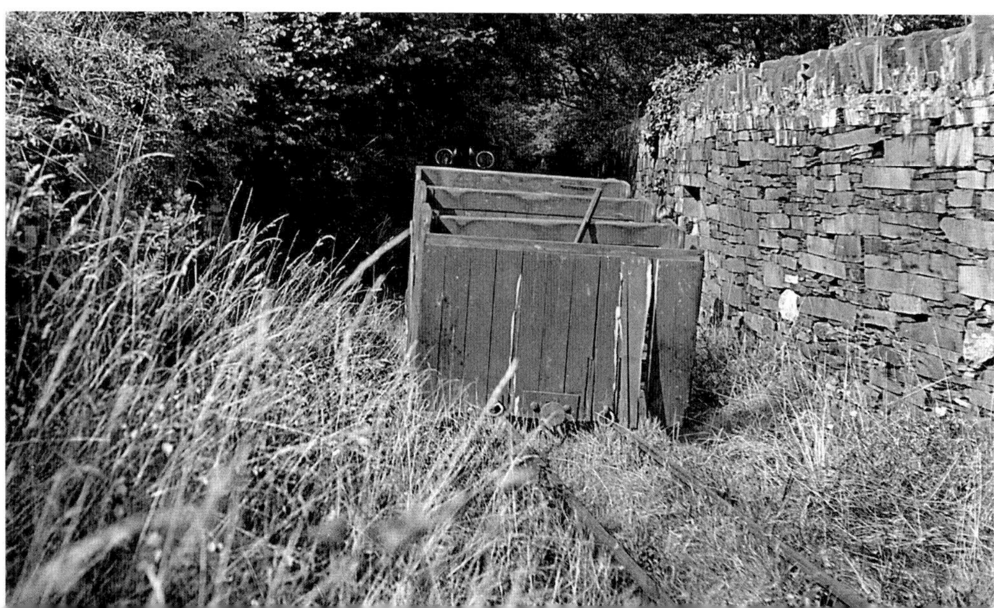

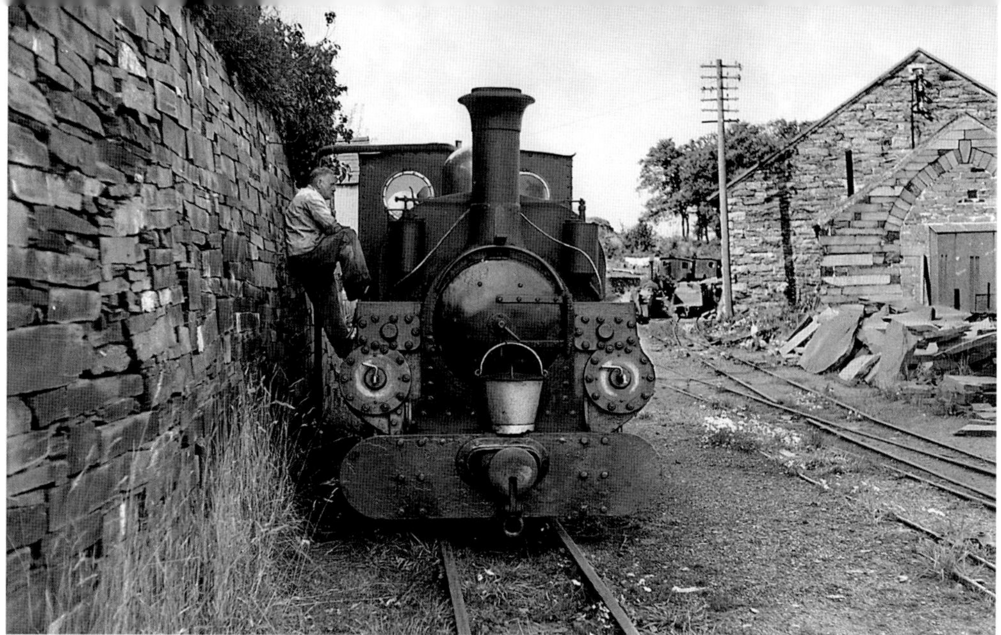

Whereas the earlier Penrhyn Railroad had three inclines (hemp rope-worked initially) along the route to Port Penrhyn, the replacement Penrhyn Railway had none. For the first 2 miles or so from the quarry, it closely followed the old route in the valley of the Ogwen before diverging to the west and the valley of the Cegin. By means of this circuitous route, it was possible for the Penrhyn Railway to maintain a grade largely favourable to the load; Spooner did have thoughts about running slate trains downhill by gravity alone (as on the FR). *Blanche* has arrived at Coed-y-Parc on 1 September 1961 with a train of slate empties, and to the right is the original Felin Fawr Slab Mill of 1803 (see also page 12). The main line summit was here, a water supply that *Blanche* is taking advantage of, and also an oil house where wagons were oiled for the downward run. From the Port House steps to the oil house was 5 miles, 7 furlongs, and 9 chains, involving a climb of some 492 feet at an average grade of about 1 in 64. The bucket hanging on the smokebox door was for sand, it was part of the fireman's duties to sprinkle sand on the rails by hand en route when required. Although the gauge was a nominal 2 feet, the actual gauge was slightly narrower than the public lines of the Festiniog Railway to where *Blanche* was sold in 1963, with the FR re-gauging this locomotive in 1964.

Opposite below: The Penrhyn Railroad included three inclines where loaded wagons going downhill pulled empties up by gravity. On the approximately level lengths between the inclines were passing loops, 'passbyes' in the terminology of the period. After 1851, the average number of horses in use was twenty-six, and they hauled 50,000 tons annually (over double the 1819 figure). The Penrhyn Railroad was at capacity and after half-a-century or so of dominance was being left behind. Steam power had been in use on the Padarn Railway since 1848, and Charles Spooner (Festiniog Railway) came up with various proposals for Lord Penrhyn. The outcome was the creation of the new steam-operated Penrhyn Railway that was fully open by 6 October 1879; the Penrhyn Railroad's last train ran on 2 October 1879.

A workmen's train began running at the beginning of 1880 using four-wheeled roofless and doorless vehicles (see pages 88 and 89); to call them coaches would be an overstatement. On a railway open to Board of Trade inspection, they would never have been permitted, but the Penrhyn Railway was a private undertaking with Lord Penrhyn having personal control. For their journey along the Penrhyn Railway on 1 September 1961, Ellis's party were accommodated in one of these vehicles. Boyd refers to their indifferent riding qualities and Ellis's looks to have suffered a derailment plus damage in the process. *Blanche's* cab windows can be seen above the vehicle, but the location of the derailment is not known, and there is no record of it in Ellis's notes. Workmen's trains last ran regularly in February 1951, but they were used for a short time during May 1957 when there was a Crossville bus strike.

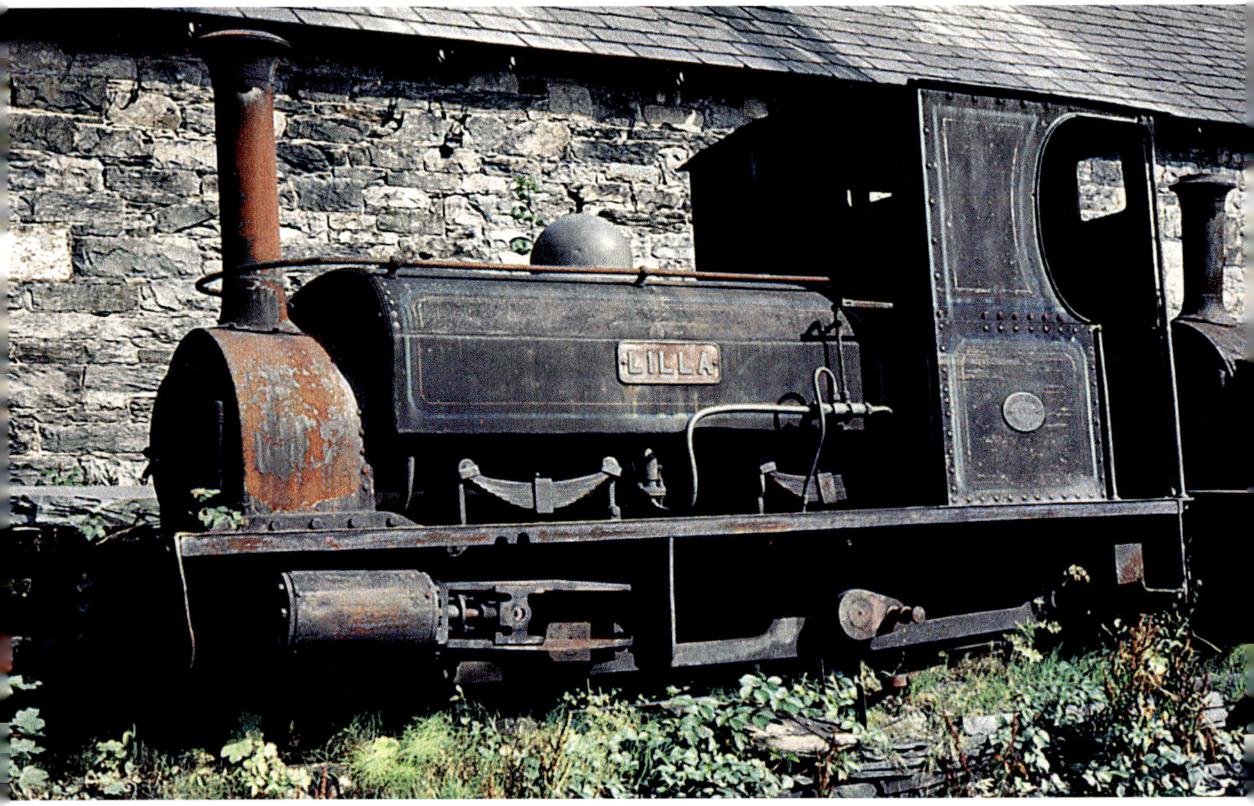

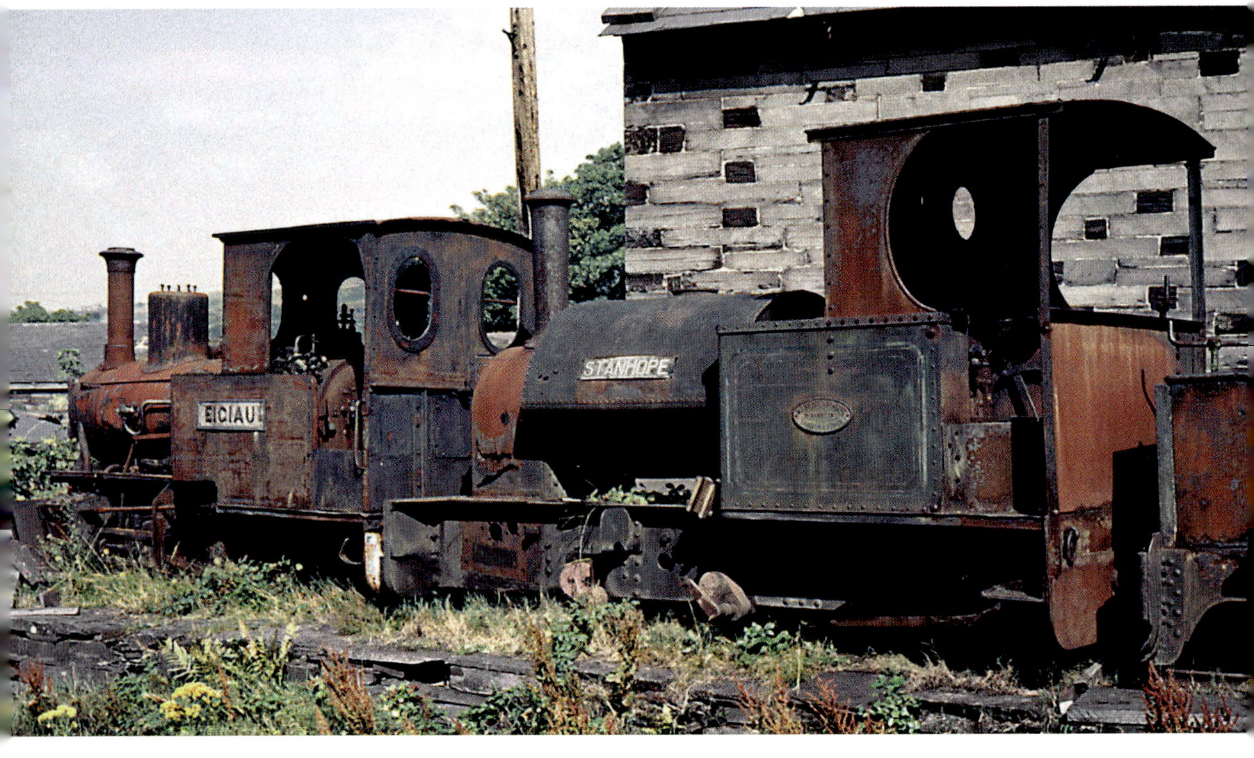

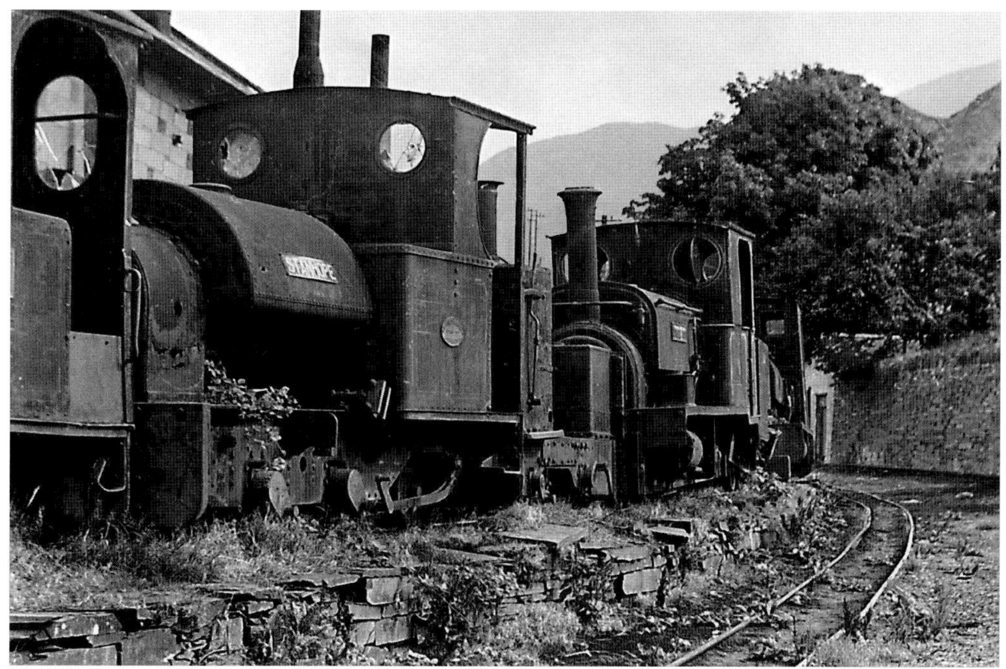

Above and opposite page: The original Felin Fawr Slab Mill of 1803 seen on the right of the previous view is the same building that appears in the background of these three photographs. Although the date of the monochrome image is unknown, the two colour images are believed to have been taken on 1 September 1961. Following the First World War, there came a boom period for domestic house building and thus slate production, with Penrhyn producing 25 per cent of the entire British output (as also Dinorwic and Blaenau Ffestiniog). Yet the Penrhyn Railway had been starved of maintenance during the war years and could not cope. Previously, newly built locomotives were purchased, but from now on, all would be second-hand. *Lilla*, in the first photograph, was purchased in May 1928 from Cilgwyn Quarry, Nantlle; it had been built by Hunslet in 1891. In 1955, *Lilla* was stored, 'laid up' in March 1957, but privately purchased in 1963. Two more second-hand locomotives are seen in the second photograph. The nearer is Kerr Stuart-built *Stanhope* that arrived in December 1934; it was 'laid up' in 1948 and officially scrapped by January 1955. *Stanhope* was also privately purchased. German-built *Eigiau* arrived in 1928, was 'laid up' in 1949, officially scrapped by 1955, but is another locomotive that survives today (see pages 14 and 101). The black and white photograph includes *Eigiau*, *Stanhope*, the De Winton, and *Jubilee 1897*.

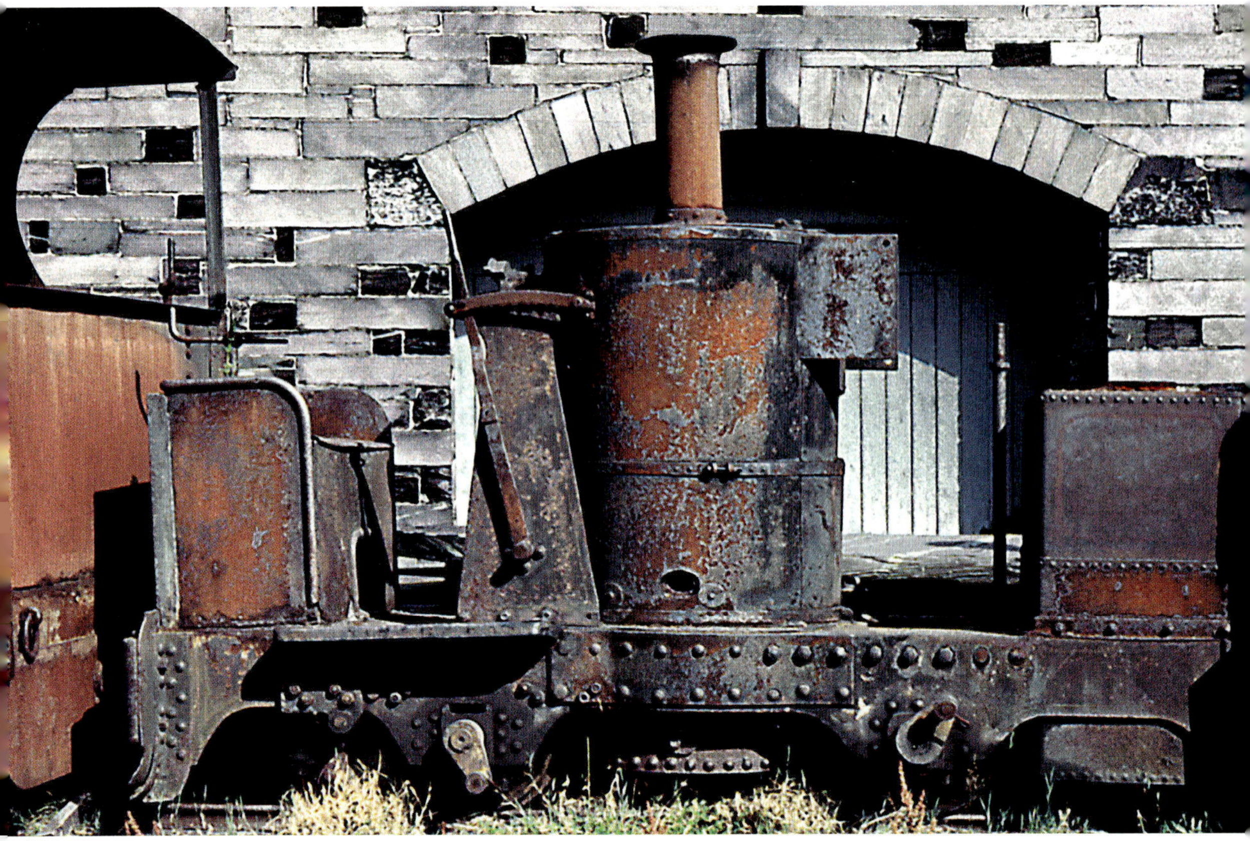

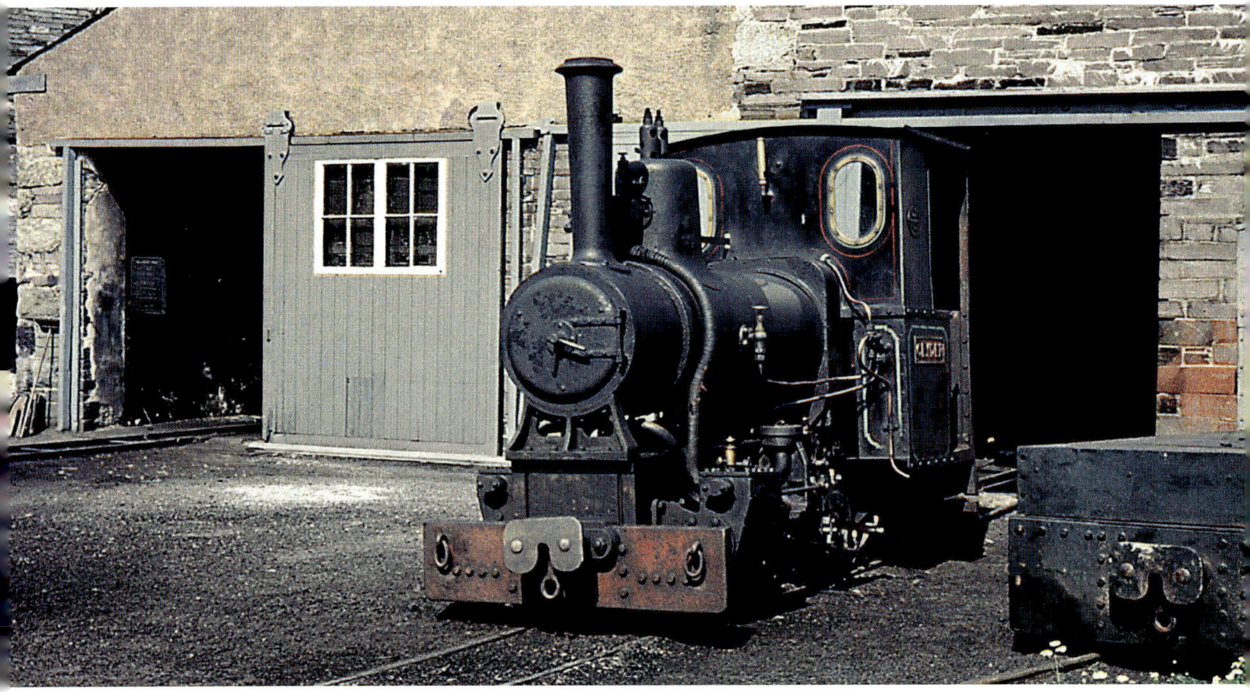

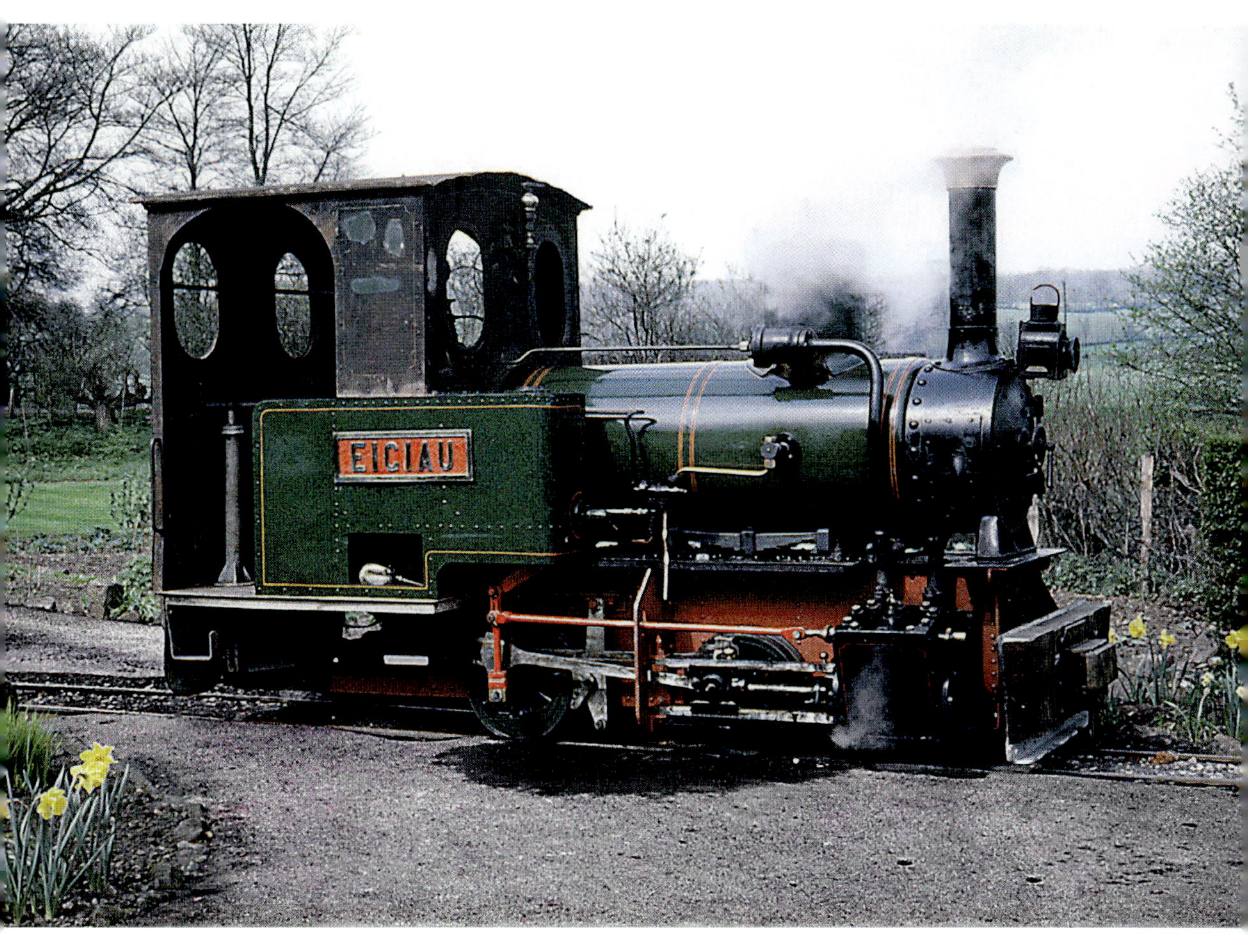

Above and opposite page: It was company policy to renew fireboxes rather than boilers and the practice of reducing boiler pressure began in the late 1920s. In 1955, the line's chief engineer said he had been 'putting off the boiler question for some years'. It had become clear that reducing boiler pressure alone was not enough, and instead, engines were withdrawn. Initially, this was regarded as temporary, but it foresaw the approaching end. Another locomotive photographed rusting away by the side of the original Felin Fawr Slab Mill of 1803 is the noticeably different *Kathleen*; the date is believed to be 1 September 1961. This is one of seven vertically boilered engines that the Penrhyn purchased, all built locally at Caernarvon by De Winton. *Kathleen* (originally named *Katie*) was purchased in 1877; it is listed as 'dismantled 1939', but survives at the Vale of Rheidol Railway, Aberystwyth (see also page 13). The Andrew Barclay-built *Glyder* in the second photograph is another of the second-hand locomotives; it was purchased in January 1938. *Glyder* is seen outside the Coed-y-Parc Workshop on 1 September 1961 and was one of the very last working locomotives on the system (see also page 12). It was shipped to the USA in 1965 but is now back home in the UK at the Beamish Museum. Partly visible to its right is a brake van converted in 1956 from the locomotive *Sanford*. Finally, *Eigiau* is seen again, but this time in the spring of 1964 restored to working order in GWR green. It was purchased by a Worcestershire farmer and moved in early 1963 to Coley Pits Farm in Wychbold, Droitwich.

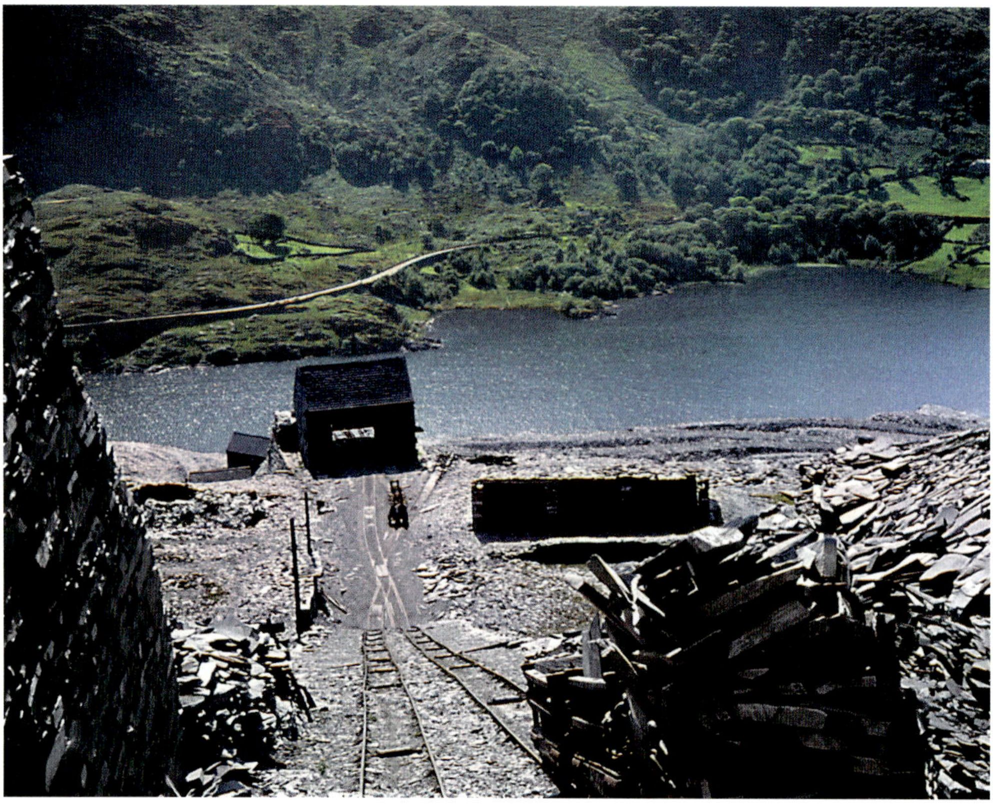

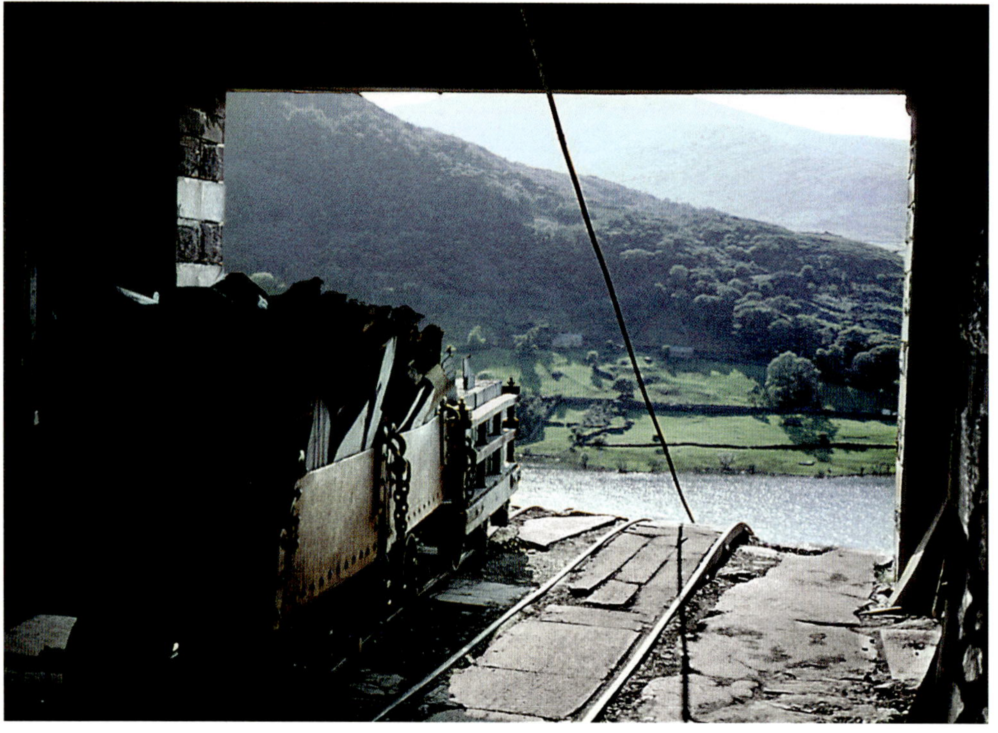

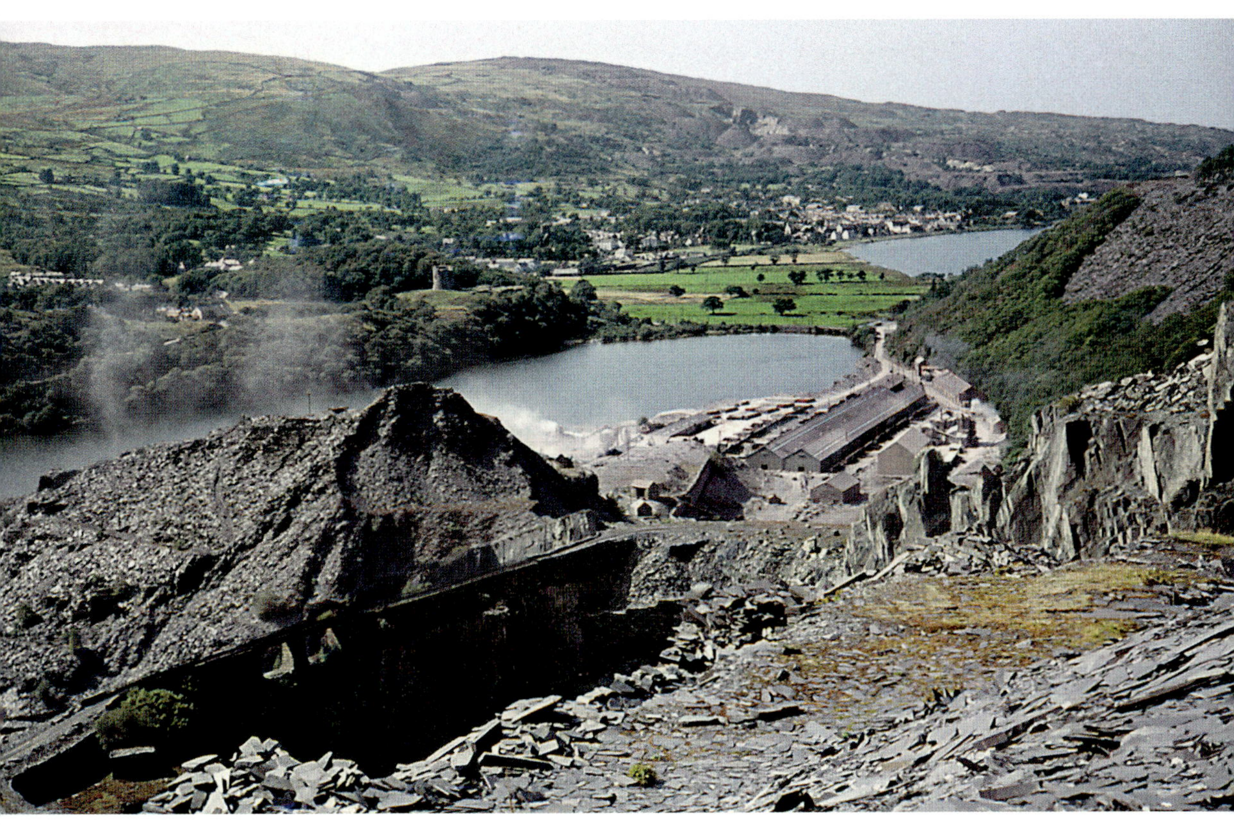

Above and opposite: The north side of Elidir Fach was quarried by the Pennants and slate transported to the Menai Strait by the Penrhyn Railroad/Railway that we have seen over the last few pages. On the south side of that same mountain, slate was quarried by the Assheton-Smiths and also transported by rail to the Menai Strait, but by the Dinorwic/Padarn Railway. Elidir Fach has been described as 'a colossal plum cake out of which two boys are each trying to take the largest slice he can'. In the very early days, groups of men divided their time between farming and quarrying as the seasons demanded; the proportion of quarry-time increasing as demand for slate increased. Initially, Assheton-Smith continued the practice of charging rent before later moving into quarrying personally. Another similarity with the Penrhyn system was the construction of 'The Slate Road' in 1812 for better transportation to the Menai Strait at Felin-Heli (Salt Water Mill), today known as Y Felinheli. The remainder of this volume will now study in some detail the Dinorwic system. The Dinorwic quarry complex ultimately had two enormous wire-rope main incline systems, and part of the most easterly (Braich) is seen in the first two views. Lyn Peris is visible in all three photographs, but Llyn Padarn is in only the third to the far right; all are undated but understood to have been taken during the summer of 1961 (see also introductory page 15).

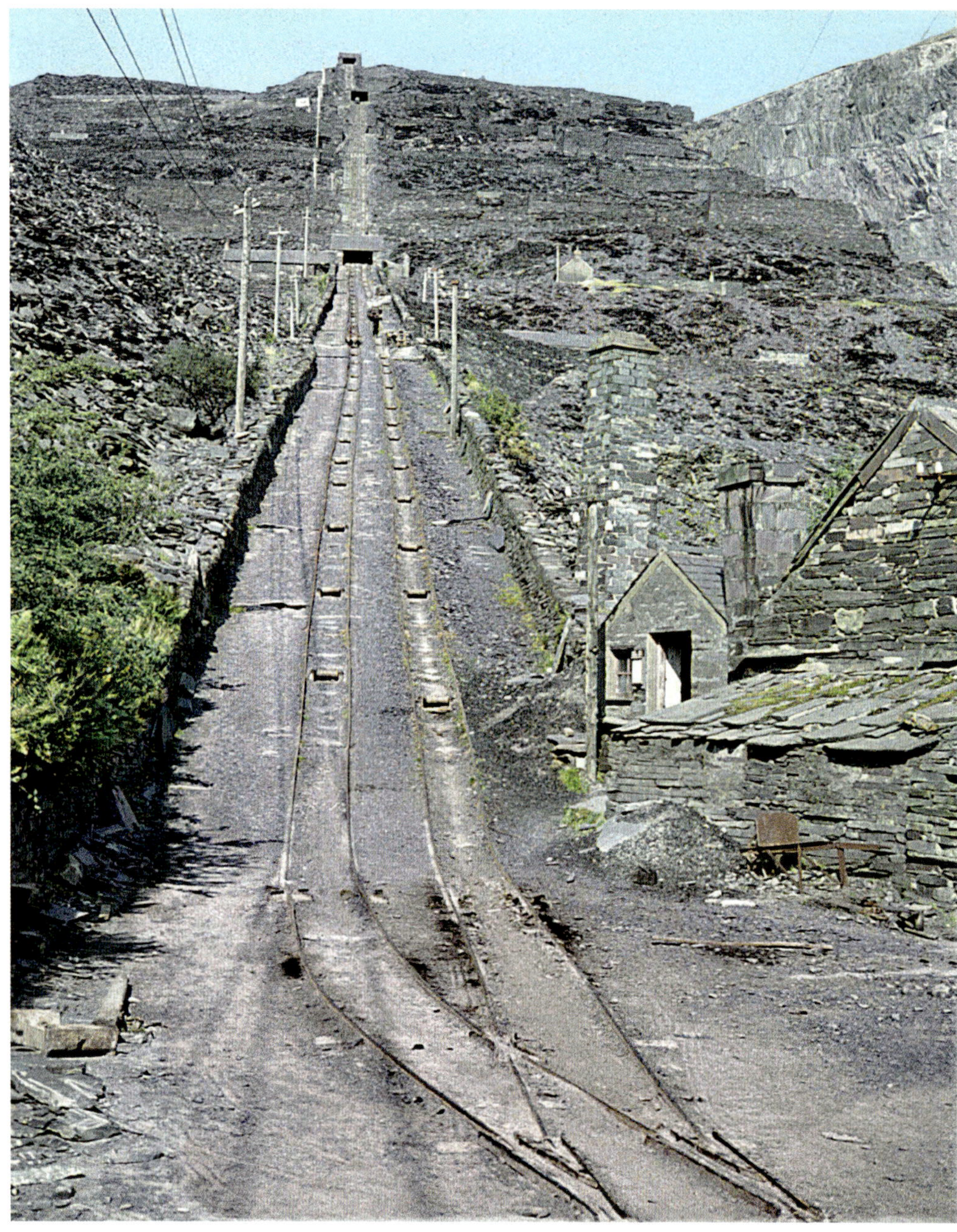

Garret was the most westerly of the Dinorwic quarry main incline systems, believed to be seen in the summer of 1961. At one time, there was a four-track incline at Dinorwic. Slate was even extracted from below lake level, and by 1858, the workings extended 1,800 feet from top to bottom. Galleries branched off to west and east; they were at intervals of 75 vertical feet, and some gallery lines passed above or below the inclines. By 1858, there were about 23 miles of tramways and wire-roped inclines, the eighteen inclines averaging 600 feet in length.

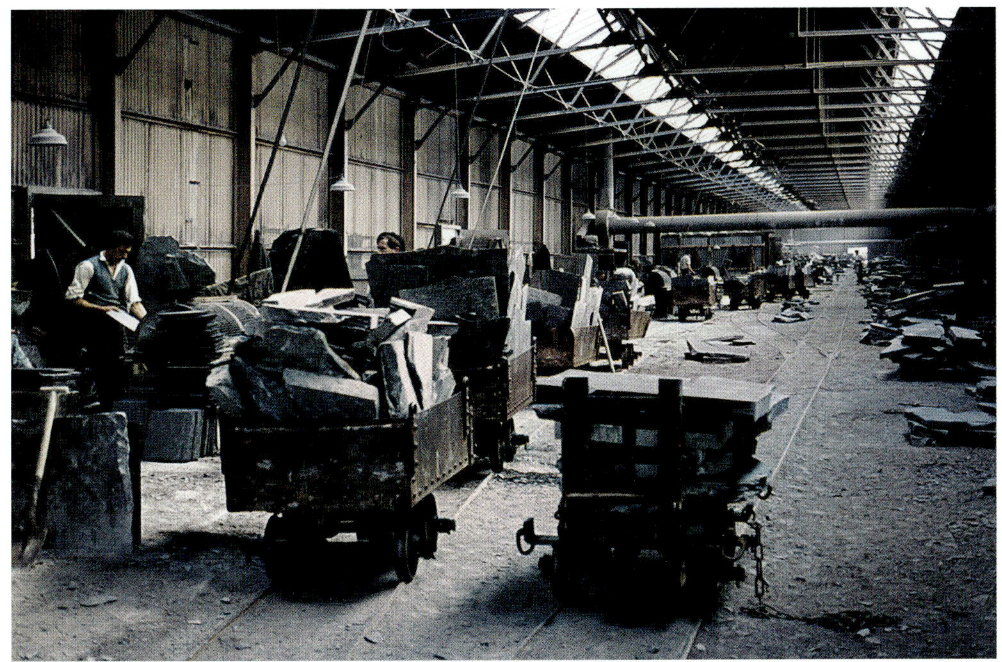

Above and below: Whether at Penrhyn or here at Dinorwic, extracted rock might be split and carried as slabs to the mill or taken away as rubbish; some 90 per cent of the extracted stone became rubbish, explaining the massive tips of spoil. Work is underway in the first photograph, converting extracted rock into commercial products. The location of the second photograph is close to the original terminus of the Padarn Railway at Muriau (also seen in the distance on page 103). Note the hawser on the locomotive's buffer connecting to wagons on the adjacent track, often used if the track could not support the engine's weight. Both photographs are thought to date from the summer of 1961.

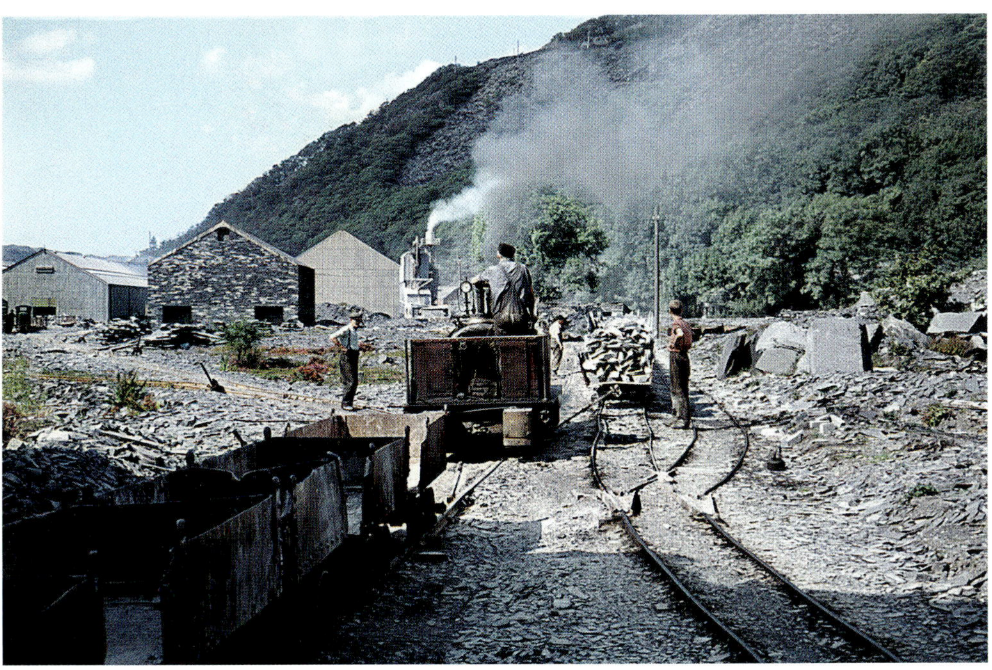

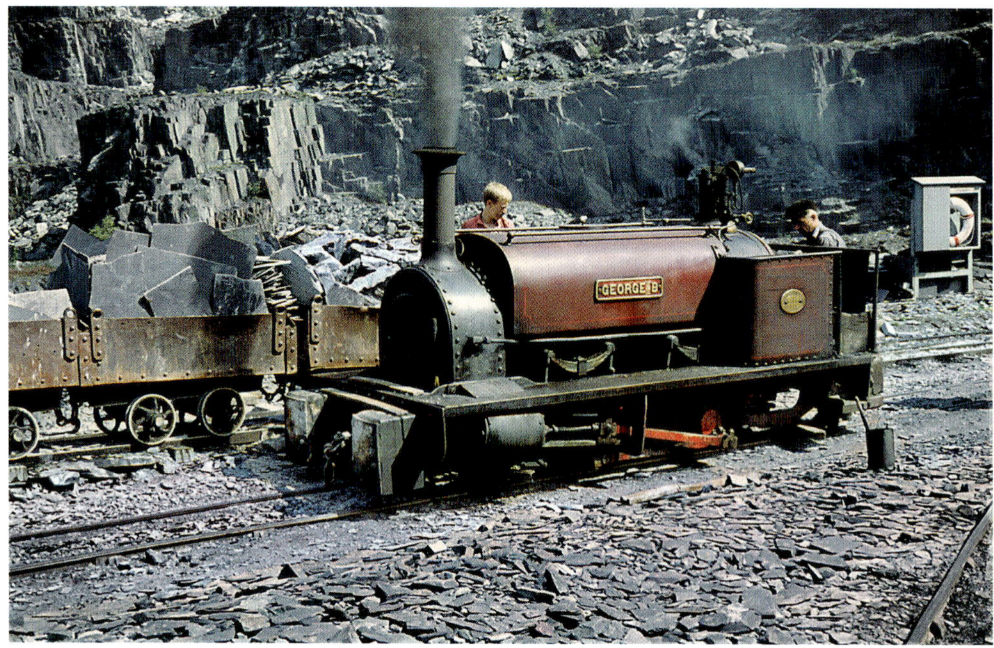

Above and below: Much of the steam locomotive fleet was made up of four-wheeled locomotives with outside cylinders from the Hunslet Engine Co. of Leeds, the bulk to one basic design. Unlike at Penrhyn, Dinorwic did not purchase many second-hand locomotives. Another difference from Penrhyn was that additional boilers were purchased when heavy repairs were required. The names of locomotives came from members of the Assheton-Smith family, their homes, racehorses, ships, and geographical locations. The engines were identified by their names, and *George B* (there had been a *George* in earlier years) plus another unidentified locomotive are believed seen in the late summer of 1961.

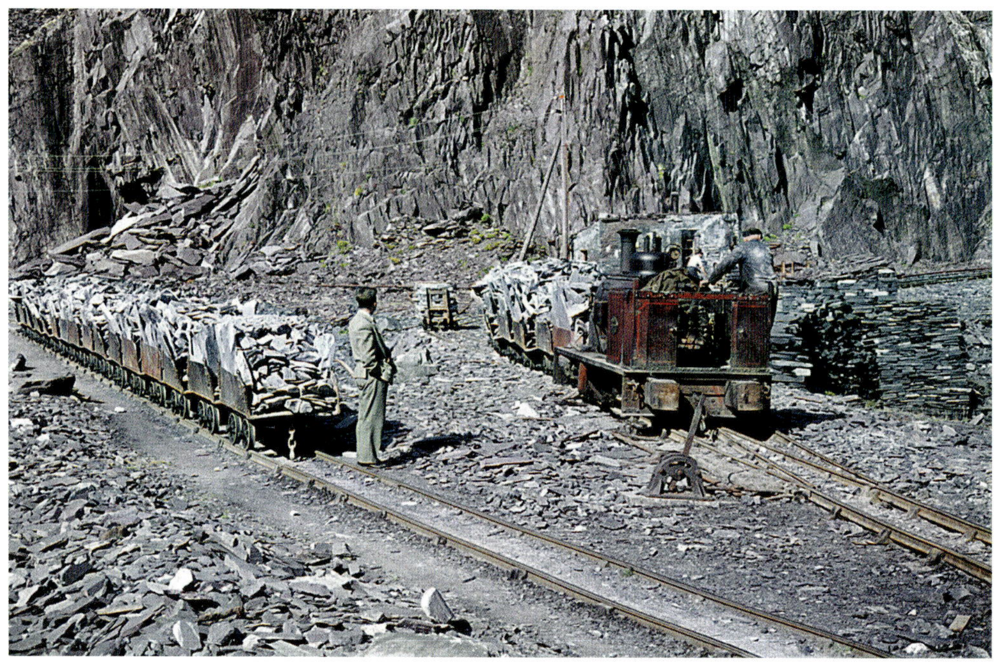

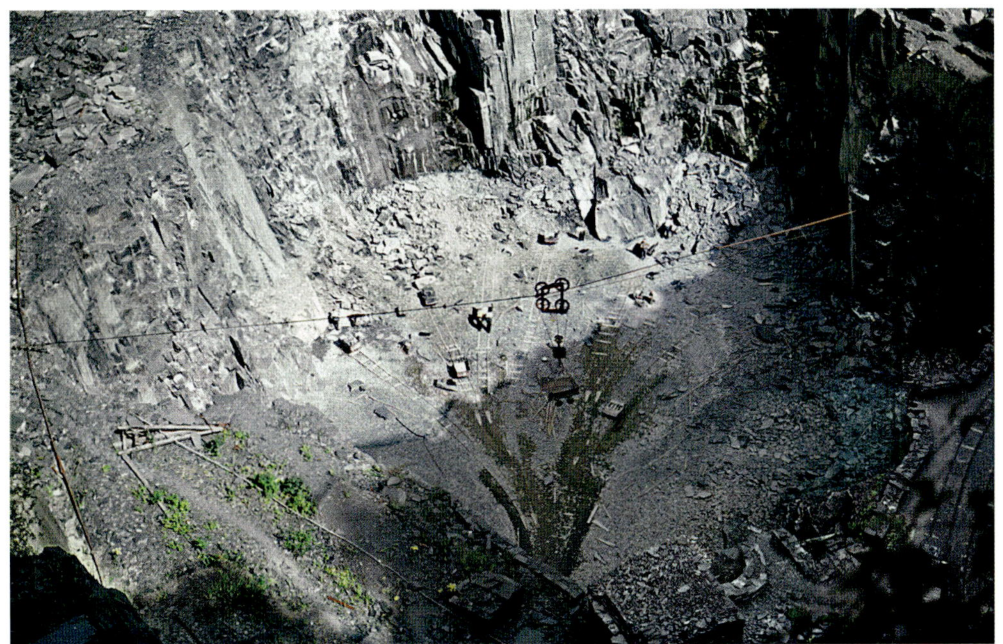

Above and below: The narrow-gauge tracks at Dinorwic quarry were 1 foot 10.75 inches wide (between the rails) and all wagon stock was double-flanged. The loosely mounted wheels could shift laterally on their axles and ideal for the roughly-gauged tracks in working areas. Certain quarry-confined wagons had lifting rings to enable them to be raised from pits by overhead wire ropeways called 'Blondins'. A suspended wagon can be seen in the first photograph. *Sybil* was not a Hunslet-built locomotive, instead coming from Bagnall of Stafford in 1906, its hawser chain for shunting prominent. It was said that around this time, quarry staff did not know of an official livery. Both photographs are thought to date from the late summer of 1961.

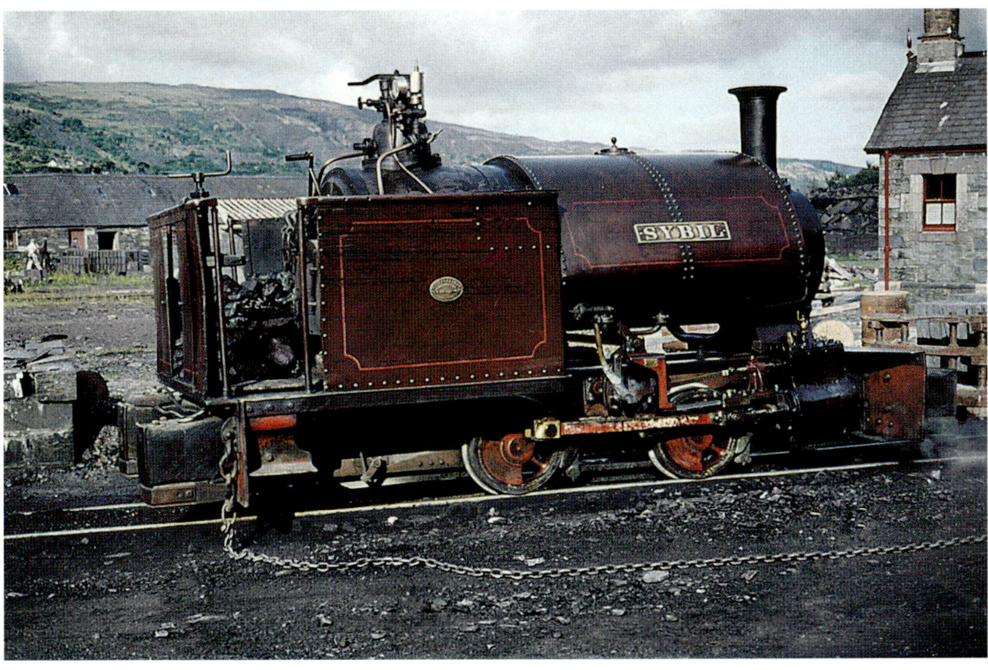

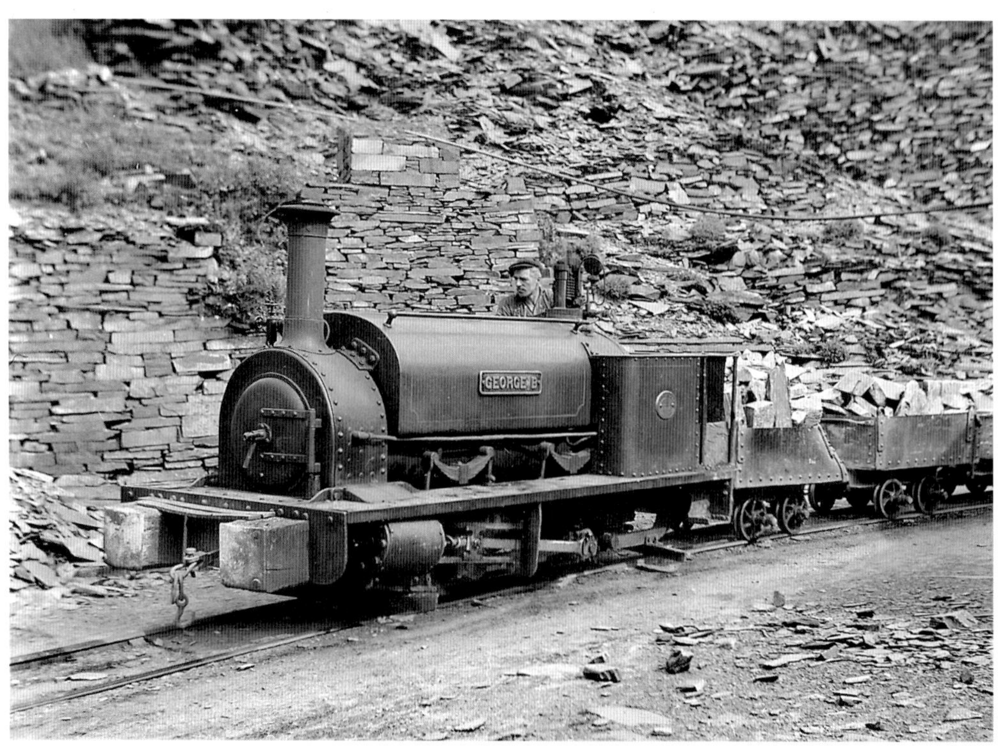

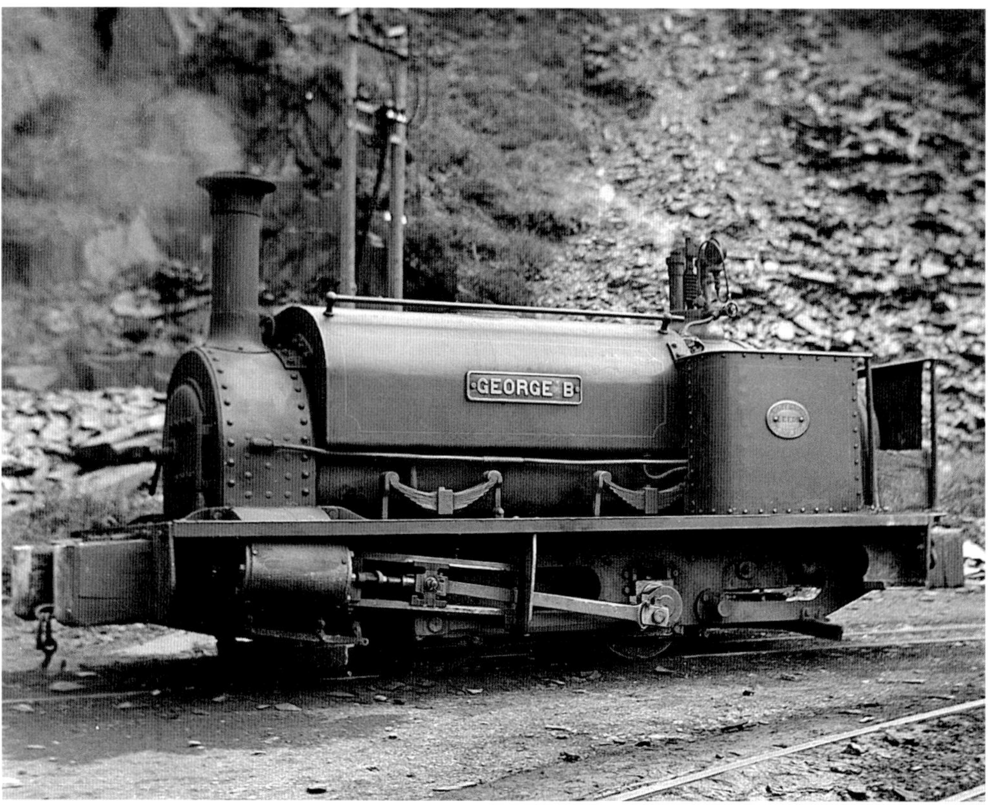

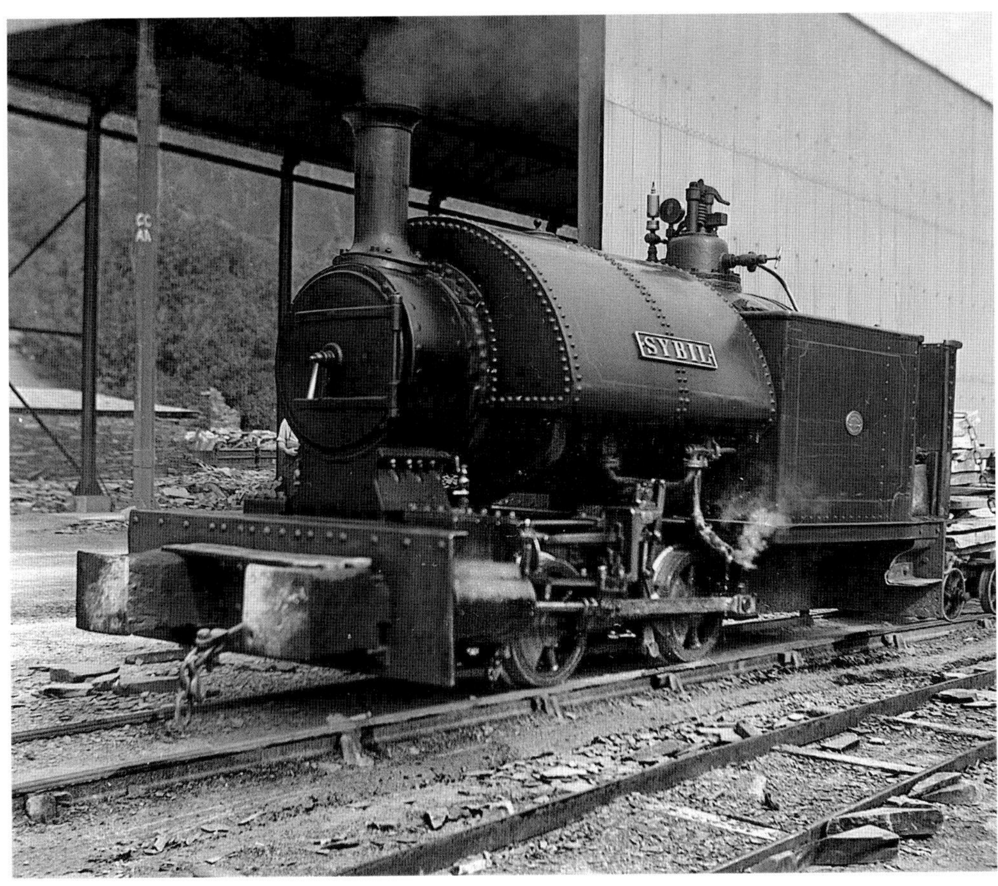

Above and opposite page: These three black and white photographs plus the next two, although undated, appear to have been taken during a different visit to the Dinorwic system from those we have seen so far. They have been catalogued in a totally different series by Ellis and there are no accompanying notes, but they feature two locomotives seen before. *George B* is a member of the 'Alice' class and dated from 1898; it was first named *Wellington*. The first of this class was constructed in 1886. They had shackle-and-hook couplers together with large wooden buffers sheeted in steel plate, one face rounded with the other flat and useful during rope or chain shunting. The slab on the footplate was to keep the coal in place and also visible on other pages such as 106. The 'Alice' class totalled thirteen locomotives with the last constructed in 1904. *George B* was sold in 1965 but has only recently been restored to working order on the Bala Lake Railway. Overall, *Sybil* was not a popular member of the fleet as its marine boiler would not make or maintain steam, and required more careful firing than the Hunslets. *Sybil* was sold in 1965 and after spending many years in Cornwall is now on the West Lancashire Light Railway. Rough working conditions at the quarry face required a rail gauge with some latitude, the wagons having double-flanged wheels free to slide on their axles; it was defined as the distance between rail centres and was 2 feet. Yet with the advent of steam locomotives and their single-flanged wheels, the gauge was restated in terms of the distance between the rails, this being 1 foot 10.75 inches.

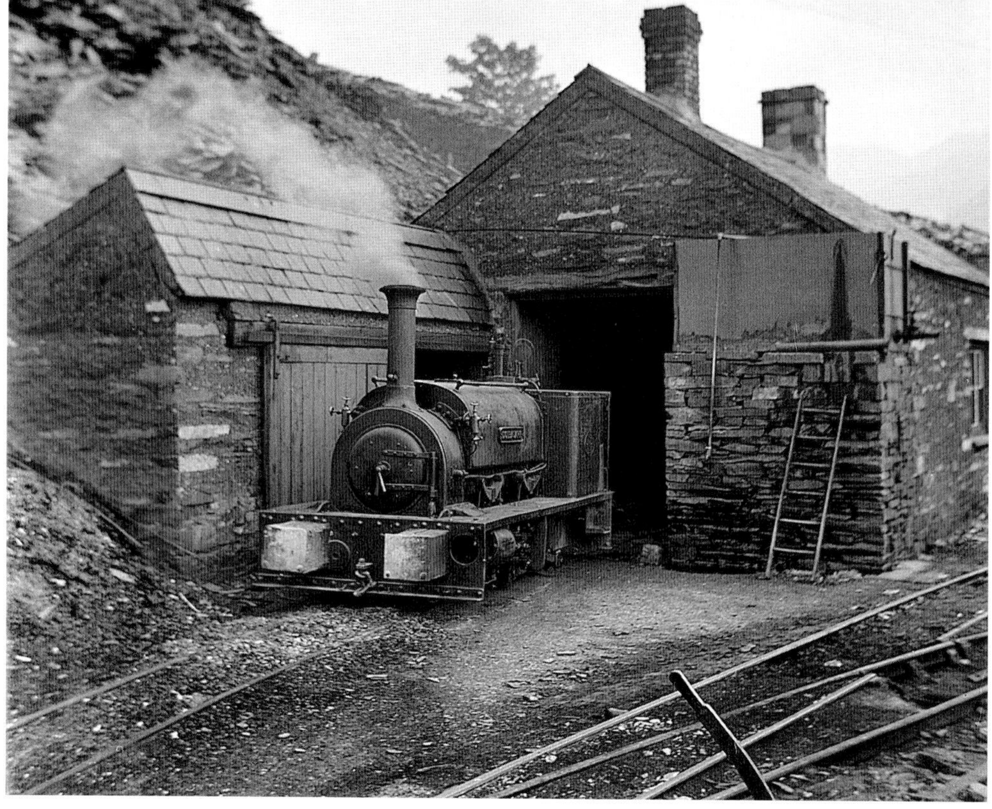

Above and below: Dolbadarn features in both of these undated photographs and was built in 1922; it was initially No. 2 and was a member of the 'Port' class. Three 'Port' class locomotives were purchased from Hunslet. When built it had a cab, but after transfer to the quarry from the port in 1935 this was removed due to the more restricted clearances. The 'Port' class had deeper and fuller buffer beams in comparison to the 'Alices'. *Dolbadarn* was originally fitted with safety valves and a hooter on a domed boiler. *Dolbadarn* was sold in 1969 but is still close to its old home, on the Llanberis Lake Railway, once more with a domed boiler.

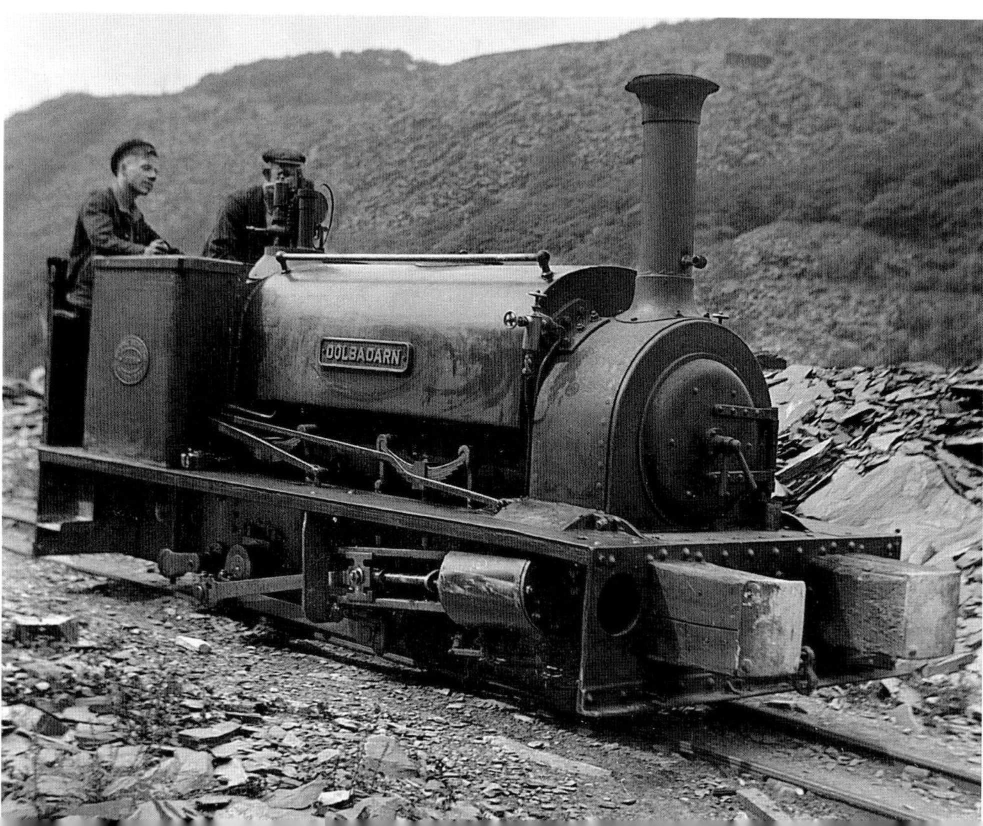

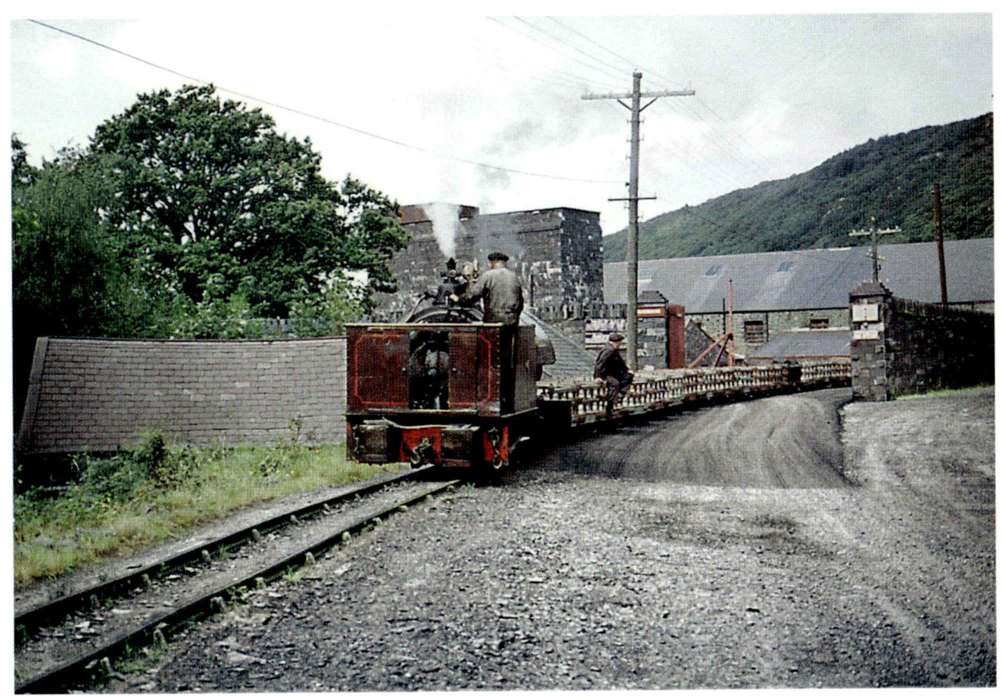

Above and below: Nominally independent, the Padarn–Peris Tram Line ran from by the exchange sidings, alongside the road past the works, then by the road junction to Llanberis village, and on to Hafod Owen. This was the route used for slate traffic between the bottom levels of the Big Quarry and the transfer facility at Gilfach Ddu. These photographs of *Sybil* approaching past the works and then heading away towards Hafod Owen with a load of empties are thought to date from the summer of 1961. Until the early twentieth century, the line ran in a tunnel here, but waste tipping enabled this link to be created bypassing the tunnel. The fortress-like works are today home to the National Slate Museum.

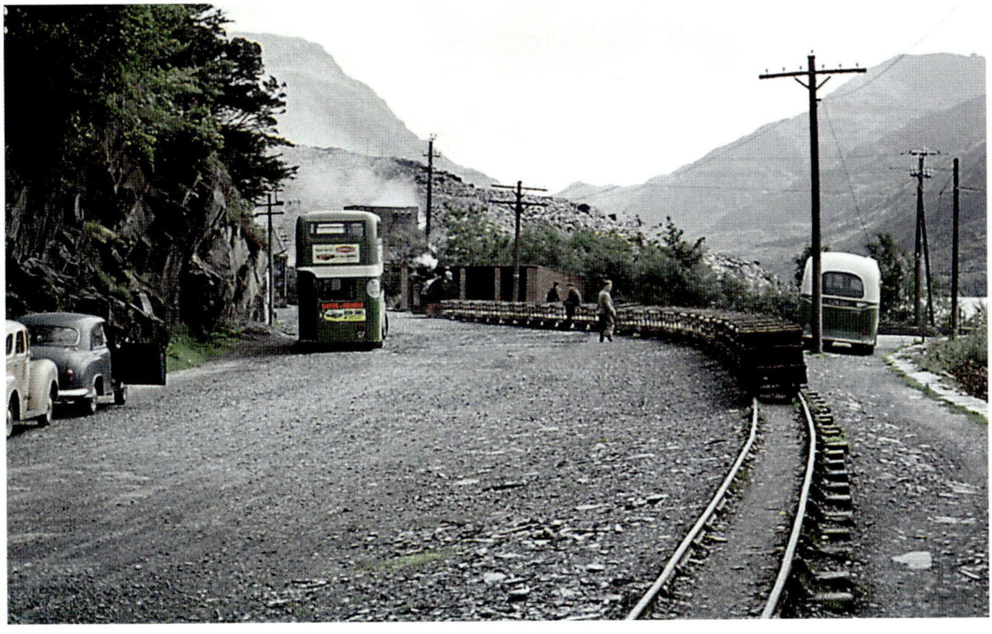

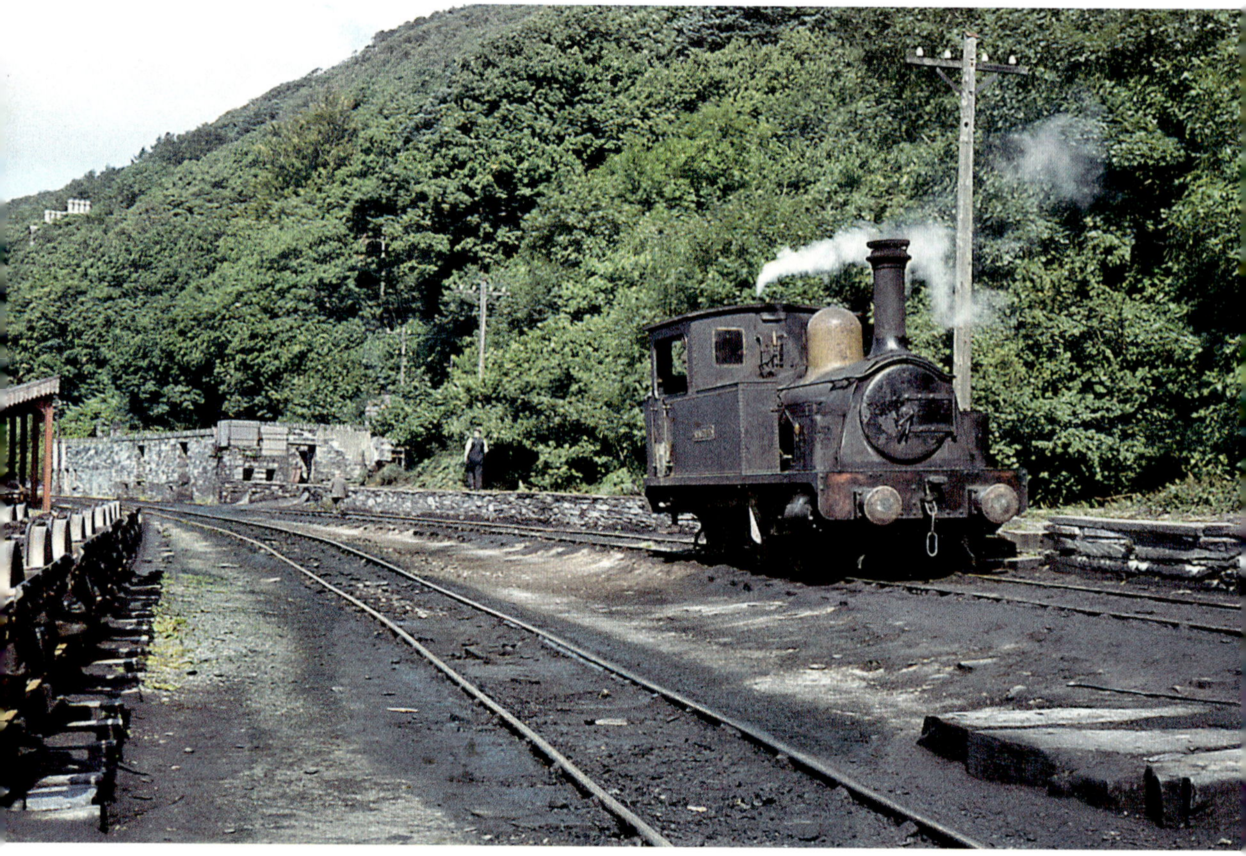

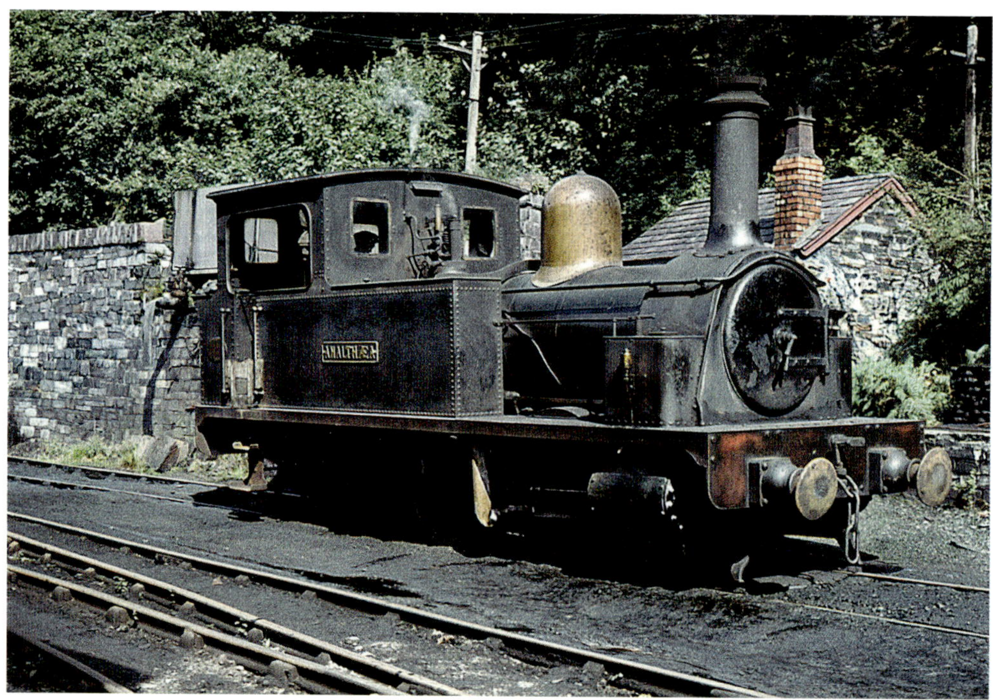

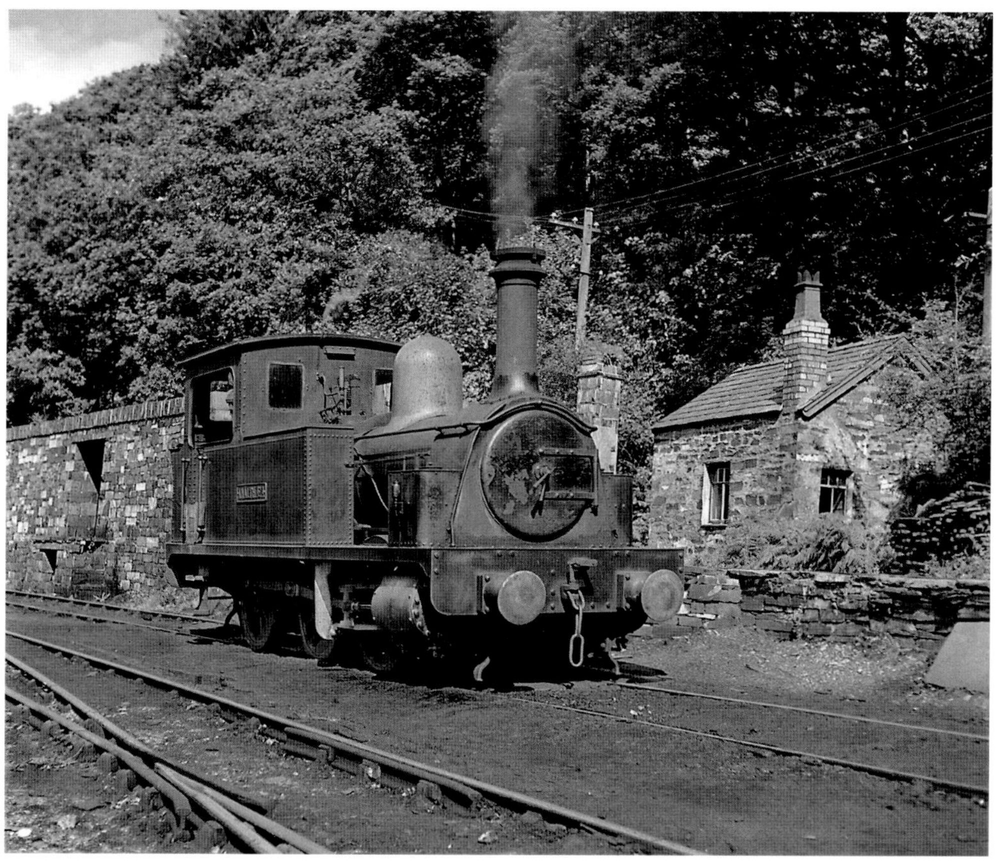

Above and opposite page: As with the Penrhyn system, here at Dinorwic, thoughts turned to something more efficient than the cartage over the 1812-built 'Slate Road'; it cost more to transport slate to the coast than it did to ship onwards to Liverpool. The 7-mile-long horse-worked 1824-opened Dinorwic Railway was the answer, built to a nominal gauge of 24.5 inches measured over the rail centres. It did, however, involve three rope-worked inclines, one of which carried the slate uphill. Yet the Dinorwic Railway proved inadequate almost from the start, and only a few years later, schemes were being considered to supplant it in the early 1830s. There were even thoughts about linking up with their rival and shipping through Port Penrhyn. The solution was replacement by the 1843-opened Padarn Railway (initially Rail Road), although from 1880 its official name became the Dinorwic Quarry Railway. Whereas the Penrhyn Railway used the same narrow-gauge tracks all the way through from the quarry face to Port Penrhyn, it was not the case here; these tracks are 4 feet—a rare gauge. A 'pick-a-back' or transporter system was used whereby four quarry-gauge wagons were carried on one 4-foot-gauge wagon (horse-worked for the first few years). Trains made up of transporter wagons plied between here at Gilfach Ddu and Pen-Scoins where they were unloaded to descend a gravity-worked quarry-gauge incline to Port Dinorwic (today known as Y Felinheli) on the Menai Strait. To work the transporter trains latterly, three tank engines were built by Hunslet of Leeds, and *Amalthæa* (correctly spelt with a diphthong as on the locomotive's nameplate) features in all three photographs. Ellis visited the line on two occasions—the end of August and the beginning of September 1961.

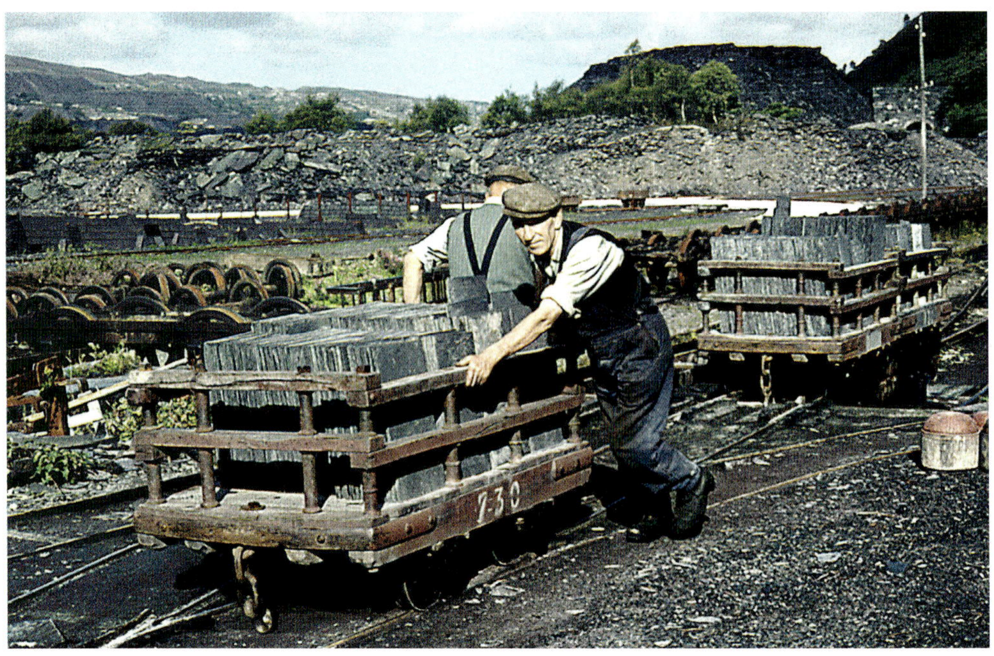

Above and below: Two more photographs at Gilfach Ddu taken on the same visits. First, slate-filled quarry-gauge wagons are being loaded at the transhipment platform onto the 4-foot-gauge transporters. There were once over 700 of these slate wagons, many built locally at Gilfach Ddu. On their side was the tare weight (7 cwt and 3 quarters) to assist working out the weight of finished slate. On the right of the second photograph, *Amalthæa* is at the head of a line of transporters loaded with quarry-gauge wagons. To the left in the distance with a sloping roof is the former Workmen's Train station shed.

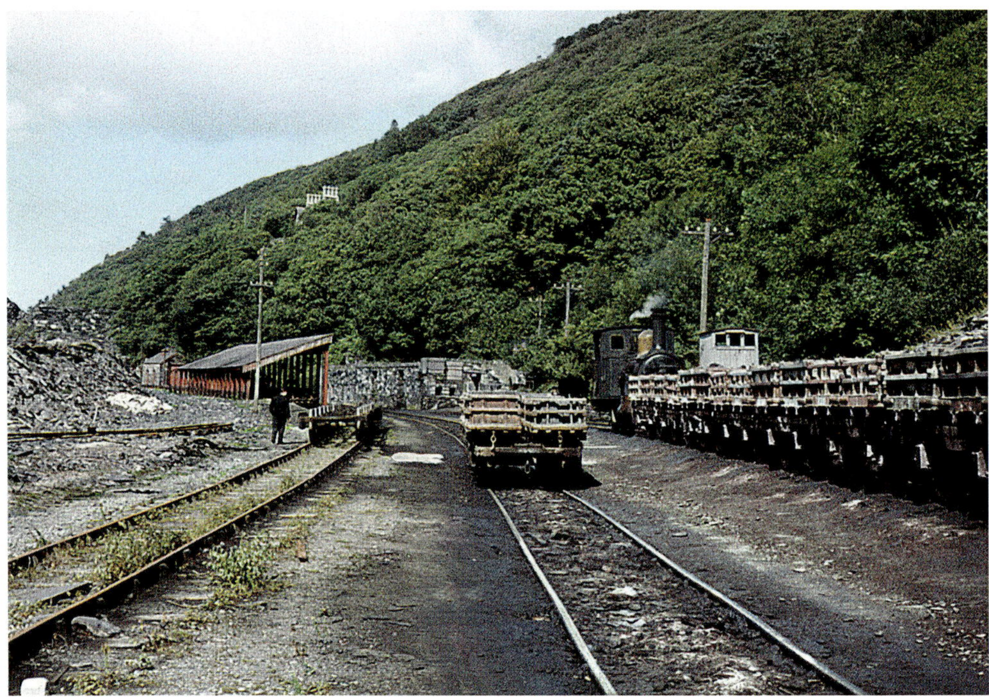

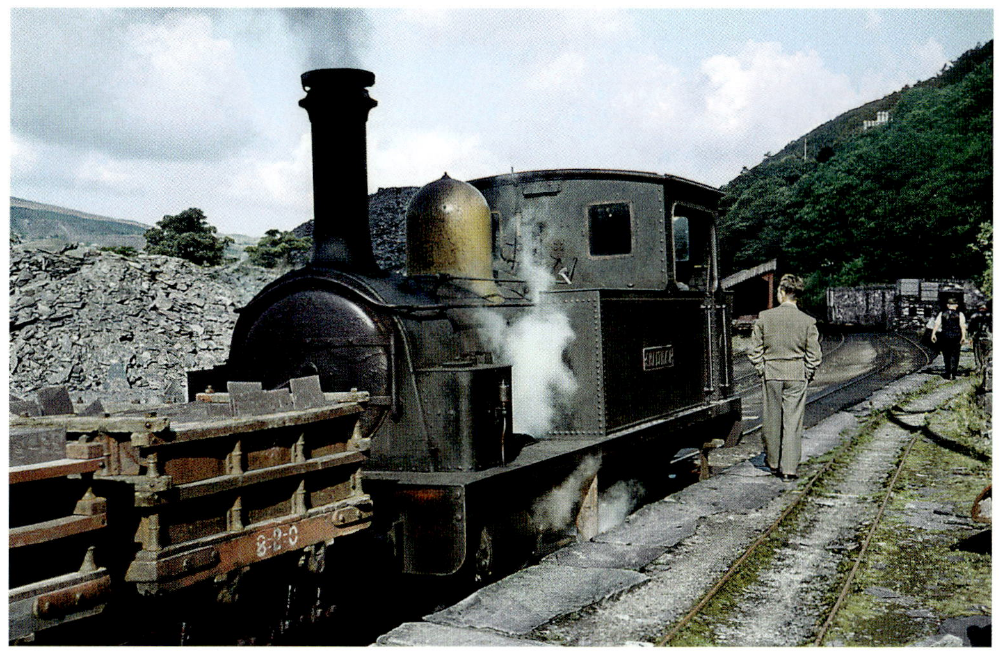

Above and below: The three 4-foot-gauge Hunslet 0-6-0s were *Dinorwic*, built in 1882 (W/N 302); *Pandora*, built in 1886 (W/N 410); and *Velinheli*, built in 1895 (W/N 631). *Pandora* was renamed *Amalthæa* in 1909 and is seen on Ellis's same visits in 1961. Each worked about three months at a time. It was possible to run the daily traffic with one locomotive, the second as stand-by, and the third undergoing overhaul. They could be mistaken for conventional standard-gauge locomotives, but noticeable were the side wings to the smokebox with sandboxes alongside and more closely centred buffers than usual. They had jaw-and-link couplings, which could be released from the footplate by a treadle. None survived to be preserved.

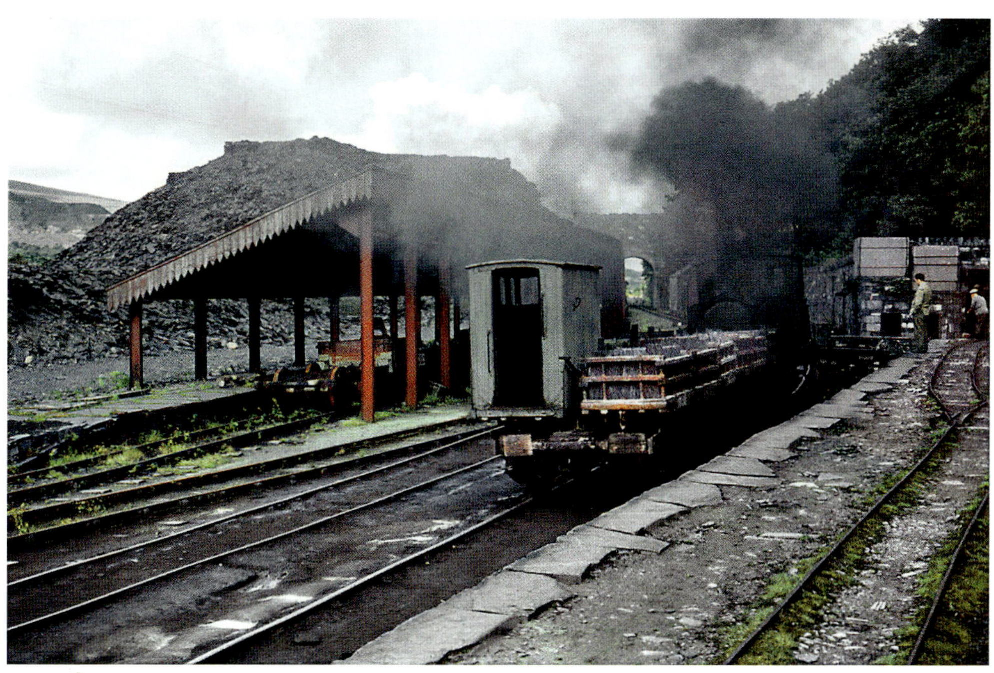

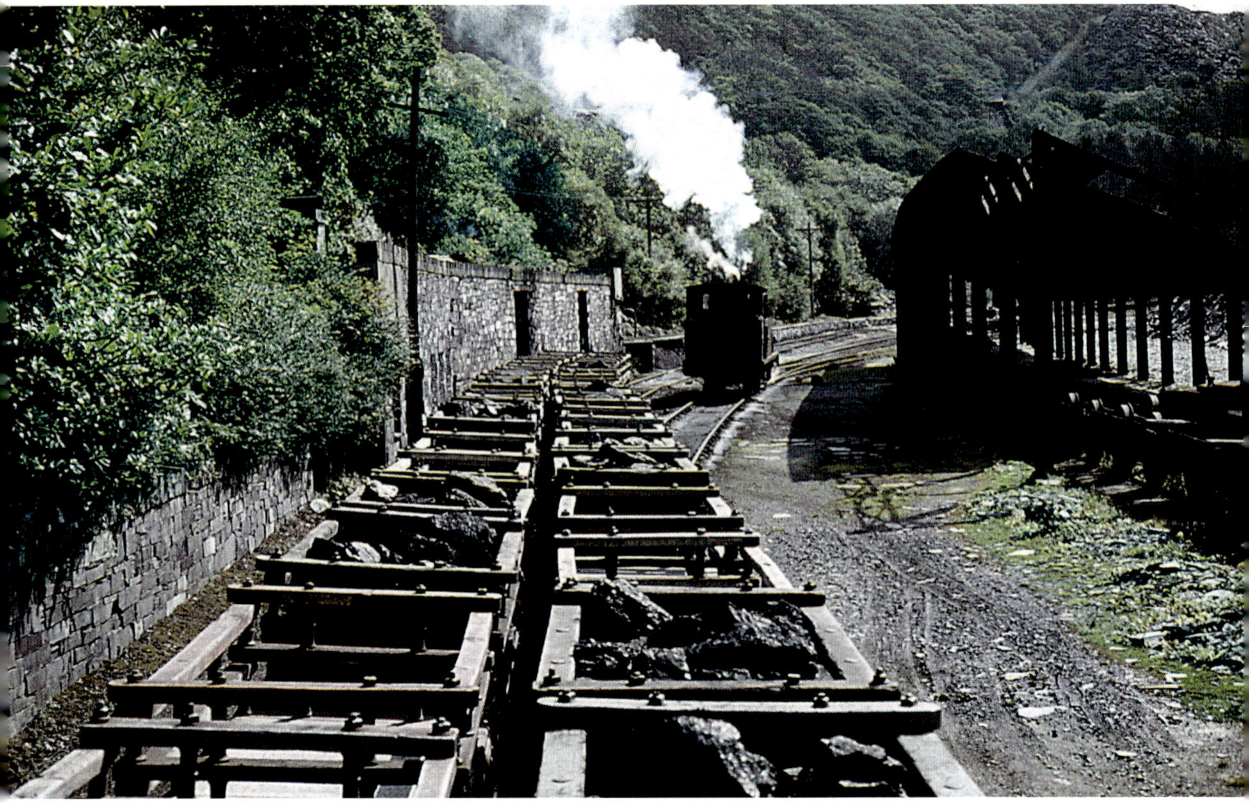

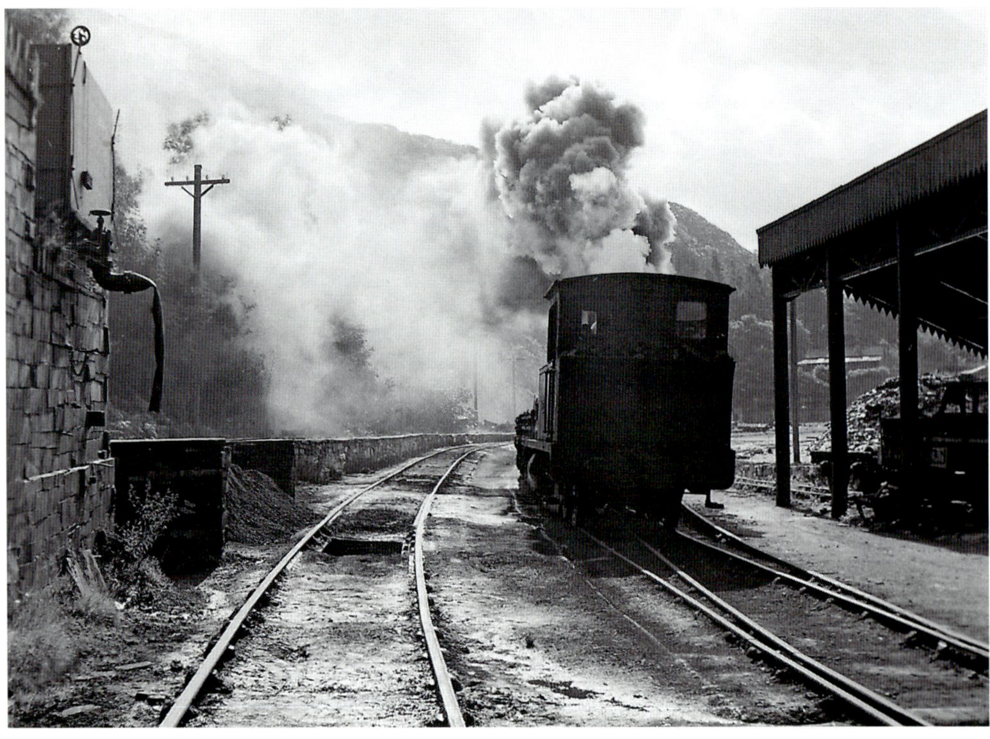

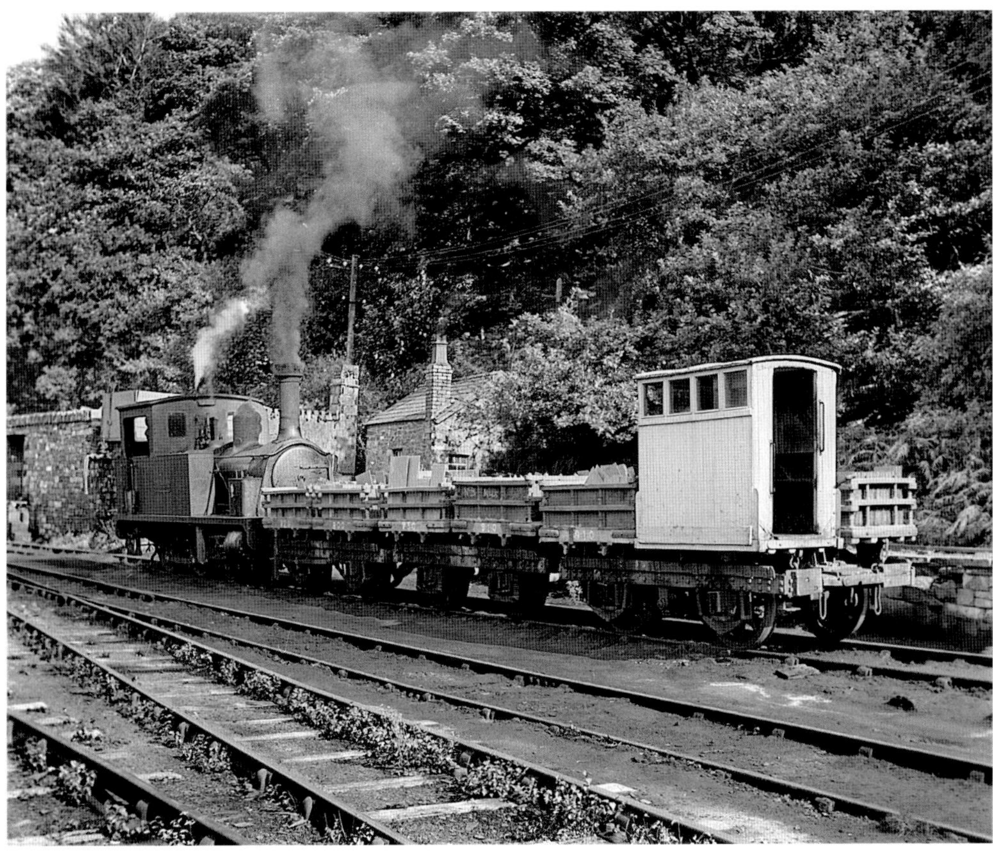

Above and opposite page: The first photograph shows an arrival at Gilfach Ddu from Pen-Scoins. It is difficult to see but the wagons are being drawn forward by *Amalthæa* using a chain. To the right are transporter wagons stored in the one-time Workmen's Train station shed; the Workmen's Trains had ceased running in November 1947 (but briefly restored during Crossville bus strikes). As on the Penrhyn Railway, the load was not always just empty slate wagons making their way back to the quarry. Coal was used for quarry plus locomotive purposes and certain slate wagons were given sheet iron sides to serve as coal wagons. It was taken up to the various levels from the walled coal yard (where it was kept under lock and key) that is to the left of *Amalthæa*. At the far end of this same wall was a water tank for locomotive purposes and best seen in the first monochrome photograph. All three photographs are believed to date from about the end of August 1961 and the last Padarn Railway train ran on 27 October 1961, less than two months away. The final photograph is perhaps a sign of these times, as business fell away the trains became shorter. The sentry-box-like shelter mounted on wheels is the guard's van. An indication of the different variations of slate wagons built over the years is that of the five visible, close examination reveals four of them have different tare weights on their sides.

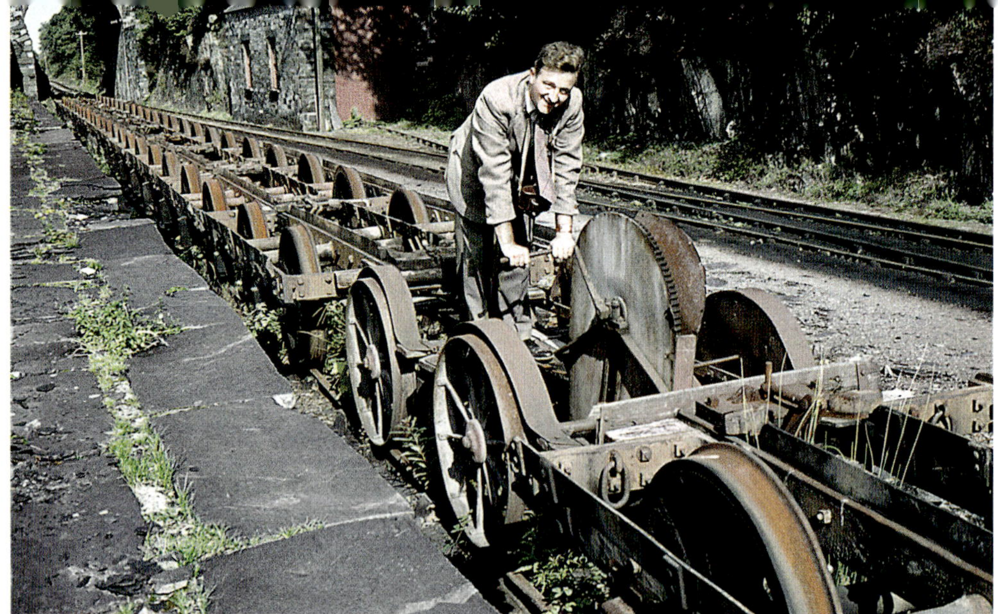

Above: This final photograph at the Gilfach Ddu complex shows a row of transporter wagons plus one velocipede. The view is looking towards Pen-Scoins and was taken around the end of August 1961. In the background, the arch was built in 1900 and carried a tramway for rubbish from the Vivian Quarry. The disused locomotive shed dates from about 1901 according to Boyd; the traffic locomotive was kept at Pen-Scoins nightly and at weekends. Even at the time of this photograph, the 4-foot-gauge transporter (or host) wagons were believed to be over a century old, the first seems to date from 1841 and ultimately the stock appears to have totalled over eighty. 'Rails' to carry the quarry-gauge (nominal 2-foot) slate wagons were just cast bars incorporated into the wagon frame. The level of these 'rails' is well below the top of the transporter wagon wheels to give a low centre of gravity and thus stability when loaded; however, this required a change in slate wagon design from 1841. The customary full axle for individually mounted wheels had to be abandoned, and instead, the slate wagons had separate axles not extending across the truck, to clear the wheels of the transporters. Ellis's friend is standing on a velocipede; these contraptions had been introduced before 1855 for quarrymen to get to and from work from the outlying districts, and at the height of their popularity, they carried some 500 men daily. This is a 'Turning Car' driven by handles and there were also 'Kicking Cars' worked by foot treadles; a sixteen-man team could be carried but not all were able to work the machine at the same time. They operated outside the hours of the first and last slate trains and latterly there were fifty-two vehicles. Introduction of the Workmen's Train in August 1895 brought about their demise, although one or two survived for permanent way gang use.

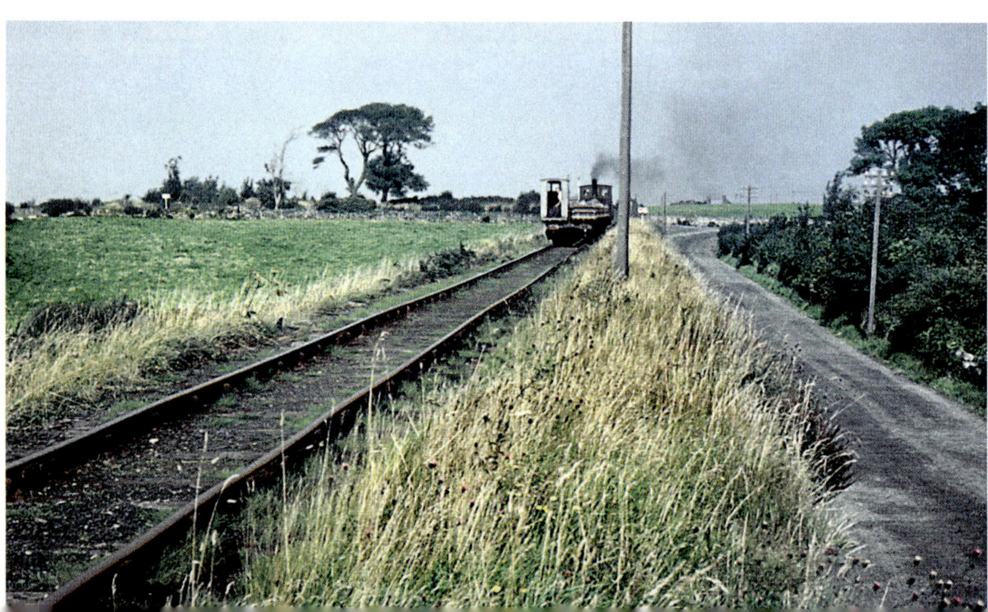

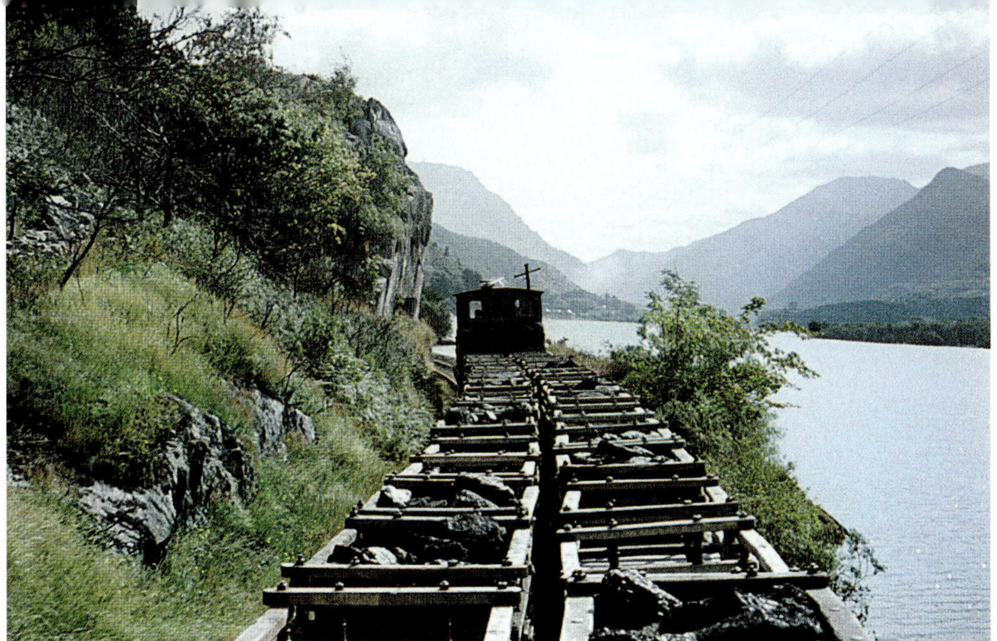

Above, below, and opposite below: The Padarn Railway opened at the beginning of March 1843, replacing the earlier horse-worked Dinorwic Railway, although for the first few years, the Padarn Railway was also operated by horses. Land by the side of the railway was given over to growing gorse as food for the horses; there was to be no wasted border. In the first photograph, a loaded train is making its way to Pens-Coins on an embankment between Pensarn and the road crossing at Cefn-Rhyd. Barely visible in the distance to the right is the unusual footbridge also to be seen on page 123. Just before this footbridge was a passing loop from the horse-operated days, these used to be at about 1-mile intervals. Steam operation began in 1848, and as it was usual for only one locomotive to operate on any one day, there was no need for passing loops (or stables). Secondly, a Gilfach Ddu-bound train is by the side of Llyn Padarn, and many of the wagons are loaded with coal. The final photograph shows a train from Pens-Coins at the Pont Pen-y-Llyn level crossing; in 1895, there were ideas about replacing this nasty level crossing for road users. There were crossing gates here (from 1926), protected by the fish-tailed semaphore signal with spectacles on each side of its lamp, plus a signal hut. The gatekeeper was connected by telephone and would open the gates five minutes before the train was due (see also page 17). All three photographs are from Ellis's visits to the Padarn Railway at the end of August and the beginning of September 1961.

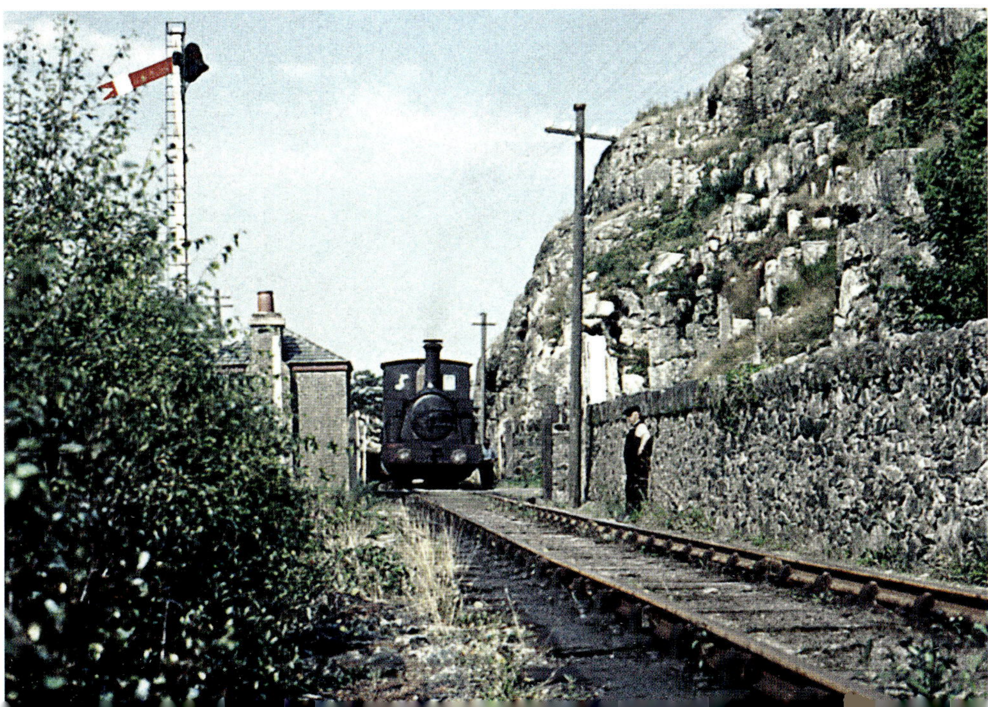

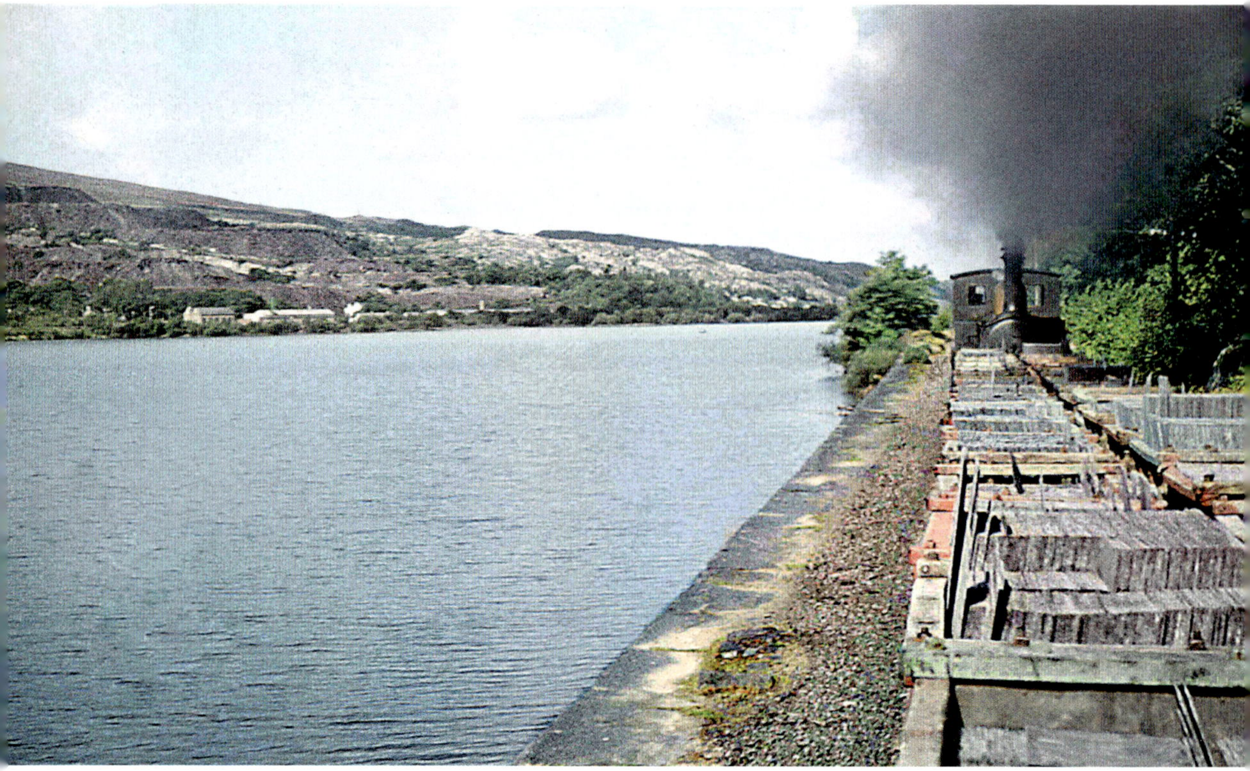

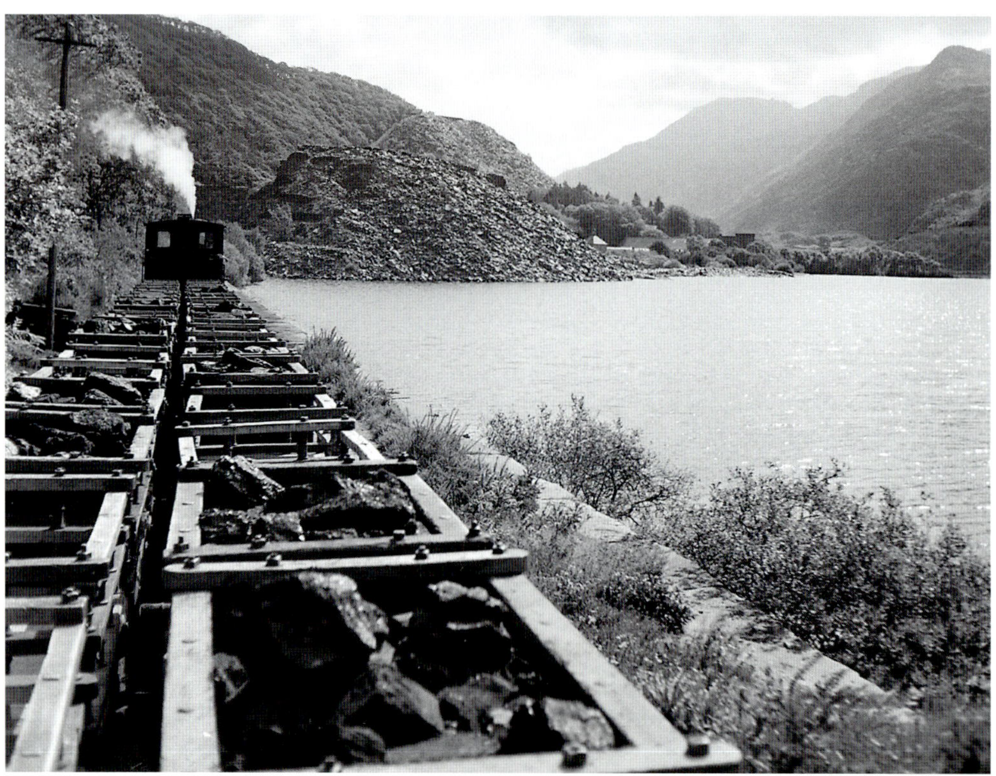

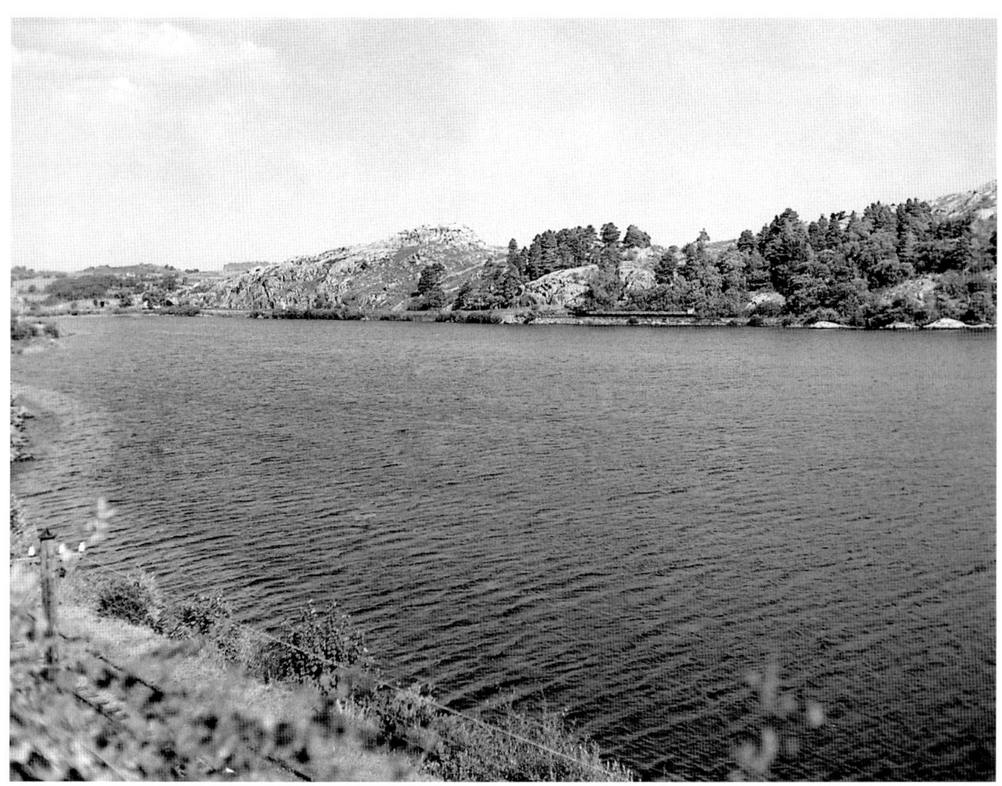

Above and opposite page: On page 96, it was explained how the imposition of a 'Horse Tax' at the end of the eighteenth century considerably increased transportation expenses for the Penrhyn system, as also here at Dinorwic; much thought was then given to reducing the need for horses. The war against France also increased the cost and scarcity of horses; the railway purchased them from as far afield as Anglesey, the Conwy Valley, and even Knutsford, Cheshire. In the early days, the Dinorwic Slate Co. transported slate 'in hampers on horseback', but in the late 1780s, they built an incline to near Y Cei, an established quay on the shore of Llyn Peris. From here and the newer Cei-Newydd on Llyn Padarn, barges took slate across the lake to its western end, and the company's stockpiles at Cwm-y-Glo and Pen-y-Llyn for onward transport to Caernarvon and Port Dinorwic. The barges were successfully used and kept Dinorwic free (at least in part) from the 'Horse Tax'.

Llyn Padarn is seen in all three photographs, first with a loaded slate train on its way to Pens-Coins. The second shows a train including loaded coal wagons returning to Gilfach Ddu; very noticeable is the Vivian Quarry's large waste tip encroaching into the lake. In mid-Victorian times, ideas about waste were that it should go in the lake; however, one commentator at the time did say it 'threatens to reach the opposite shore' and was 'terribly destructive of the picturesque'. The final photograph is looking across Llyn Padarn with a Pens-Coins-bound train on the far shore not far from the Pont Pen-y-Llyn level crossing (see also page 15). All these photographs are from Ellis's visits to the Padarn Railway towards the end of summer in 1961. Today, the heritage Llanberis Lake Railway runs alongside Llyn Padarn on the trackbed of the Padarn Railway.

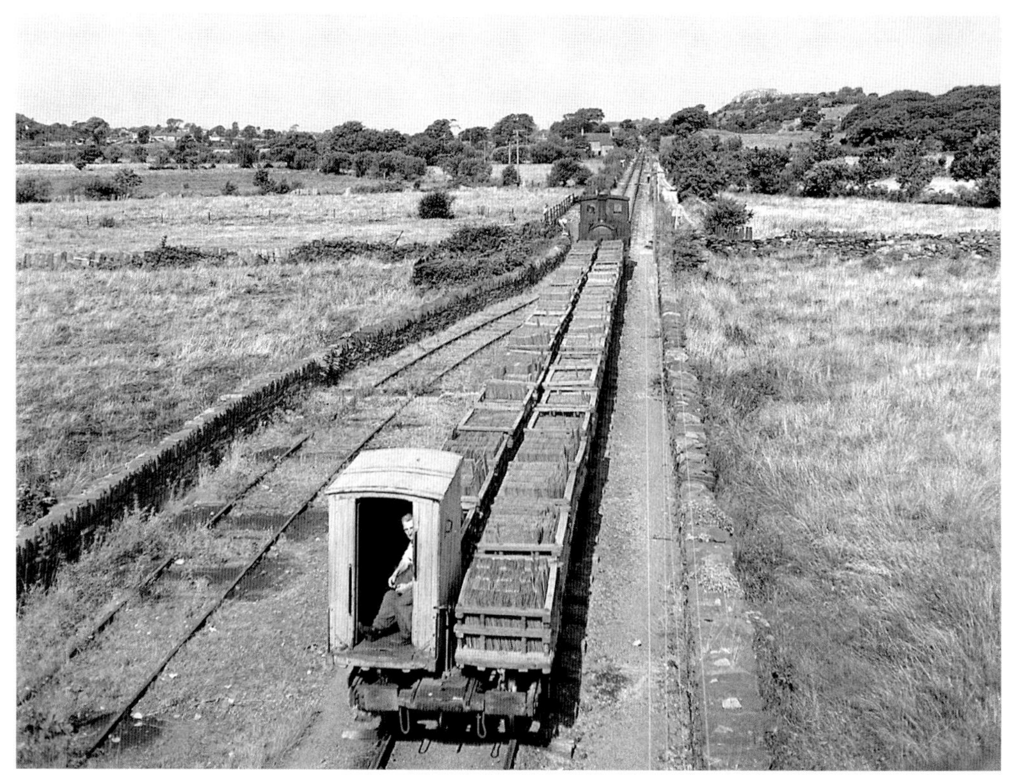

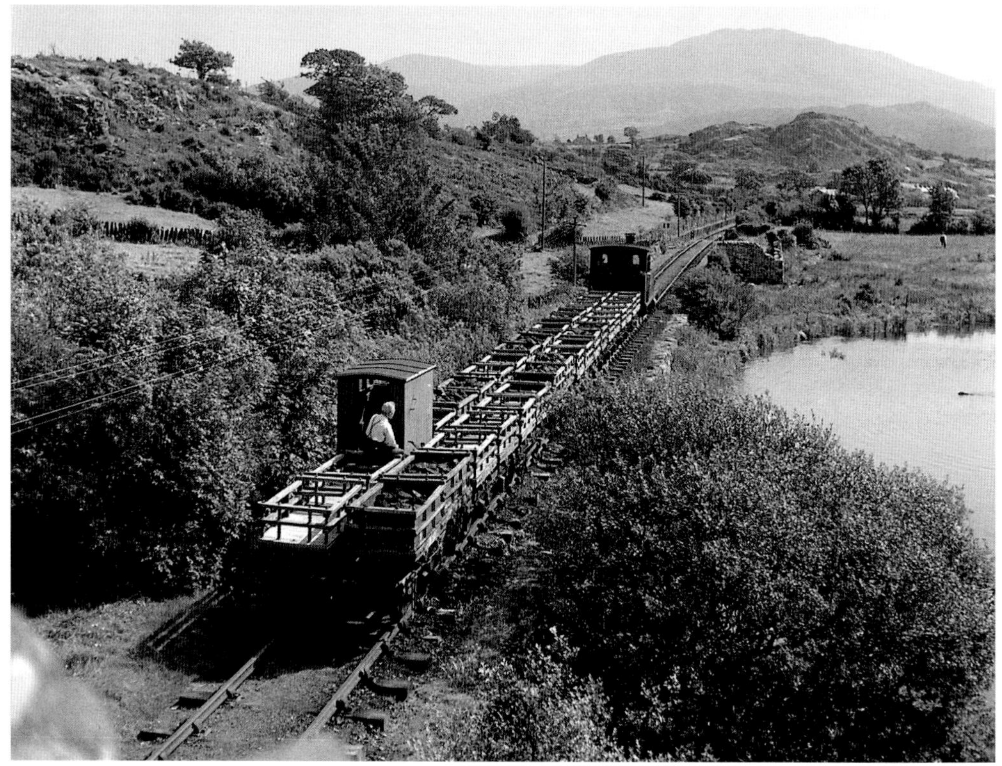

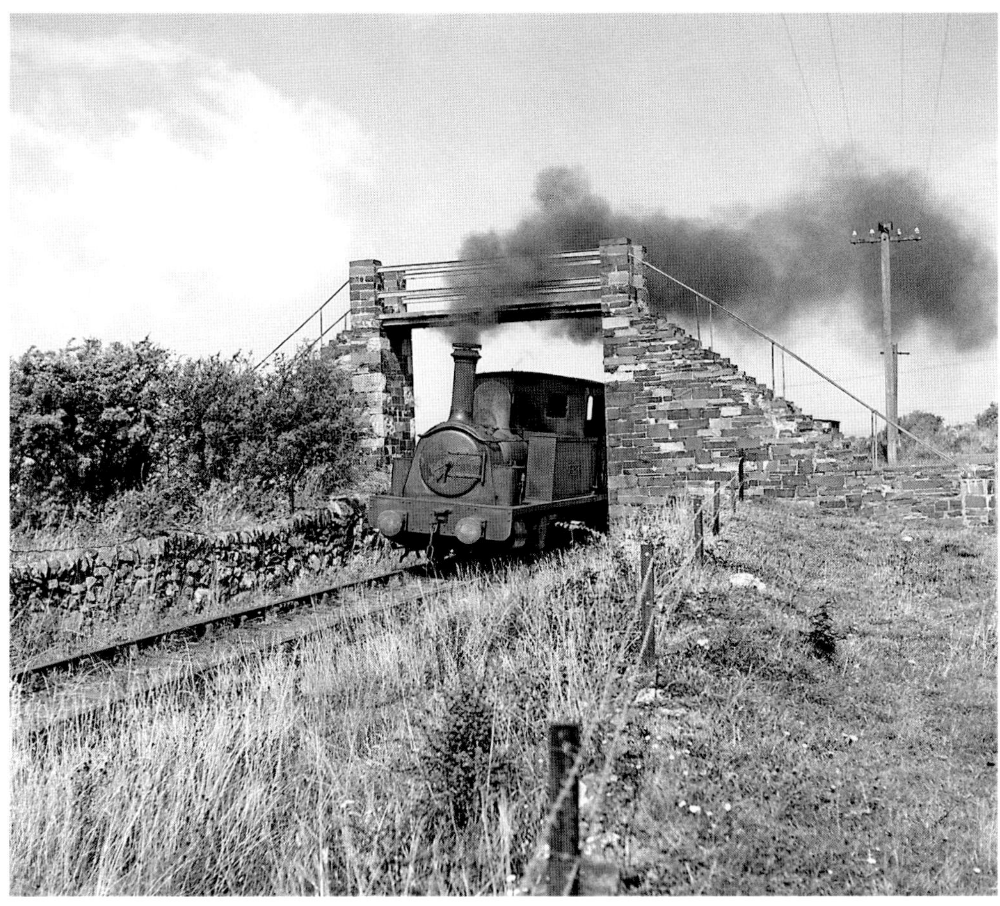

Above and opposite page: The precise date is known for these three photographs along the Padarn Railway—Friday, 1 September 1961. The last train ran on 27 October 1961, and it officially closed on 3 November 1961. The first shows a well-loaded slate train from the road bridge at Pen-y-Llyn heading for Pens-Coins with *Amalthæa* at its head (this photograph was published in the February 1962 edition of *Railway Magazine*). *Amalthæa* was the only 4-foot-gauge locomotive at work during Ellis's visits. Until 1870, there was a level crossing at Pen-y-Llyn. To the left was once the location of a corrugated iron shed that housed four carriages for the Workmen's Train. The second view is a mixture of empty slate and loaded coal wagons making their way back to Gilfach Ddu, and again, the bridge this is taken from was once a level crossing. A dog looks to be swimming in the Afon Rhythallt and has caught the guard's attention. Ahead of *Amalthæa* to the right are the remains of Pont-Rhythallt station. It had produced the most custom for the Workmen's Trains. Barely visible even further ahead, the terraced housing marks the location of stables from the horse-worked early days. The footbridge in the final photograph is just south of Bethel; Boyd was unable to find a reason for building so substantial a structure. It was called 'Charlie's bridge' after the name of the mason who built it and still exists today. The service is the noon train to the quarry with *Amalthæa*.

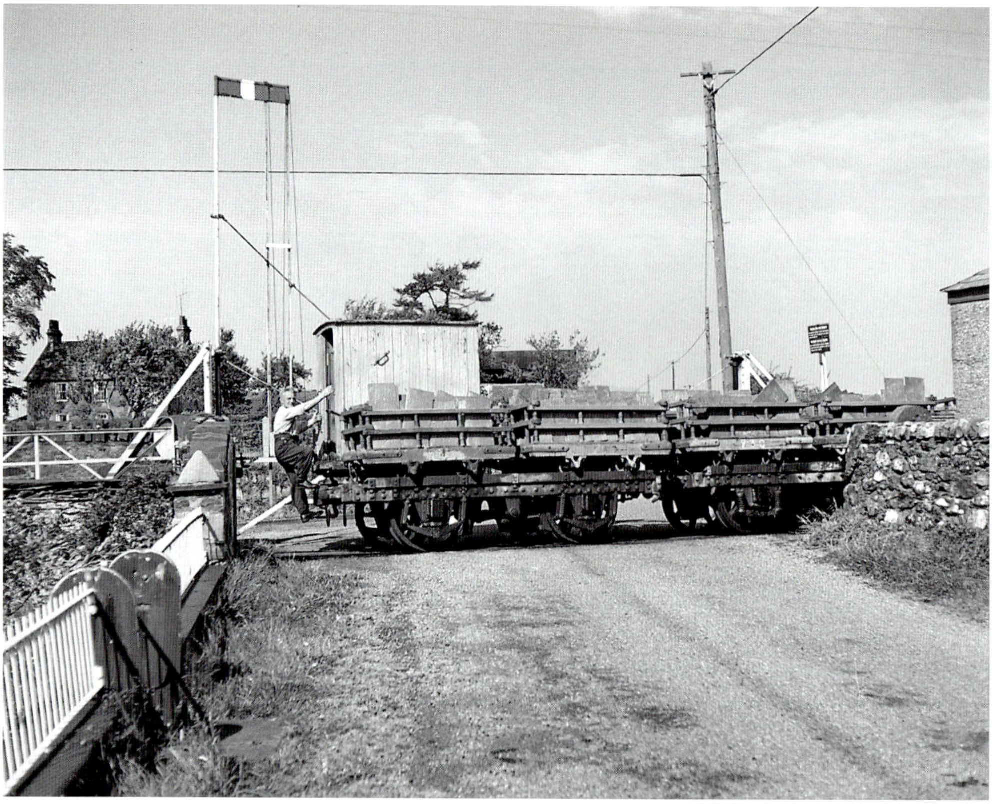

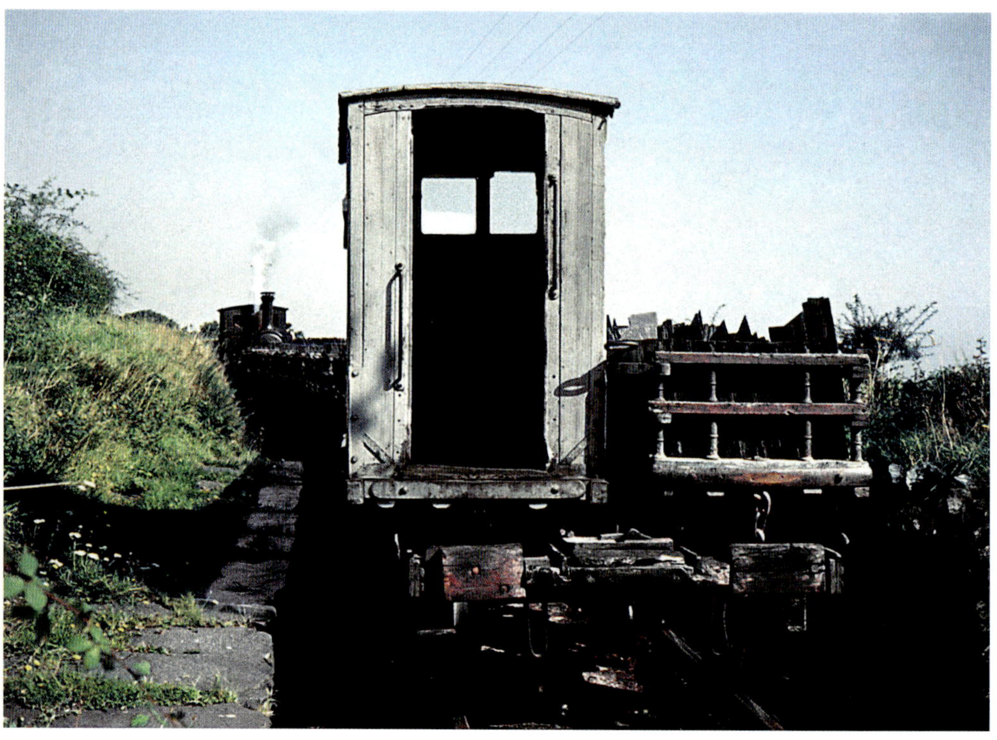

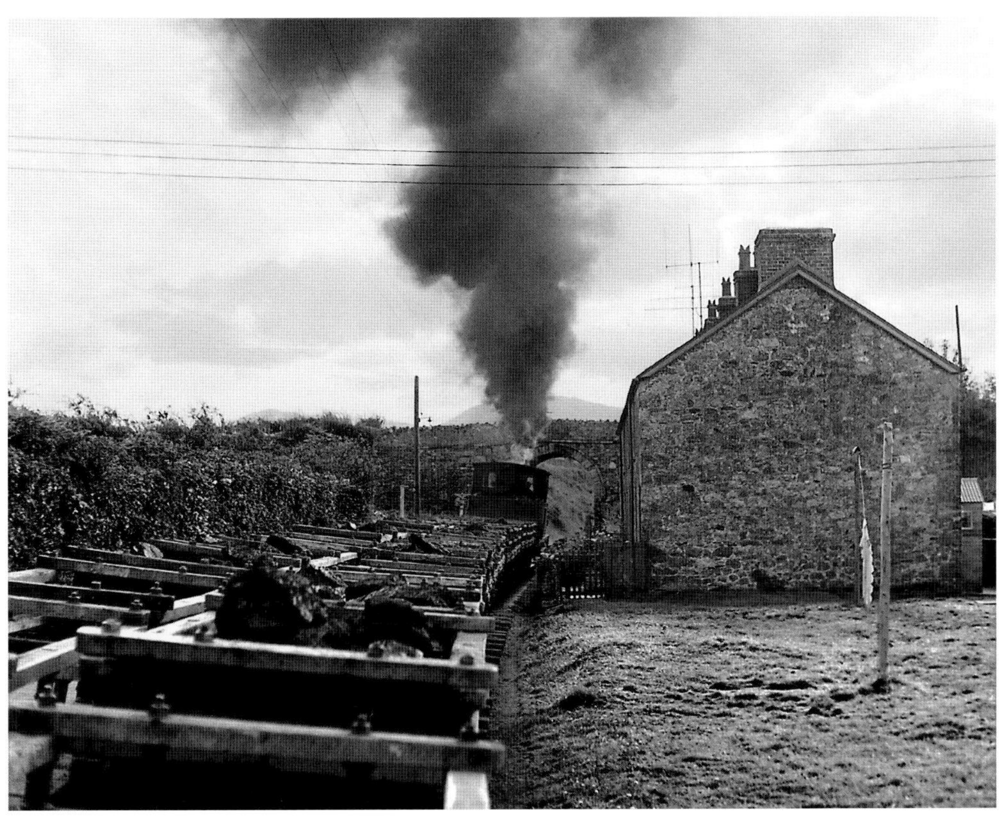

Above and opposite page: Another three photographs from Ellis's two visits to the Padarn Railway at the end of August and the beginning of September 1961. The first two are at the Cefn-Gwyn gated road crossing, about 1 mile from Pen-Scoins, where this loaded slate train is bound. Note the warning sign indicating the gate was across the road, taking the form of a red rectangular target board with a white stripe, lifted high above the crossing. To the right of the crossing is an enamelled bilingual warning sign, a common feature along the line. Being a private railway, it had not always carried out preventative measures as might be imposed by the Board of Trade on a public railway; the company was anxious to avoid any embarrassing enquiry. The long, wagon brake handle can just be seen poking out between the guard's van and adjacent slate wagon at about the level of the guard's shoulder. To apply the brake, the guard would stand on this, holding on to the van's exterior grab-handle for support. Can you make out the tare weight (7 cwt and 3 quarters) marked on the side of one of the slate wagons? In the colour photograph can be seen the small 30-foot-long platform on the west side of the line to the north of the crossing. The shadow of the wagon brake handle is visible on the back of the guard's van. The final photograph was taken just after departure from Pen-Scoins bound for Gilfach Ddu, approaching a terrace of cottages built in 1896 (see page 127).

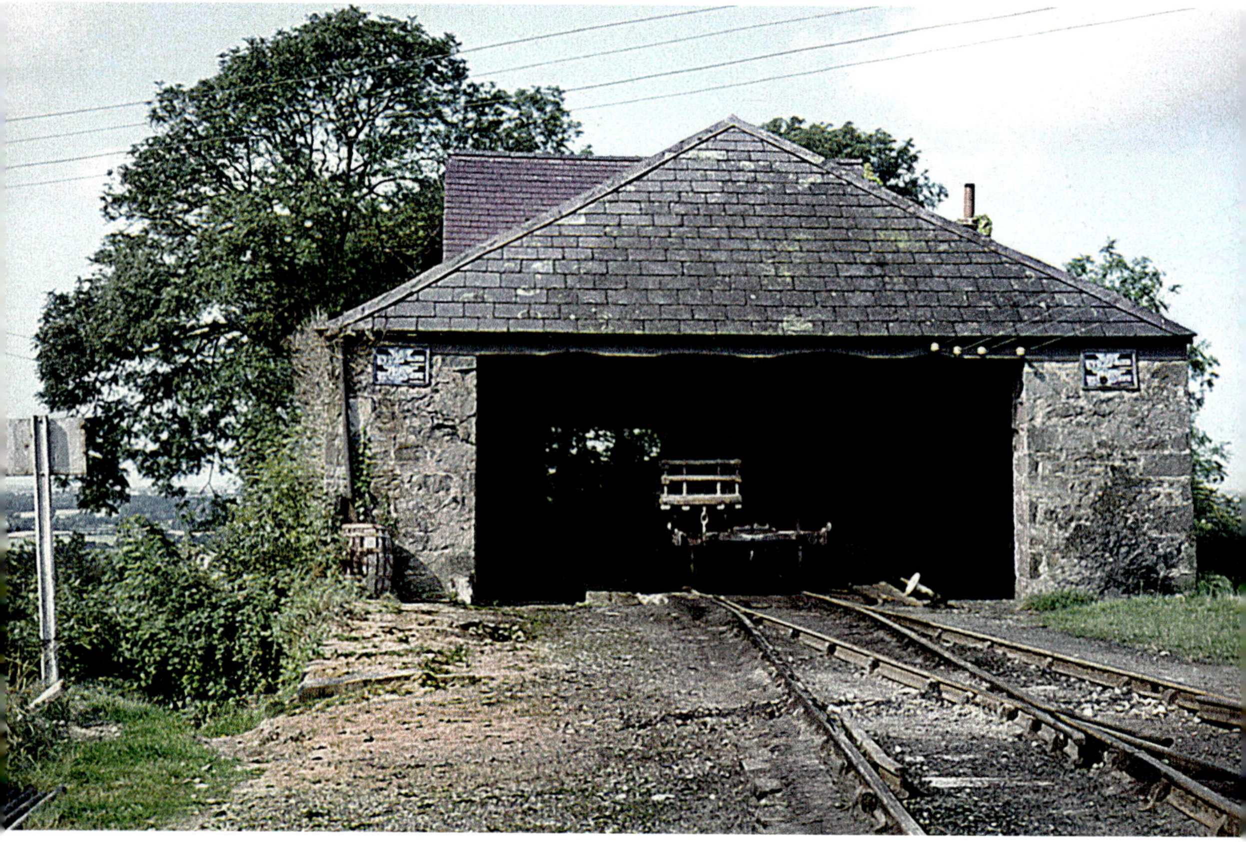

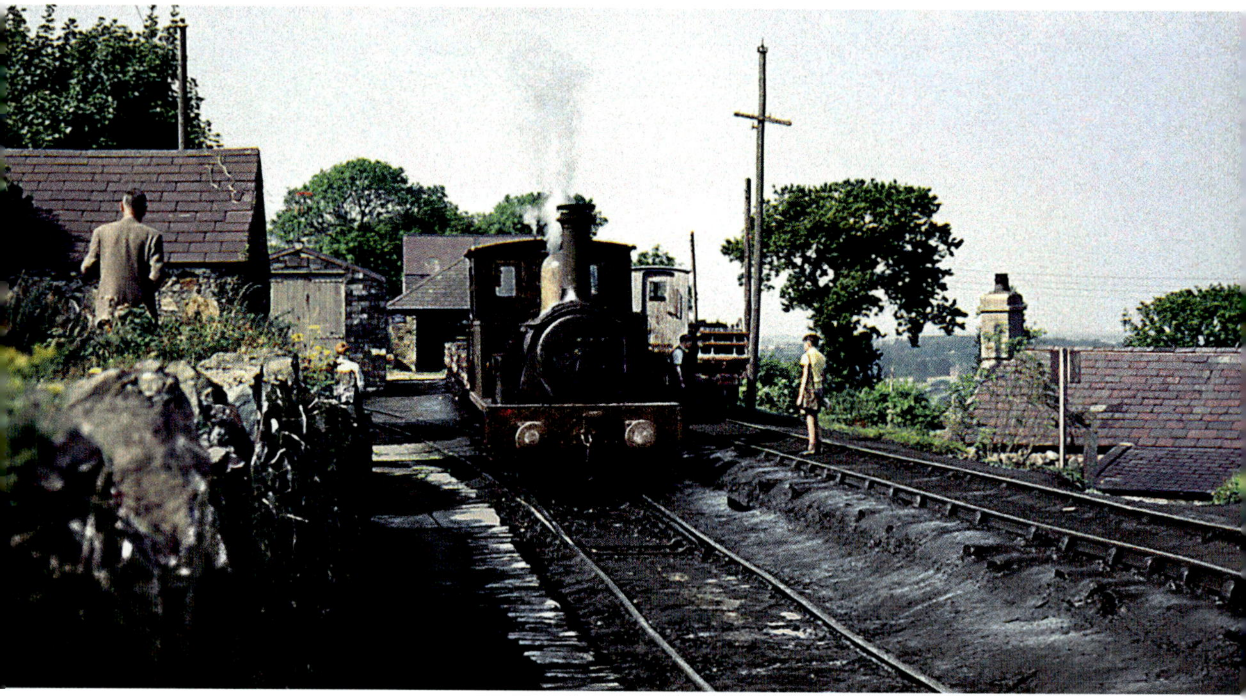

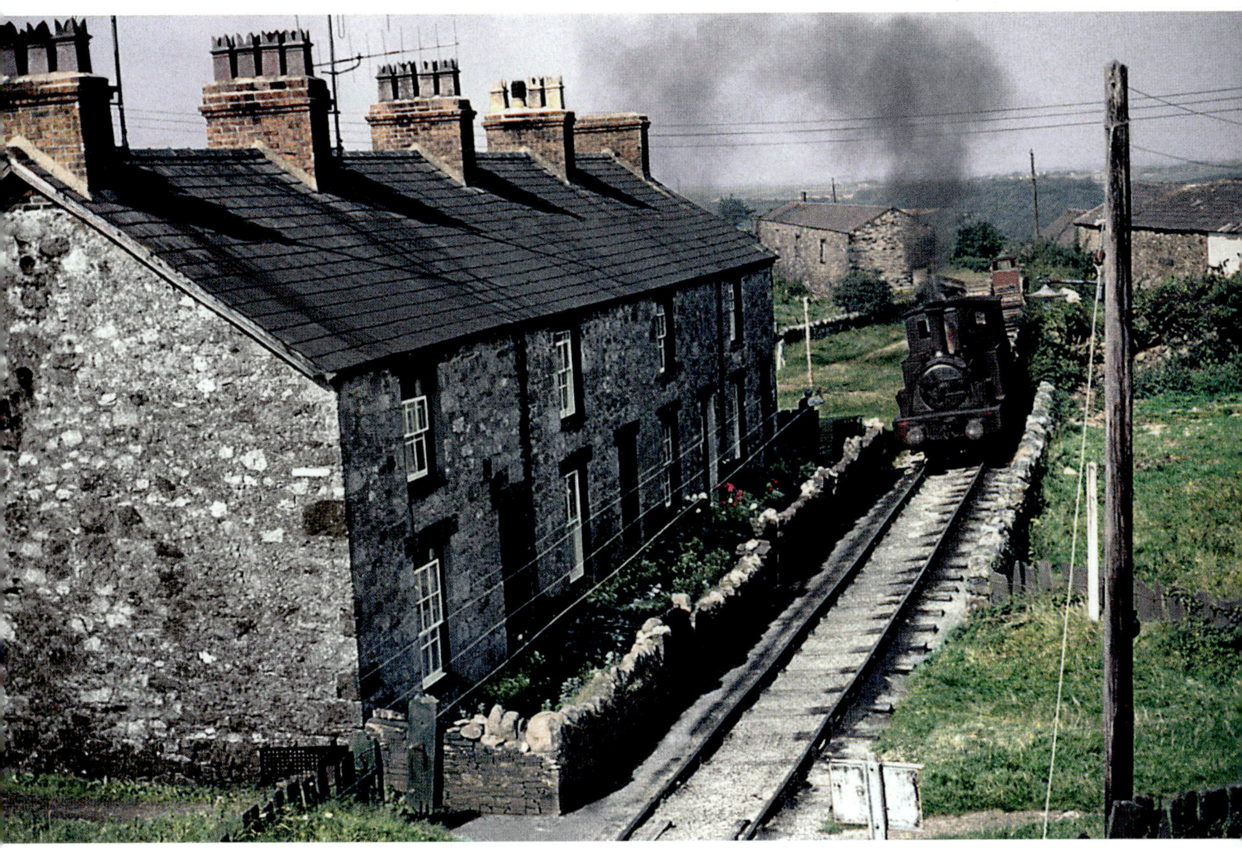

Above and opposite page: Pen-Scoins was the terminus of the 4-foot-gauge tracks, and here, the opposite procedure to that at Gilfach Ddu was enacted in the first photo. Loaded quarry-gauge slate wagons were taken off the transporter wagons in the transfer dock/drumhouse, then lowered to the port on a narrow-gauge gravity-worked incline. In the second photograph, the two tracks can be seen to be at different levels. Transporters with quarry-gauge wagons full of slate are on the higher track, to the north, and run down to the transfer dock/drumhouse for unloading assisted by the height difference. After this, the empty transporters are loaded with empty slate wagons brought up the incline from the port. The transporters, now loaded with empty quarry-gauge wagons, run down the left-hand lower southern track, again assisted by the height difference, to be picked up by *Amalthæa*. The locomotive only worked at the east end and did not approach the transfer dock/ drumhouse. The bearings of the transporters were liberally lubricated with thick oil; this made the trackside in the second photograph a solidified causeway of oil droppings. All three photographs are again from Ellis's visits to the Padarn Railway in the late summer of 1961.

As a train full of slate neared Pen-Scoins from Gilfach Ddu, it would uncouple itself on the move by means of the treadle-operated jaw-and-link couplings. The driver would then pull away sharply over the points to the south line, and the guard would put all his weight on the brake lever (page 124). Once the engine was on the southernmost track, a pointsman would throw the points and the loaded transporters would take the northernmost track, the pointsman then jumping on the step of the first wagon to also depress its brake lever. This is called fly-shunting and would not be permitted in today's health-and-safety-conscious world; in fact, even by 1961, it had long since been illegal on main lines, but it did enable a very simple track layout at Pen-Scoins; it was not used at Gilfach Ddu due to an adverse gradient (see page 116). To conclude this book is a lovely photograph of *Amalthæa* with empties bound for the quarry. It has just departed Pen-Scoins and is passing by Penscoins Cottages that are still lived in today; the trackbed here is now a roadway.